Everyone Mattered

Everyone Mattered

*The life and times
of
Dame Kitty Anderson*

The Chandos Press

The Chandos Press, The North London Collegiate School,
Canons, Edgware, Middlesex, HA8 7RJ

First published in 2003 by The Chandos Press

Copyright © 2003 The North London Collegiate School

The North London Collegiate School has asserted its moral right
under The Copyright, Designs and Patents Act, 1988,
to be identified as the author of this work

All rights reserved. No reproduction, copy or transmission of this
publication may be made without written permission. No paragraph of
this publication may be reproduced, copied or transmitted save with
written permission or in accordance with the provisions of the Copyright
Act 1956 (as amended). Any person who does any unauthorized act in
relation to this publication may be liable to criminal prosecution
and civil claims for damages

A CIP catalogue record for this book
is available from the British Library

ISBN 0-9545311-0-8

Cover Design by DM Design Consultancy

Printed and bound by
◆ DIMOND PRESS
Pembroke

Foreword

When I became Secretary of the Old North Londoners' Association six years ago, I was bombarded with requests to organize the writing of a biography of Kitty Anderson— perhaps because I myself am a 'DA girl'. The Sesquicentennial publication *And Their Works Do Follow Them* by Nigel Watson was already in the pipeline and initially I explored the possibility of producing a similarly grand hardback book to celebrate Kitty Anderson's centenary in 2003. It soon became evident that such a book would be much too expensive for a relatively narrow market and being inexperienced in the world of publishing, I felt I had drawn a blank. Then a conjunction of events occurred which made me think it might be possible after all.

First of all, Ennis Brandenburger, Old North Londoner and a former Governor of the school, showed me a paperback book that had been produced by one of her contemporaries at school, Charmian Cannon, at an affordable price. Secondly, I heard that Barbara Ker Wilson, Old North Londoner and a professional editor, was prepared to take on the editorial job. Thanks to modern technology, her residence in Australia did not seem to offer any obstacles to the process.

So with the blessing of the Governors, much hard work by all the contributors and the kind cooperation of the School Archivists we are able to offer this biographical and reflective account of Dame Kitty Anderson, whose influence affected so many people's lives.

Joan Lundie

Introduction

This book is published to celebrate the 100th anniversary of Dame Kitty Anderson's birth in July 1903. It has been a century which has seen many changes: in the role of women and in the equality of opportunity which they have come to expect, along with developments in technology and communication that have enabled this publication to be assembled and edited on both sides of the world. At NLCS, Dame Kitty, or Dr Anderson as she was when she first became the school's fifth Headmistress, saw in the period of her Headship the change from wartime austerity to the liberation and pop culture of the 1960s.

It has become the custom at NLCS on Founder's Day for the current Headmistress to talk about her predecessors. Inevitably Frances Mary Buss features more often than her successors, but in 1999 I chose Dame Kitty as my subject and I enjoyed then looking through much of the School's archive material and learning about her. I formed the impression of a studious woman who, nevertheless, could find enjoyment in clothes, especially hats, and who was remembered above all for her infectious enthusiasm (described by one of her pupils as 'a kind of psychic champagne'). In school she encouraged a curriculum that allowed girls to find out for themselves and warned against too many examinations — views that strike a very topical note today. Dame Kitty found time to lead her school and also to serve on numerous educational committees, ensuring that NLCS continued to play a role in influencing the education of children beyond the walls of the School. She had the courage to disagree publicly when she felt educational commonsense was being sacrificed to political ideology. Far-sighted, she recognized that the educational developments in the 1950s would require improved facilities at Canons, and an appeal for a Buildings and Endowment Fund was launched. The Inspection Report of 1958 referred to ' … the strong tradition of a liberal and scholarly education and which at the same time adapted itself successfully to the needs of the age with the vitality and vision which were characteristic of its founder'.

I am glad that it has been possible to publish this book about Dame Kitty and to include personal memories of her. No one who knew her feels that the rather stern portrait in the school's Entrance Hall does her justice. Her students found her to be warm and caring, with a memorable smile and the ability to make each individual feel important.

Bernice McCabe

Canons — December 2002

Contents

A loving family — Walter Anderson

1   THE EARLY YEARS — FROM SALTBURN-BY-THE-SEA TO LONDON
Kay Moore   page 3

Her kind smile and lively eyes .... Jane Bidder
At NLCS we were given the idea we could do anything ... P. Jane Ross
A ghost laid to rest .... Esther Rantzen

2   'SEVENTEEN IS MUCH TOO YOUNG' — KITTY ANDERSON, STUDENT OF HISTORY
Caroline M. Barron   page 17

A great persuader all her life .... Norma Rinsler
'On no account should this girl go to university' ... Barbara Ker Wilson
Crunch time .... Susan Bennett

3   CRAVEN STREET, BURLINGTON, KING'S NORTON — KITTY ANDERSON'S TEACHING CAREER BEFORE SHE ARRIVED AT THE NORTH LONDON COLLEGIATE SCHOOL
Katharine McMahon   page 43

A shock for the Sixth Formers! .... Margaret Wicks
From orange-peel teeth to Senior Prefect .... Joan Lundie
She respected us .... Mary Wilson
Bright powder paint and baking tins for buns .... Margaret Glover

4   'I HAVE AT LEAST GOT A HAT' — DR KITTY ANDERSON AND THE NORTH LONDON COLLEGIATE SCHOOL: 1944-55
Ann Thomas   page 59

'I delegated everything except knowing people' .... Mavis Greathead
Short, rather plump, with a ready smile .... Ann Holmes
Things were going to be different .... Margaret Keeble
'Scintillating' .... Pamela Melnikoff

5   EVERYONE MATTERS — A DECADE OF CHANGE: 1955-65
    Olive Mellor   page 79

    She was actually in tears .... Adele Beverley
    'Hello, hello' .... Margaret Bates
    Her enthusiasm was infectious .... Janet Wells
    The first role model in my life .... Ann Beaton
    For me, NLCS and Dame Kitty are one .... Carolyn Spittle
    A dance dress with detachable sleeves .... Laura Fransella

6   IDEALS AND PRACTICE — SOME POSTWAR LIMITATIONS
    AND STRESSES DURING THE TIME DAME KITTY ANDERSON
    WAS HEADMISTRESS
    Erica Brostoff   page 103

    The quick firm step .... April Halton
    'With admiration, gratitude and affection' .... Margot Edmonds
    Dame Kitty's extended family .... Barbara Dorf
    What mattered .... Eleanor Bron

7   IF IT AIN'T BROKE DON'T FIX IT
    Kay Moore   page 127

    Not somebody to be trifled with .... Ann Digby
    Two reprimands .... Helen Lloyd
    The School Dance Outrage .... Gillian Cross
    'Please try something different next week' .... Ruth Padel

8   A HIATUS IN TRADITION — DAME KITTY ANDERSON
    AND SCIENCE TEACHING AT THE NORTH LONDON
    COLLEGIATE SCHOOL
    Margaret Ghilchik   page 139

    'DA's coming!' .... Angela Cannon
    The University of Life also had much to offer .... Mary Coulter
    She was always 'DA' .... Rosemary Rees
    We were well prepared for the modern world ...... Philippa Robinson

9 'IN SPITE OF THE MANY OTHER CLAIMS ON YOUR TIME' — THE ROBBINS COMMITTEE AND DAME KITTY'S CONTRIBUTION TO OTHER NATIONAL BODIES
Joan Clanchy   page 155

She was a Labour supporter .... Vera Woolf
We basked in her reflected glory .... Linda Williams
The atmosphere at Canons .... Joy Taylor

10 'TRUST SCHOOLS WHICH I FEEL ARE MY SCHOOLS' — DAME KITTY AND THE GIRLS (PUBLIC) DAY SCHOOL TRUST
Janet Sondheimer   page 171

11 'I LOVE RETIREMENT' — THE LAST YEARS
Barbara Ker Wilson   page 175

Not the kind of remark you expect to hear .... Barbara Faux
Our friend at all times .... Lisa Thaler
A long association: England and India .... Chaya Ray
A verve never to be forgotten .... Maya Ray

EPILOGUE .... Enid Ellis
                                                                   page 195

~

Acknowledgments

Several of the biographical essays in this book include their own acknowledgements. All have plundered the NLCS Archives and their authors have been most ably assisted in this by the two School Archivists, Karen Morgan and Ellen Curran, who have helped not only with the research of information but with the quest for photographs. Thanks on this count also to Angela Cannon, who has allowed us to use some of her personal photographs. Kay Moore acknowledges special help she received from Robin Cook and the Cleveland & Teesside Local History Society, and Barbara Ker Wilson expresses her thanks to John and Wendy Jameson, Dame Kitty's neighbours in Northallerton, who supplied details for her essay.

We are most grateful to Julie Alberg (née Mills), the designer of Online, for her cover design for the book, and to Norma Rinsler (née Lee) for expert proof reading — and overall to the many contributors and collaborators who have worked together to bring this project to completion.

The Anderson family, 1916
Lizzie and Herbert with their three children,
Walter aged 8 months, Bert aged 5 and Kitty aged 13

A Loving Family

I was delighted to learn that the Old North Londoners' Association was planning a book about my sister Kitty; I would like to write something about her family background.

Kitty was born in 1903, my brother Bert in 1911 and myself in 1916. Kitty always showed a loving care for all the members of her family. Until about 1939, she would always travel north to spend part of her holidays at the family home in Saltburn.

She had a very high regard for our father, John Herbert Anderson, and would always seek his advice on matters arising in her career. My father was the eldest son of a large family with limited means, living in the Lancashire town of Padiham. He left school at an early age to work in the local Co-operative Shop. It required a considerable effort on his part to improve his education by going to night school, and ultimately qualifying as a chartered accountant.

Our mother, whose maiden name was Lizzie Dawson, was born in Wigan, the youngest daughter of a family of five. Her father was a commercial traveller. She was a good pianist, artistic and well-read.

Our parents died in 1948/49 but Kitty's links with the family continued. She gave a lot of guidance to my brother Bert and myself in bringing up our families. Bert and his wife, Muriel, had three sons — Richard, David and Geoffrey, and my wife Audrey and I had one daughter, Mary. Part of Mary's schooldays were spent at Cleveland Grammar School, Redcar, which ultimately replaced the Saltburn High School for Girls which Kitty attended.

My nephew David knew Kitty particularly well because he stayed with her for six years while studying medicine. He recalls how, after supper in the evening, Kitty would regularly work from 11pm to 3am, then be up at 7 o'clock the next morning. She seemed to require very little sleep. Another recollection of David's is that when they went shopping together in Edgware on Saturday mornings, if they met any Old North Londoners, Kitty would greet them by name — even if they had left school many years ago.

Kitty always got on very well with my wife Audrey and her parents, who were Londoners. When my father-in-law died, my wife's mother, Nanna, moved north to live with us but did not settle too well to our colder climate. When the opportunity arose Kitty invited her to become her housekeeper in Edgware. Nanna gladly accepted this offer and stayed with Kitty for a number of years.

Walter Anderson

(Sadly, Walter died on August 27th 2002)

1

The Early Years — from Saltburn-by-the-Sea to London

KAY MOORE

The Education Act which created England's maintained secondary schools was passed in 1902; Kitty Anderson, born a few months later on 4 July 1903, came to believe this timing was significant to her own opportunities, choices and successes.

Within the wider context of early Edwardian England, what other factors might affect her future course? King Edward VII had ascended the throne in 1901; if Kitty had been born two years earlier, she would have been a Victorian, with the Boer War not yet resolved.

Britain in 1903 was not the sunlit pastoral of popular recall: following a great wave of immigration from the land into the towns during recent decades, less than a quarter of the population now lived in country areas. The total population was 44 million; London, at 7 million, was the largest city in the most urbanised country in the world. Two new words, 'conurbation' and 'suburbia', had entered the language. Yet half an hour on a bicycle would take you from central London to the countryside. (Camden's air was becoming less clean, its green spaces were being eroded, but the Underground would not reach Golders Green until 1907 and that area was full of farms and orchards.) Electricity had recently been installed in cities, alongside the older supplies of gas and water; there were still 250,000 horses in London, plus their allied trades — they were the main form of transport, supplemented by the new motor buses. There were a few newfangled cinemas in addition to the established theatres and music halls.

Middlesbrough, in the north-east, where Kitty's father would come to work in 1913, was a working-class iron and steel town, with few public spaces to encourage healthy recreation; but children played marbles, pitch-and-toss, football, and bowled hoops and swung skipping-ropes in the streets; indoors, there were home entertainments centred around the piano, for those fortunate enough to possess one, and people also enjoyed music halls, choirs, brass bands and the concerts, lantern shows and debates organised by church and chapel. Touring opera and theatre companies regularly performed — and the Co-op organised lectures on Shakespeare.

Lady Florence Bell, an amateur Yorkshire sociologist who published her findings in *At the Works* (1907) estimated that 75% of the workers of Middlesbrough read newspapers, and 25% also read books. By contrast, in one Yorkshire village she reported that 'a little group of young men would frequently walk a couple of miles to watch the expresses dash through the small station in the darkness', so few were the choices open to those unable to entertain themselves.

In village and town alike, the most accessible source of entertainment was the pub, warm, glowing with gas lamps, friendly and free: nationally, there was a public house for every 300 people. One Sunday, Lady Bell and her team counted four times as many people of all ages going into the pubs as into the churches of Middlesbrough.

Britain was riven socially by the vast gulf between rich and poor, between flaunting consumption and living on the edge of poverty. Well-to-do ladies and gentlemen had outfits for every social occasion, every leisure pursuit, for day and night. The children of the poor often went barefoot and relied on officialdom or charity to find them boots for school and clothing against the cold. Pawnbrokers' doors were rarely still.

Seebohm Rowntree's *Poverty, A Study of Town Life*, published in 1901, was based on his researches in Yorkshire (York, Leeds, Sheffield). It revealed 28% of the population living below a 'base nutritional standard' (in other words, in poverty). A typical manual worker's wage was just sufficient to raise four (but no more) children adequately. However, Rowntree writes:

> They must never spend a penny on railway fares or omnibus. They must never go into the country unless they walk. The children must have no pocket money for dolls, marbles or sweets. The father must smoke no tobacco, and must drink no beer ... Finally, the wage earner must never be absent from his work for a single day.

We have all seen enough Merchant-Ivory interiors and acres of landscaped grounds, afternoon tea-parties and lavish breakfasts, to understand the contrast between the picture Rowntree presents and the aristocratic and upper-middle class homes presented on film. In 1903, the year Kitty Anderson was born, the Balfour government set up an Interdepartmental Committee on Physical Deterioration: some notice was being taken.

Sydney and Beatrice Webb and George Bernard Shaw inveighed increasingly against inequalities; the fact that the fledgling Labour Party returned five Members of Parliament in 1900 and thirty in 1906, and that Trade Union membership was set to double, gives us a sense of a country ready for change.

Within our two key areas of education and the place of women within society, things were also on the move ... even if the 1902 Education Act originated in a desire to keep Britain competitive for world markets, rather than concern for children's development, it did provide a vital 'ladder of progression' and enabled social mobility. Caning in schools was commonplace and approved, yet the old rote learning of just the three Rs was starting to give way to a wider, less restricted curriculum. And in 1904 the Workers' Educational Association was founded, reinforcing the social changes the 1902 Act had set in train.

What of the status of women and girls? Marriage was the main career open to them, whatever their social class. Domestic service was regarded as the best training for marriage and a lifetime of housework: those with four or more children and a limited income had no time or energy for outside work; those with titles and/or wealth were destined to become decorative accessories or hostesses to their fathers or husbands. Middle-class and wealthy women were often expected to emulate the frailty, physical or mental, of the nineteenth-century 'Ideal Woman' (the 'Angel of the house'), as well as being, inevitably, excluded by lack of educational opportunity from prestigious paid careers. Violet Bonham-Carter tells a revealing story of her childhood: '...asking my governess how I was going to spend my life, she replied: "Until you are eighteen you will do lessons ... And afterwards you will do *nothing*."'

Over a quarter of women who worked were servants; in 1906 the Board of Education suggested that Science 'might be wholly replaced by an approved scheme ... in practical housewifery' for the top two classes. In 1910, elementary schools taught Domestic Science and how to make up a baby's cot, not just to be helpful, as in 2002 Parenting classes, but to prepare the pupils for their future as domestic servants or running their own homes. Yet at the same time more and more opportunities were arising for 'lady typewriters' and female teachers. Moreover, since the 1870s, birth control, with all its benefits for the freedom and health of women, was more and more widely practised amongst the working class as well as the upper and middle classes. Divorce was so costly in the 1900s that only two petitions for every 10,000 couples were put forward; but the number of formal separations was ten times larger and in practice there were many more informal ones. (Amongst peers of the realm one third of marriages in the same period ended in divorce.) Two books published in 1909 have titles that suggest women in unhappy marriages were often admirably feisty — *Modern Marriage and How to Bear It*, by Maud Braby, and *Marriage As a Trade* by Cicely Hamilton, who declared caustically: 'Boys are to be happy in themselves; the girls are to make others happy.' Wives, as always, devised their own strategies and solutions — and, outside the home, the voice of women was increasingly clamorous, increasingly heard, not just for independence but for the Vote.

In 1903 Emmeline and Christabel Pankhurst, impatient at the slow progress of Millicent Fawcett's National Union of Women's Suffrage Societies since its beginnings in 1897, founded the Women's Social and Political Union, openly more militant, determined to draw attention to the cause of Votes for Women. The Daily Mail promptly labelled its members 'Suffragettes'. When Kitty Anderson was ten, Emily Davison threw herself in front of the King's horse on Derby Day and was killed. When Kitty was fifteen, six million women — female householders over thirty, the wives of male householders and female graduates — were given the Vote. When she was twenty-five, women finally gained the Vote on the same terms as men.

Finally, what was the state of women's education in 1903, and what were its prospects? The North London Collegiate School was fifty-three years old, Cheltenham Ladies' College fifty. It was thirty-nine years since the all-important Schools Enquiry Commission of 1864 had surveyed the secondary education of girls as well as boys: Frances Mary Buss, Emily Davies and Dorothea Beale had all passionately testified before it. Five years later, Davies founded Girton College; in 1871 the Camden School was set up and the National Union for 'an educated womanhood' was formed on the initiative of Maria Grey and her sister Emily Shirreff. The following year The Girls' Public Day Schools Trust was set up. (Dame Kitty would be its Chairman from 1965-75 and then its Vice-President.) The girls who attended the Trust schools, including North Londoners, were lucky in the facilities and prospects they enjoyed. There were, however, some reactionaries: in 1879 the Oxford High School magazine reported: 'Many girls put on their gloves *in the street* and some wear no gloves going to and from school. The latter I have heard objected to more than anything and it certainly gives our enemies reason to say that the High School makes girls rough and unfeminine.'

The Trust girls rejoiced in new gyms, fencing and Swedish drill classes and 'a healthier style of dress' with shorter skirts; in tennis courts; in chemistry lessons, albeit without 'dangerous practical work'; in some fine new buildings and spacious grounds. At Oxford High School there was Logic with the Rev Charles Dodgson, at Kensington and Sheffield Greek was taught, as well as practical Botany, with microscopes lent by local doctors. Trust girls regularly won open awards to Oxford and Cambridge. In 1901, two years before Kitty's birth, the opening of Birkenhead School along the coast from her Lancashire birthplace brought the total of Trust schools to thirty-eight. Cheltenham, NLCS, the Trust schools and those like them sent many teachers to be headmistresses at the new girls' schools proliferating all over the country, both private and, following the 1902 Act, maintained.

from left to right
Three generations of enlightened women:
Kitty's grandmother, Kitty and her mother

Without the Act, Kitty Anderson would certainly have not lacked encouragement or money spent on her education: twenty-six when Kitty, his first child, was born, her father was a remarkable Lancastrian who had already progressed a long way from his own disadvantaged beginnings. He believed in the efficacy of self-discipline, hard work and education and was determined to inculcate the first two and provide the third to any child of his, girl or boy.

Herbert Anderson was born in 1877 in the Lancashire mill town of Padiham, near Burnley. As the eldest of several children of a carpenter, he needed to start earning as soon as he could. He left school young (the school leaving age was raised to twelve in 1899) and went to work in the local Co-op. In the late nineteenth century the Co-op movement did far more than provide low-price shops; it was an educational force. The young Herbert studied at night school and was soon qualified to work as clerk to a Preston accountant; eventually, aged twenty-seven, when his daughter was a year old, he completed his articles and became a Member of the Institute of Chartered Accountants.

His wife, Lizzie Dawson, came from Wigan and was a little younger than her husband. Vivacious and energetic, she was the youngest of five children. Her father was a commercial traveller. She was skilled in music making and painting and enjoyed reading. Herbert and Lizzie shared their enjoyment of books and music — he was a fine singer, at ease before an audience. Lizzie, of course, taught her daughter to cook, sew and embroider, and these skills became Kitty's pleasures all through her life.

When Kitty was born Herbert was working in Preston again. He and Lizzie had married in 1901 and settled in St Anne's, close to Lytham on the Lancashire coast. Having both grown up in late nineteenth-century mill towns, their decision to live at the seaside and raise their children there is understandable. Their lively, pretty little girl was sent first to a primary school at Ansdell, within the Borough of Lytham St Anne's; later she recalled that her enthusiasm for learning had been fostered there by a particularly good teacher. Once fired, that passion was never dampened.

A year or two later, Kitty was sent to Edenfield, a private school in St Anne's — a handsome, redbrick Victorian villa originally built

She loved dressing up — Kitty as a fairy, aged 6

for a cotton magnate, in a fine setting overlooking the estuary. Edenfield was nearer home; Kitty's brother Herbert Dawson, the Andersons' elder son, was born in March 1911, when Kitty was nearly eight, and the shorter journey was probably helpful; however, her parents' realisation that their little girl was very bright indeed was probably the prime reason for sending her to the new school. They were willing to spend money on schooling that provided facilities to stimulate and involve her.

One non-academic feature that clearly impressed Kitty at Edenfield was the Headmistress's custom of having tea on a tray brought to her study at eleven each morning. When Lizzie Anderson later met Miss Norah Craig at Kitty's Yorkshire secondary school, she told her that Kitty's ambition was to become a headmistress, precisely so that she could enjoy tea on a tray each morning (with biscuits, perhaps).

While Kitty was at Edenfield, she continued to attend the Ansdell Baptist Sunday School, until the Anderson family moved to Yorkshire in 1913. Walter Anderson, Kitty's younger brother, for years kept the copy of *Lamb's Tales from Shakespeare*, in its crimson leather binding, 'Awarded to Kitty Anderson for Regular Attendance — 1912'. The text is crossed out in several places, with simpler wording pencilled in the margin to enable her to read it aloud — to the juniors at Saltburn High School, perhaps, or possibly to her younger pupils later on.

In 1913 Herbert Anderson bought an interest in an accountancy firm in nearby Middlesbrough, and the family soon moved across the Pennines to the North Yorkshire coast — to Number 8, Exeter Street, in Saltburn-by-the Sea, a little town 'with a glorious stretch of golden sands'. Herbert's partnership did not work out; a year later he set up his own firm in Middlesbrough, J.H. Anderson & Company, a few streets away. It flourished, and it is a tribute to the closeness of the family that both Bert and Walter Anderson chose to join their father later on, as did Bert's son, Richard. Herbert's venture began against the grim backdrop of the Great War; a lifelong asthmatic, he was unfit for service.

At Saltburn Kitty tackled her own new venture: Saltburn High School, where Miss Norah Craig was Headmistress. In 1961, when Kitty Anderson received the DBE, Miss Craig wrote a piece to mark the occasion, recalling her pupil as 'working enthusiastically, playing enthusiastically' ... 'small, eager and very attractive' and 'taking a leading part acting, debating, rambling, "digging for Victory" on part of the school field'. Saltburn High

School for Girls had opened in 1907 with forty-six pupils; under its energetic Headmistress, Miss Emma Leakey, the school gained fine, purpose-built premises in 1911. By the time Kitty arrived in 1913 there were 135 girls and seven assistants, and by 1921 the number of pupils had grown to 350, with eighteen assistants. The fees were £2 a term. Norah Craig, an Oxford English graduate, was the teacher who became 'a great influence' on young Kitty. Towards the end of the war she succeeded Miss Leakey as Headmistress, and remained at Saltburn until 1925. She later became Head of Christ's Hospital.

When Kitty was in the Lower Fourth, her family was completed by the birth of Walter in July, 1916. Out of school, all the family enjoyed exploring the surrounding countryside. Catnab Hill, once a smugglers' haunt, was their summer picnic spot; Huntcliffe, the majestic 'old man of the mountains', overshadowed Saltburn and was tackled at various levels; there were spring walks in Riftswood among 'bluebells and the pungent smell of wild garlic', with numerous birds to observe. In summer 'grand and noisy fairs' arrived, with coconut shies, helter-skelters and noisy rides. Inevitably the war impinged even on this seaside haven: the Welsh Regiment requisitioned several hotels and could be seen drilling in the grounds. There were occasional Zeppelin raids. The German Navy shelled nearby Scarborough.

In 1919, the junior girls overflowed into The Red Lodge, a few minutes walk away; here Norah Craig says that Kitty 'infected the juniors with the school's fine traditions summed up in its motto "Members of one another", by spending a study morning each week in the junior school and reading the lesson at School Prayers'. That same pleasure in the company of small girls radiates from the many photos of Dame Kitty with the juniors at NLCS on Founder's Day. Unsurprisingly, perhaps, Kitty Anderson became Head Girl of Saltburn High School when she was only sixteen. Margaret Yates, who would become her lifelong friend, joined the school in Kitty's final year; in 1961, she recalled: 'even then, she quite unconsciously inspired in the Fifth and Sixth forms a kind of affectionate veneration. Yet this last word may be misleading, since Kitty was a lively, very young Head Girl, as round and pretty as a kitten; serious at times, with bursts of infectious laughter and zest in everything.' Countless Old North Londoners will recognize that sketch!

She was certainly very serious about her work: she was one of the six clever girls who in 1919 took over a Games cupboard with a window after

Matriculation, to study for their Higher Certificate in two years. Such was their zest and zeal that they begged to be allowed to take the exam a year early. Miss Craig agreed 'because, if we did well, the school would qualify for a grant for Sixth Form work and for a Library — we had no Library'. Those are Dame Kitty's words, spoken in 1972 as she looked back across the years. Again the synchronicity is intriguing: 1920 was the first year that State scholarships were awarded, and Kitty and her five sister pupils carried off all six awarded by the North Riding.

Encouraged and delighted by this outstanding success, Kitty's parents wrote to Royal Holloway College in September 1920 to inquire about a place for their daughter so that she could read History. 'I received a wire saying "Come next Thursday"… Imagine!', Dame Kitty recalled.

The London train left Saltburn station at six in the morning. Kitty had never been to London, nor had most of the other pupils at Saltburn High School. Her triumphal journey caused so much pride and excitement that the whole school got up very early and thronged the station to wave her off. Kitty's mother travelled with her daughter and her husband to the first stop; and no doubt much loving advice was given about coping with her new, independent life in the remote, unaccountable, hoity-toity South.

Kay Moore's own schooldays were spent at Oxford High School (1949-59). She went on to St Anne's College, Oxford (1959-62) then to a Graduate traineeship at Harrods for a year. After obtaining her Post Graduate Certificate of Education she joined the English Department at NLCS for five years. In 1968 she married David Moore and her two sons, Toby and Ben, were born in 1969 and 1972. In the 1970s she taught part-time at Mount School, Mill Hill, then 'came home' to NLCS in 1980, where she was appointed Head of Drama 1986-87. (She adores the theatre and organized countless outings for generations of students). She was Head of English 1988-95, and retired in 2001, the same year her granddaughter was born.

Bibliography
Tuchman, Barbara, *The Proud Tower*, Macmillan, 1966.
Thompson, Paul, *The Edwardians*, Weidenfeld, 1975.
Family History Magazine, various issues.
Girls' Public Day School Trust 1872-1972, *A Centenary Review*, 1972.
Kelly's Directory, various issues.
Cowley, Barbara, 'Childhood in Saltburn', *The Dalesman*, February 1970.

Interview, aged seven

I clearly remember my interview with Dame Kitty at the age of seven, about a year before she retired. She asked me to read an excerpt from *The Wind in the Willows* and I informed her that I had read that story the year before. She then gave me another book to read from (I believe it was *Alice In Wonderland*) and I made a similar comment. After that we had a lovely discussion about the books I was reading at the moment. I felt very comfortable with her kind smile and lively dancing eyes.

Miss Gare would have vouched for the fact that I was never a mathematical child; my strength lay in words and I was an avid writer as well as reader from an early age. I shall always be grateful to Dame Kitty for picking that up. When she retired, we were asked to write poems to commemorate the occasion. Mine was selected to be pinned on the board, and when I returned some six years ago for a reunion, I saw to my surprise that it was included in an exhibition.

Jane Bidder (Thomas) 1962-74

At NLCS we were given the idea we could do anything!

I remember my first meeting with Dr Anderson at my interview for the Junior School, Form One. I was seven. I had to read a poem about a bird. There were references to various colours in the poem — the impressions the fledgling had of egg, nest, sky and so on. I recall parts of our conversation even now, fifty years later. She seemed a kind and interesting person to a small girl, not at all inhibiting or frightening.

My memories of NLCS, where I spent ten years of my life, are very happy; I am sure the respect in which the Headmistress was held contributed in large measure to the sense of security we seemed to feel. In retrospect it seems like a charmed life: childhood games on Terrace and the freedom to roam in the extensive grounds, so many friendships, lots of clubs and societies, visiting speakers such as Anthony Wedgwood Benn and A.J. Ayer, and of course the teaching which we all took for granted. I was particularly impressed by the fact that at the end of each Christmas term, as the whole school filed out of the Hall, Dame Kitty shook each girl by the hand. There were about 850 all told, and we felt she knew each one of us personally.

Later, when I became Senior Prefect, I came to realise how much she cared about the individual, not just those girls who caused little trouble, but also the rebels and dissidents. It was probably easier in some ways to be a teenager in those years, but now, as a teacher myself, I am well aware how challenging the job is, apart from the enormous responsibilities of Headship. Even at her busiest, Dr Anderson made time to teach the subject she loved, History, and to lead discussion of Current Affairs in the Sixth Form.

In many ways the North Londoners were Dame Kitty's family. She was dedicated to the cause of women's education and a member of a number of important and influential committees. These responsibilities led to the award of the DBE in my final year, an honour that she made clear she felt she shared with the school. Characteristically, she invited Brenda Barrett, the School Captain, and me, as Senior Prefect, together with Miss Gossip, Miss Dobson and the Chairman of the Governors, Canon Carpenter, to join her at Buckingham Palace after the investiture and then to lunch, together with her brothers, at the University Women's Club. Her committee duties took her away from school quite a lot in my Sixth Form years, but gave her a high profile and a useful platform for her ideas. She advocated equality of opportunity, not just for boys and girls, but for people regardless of their background. I found it quite surprising when I taught in mixed and boys' schools later on, that there were people who actually regarded women as inferior! It seemed to me at NLCS that we were given the idea we could do anything! Dame Kitty was just as delighted by the success of a girl who became a top model as she was by academic stars. I think she was well aware of the challenges society would present to women of the future. I feel fortunate to have known her and it seems to me that her influence on the School and its pupils was very positive.

P. Jane Ross (Kenyon) 1951-62

A ghost well and truly laid to rest

I joined NLCS when I was seven. I had been attending a girls' school in Hampstead that had a fine academic record. However, my mother always hoped I'd eventually get into the North London Collegiate School — she had fallen in love with the exquisite gardens at Canons, the beautiful eighteenth-century house and the easy, happy atmosphere. But most of all she was hugely impressed by the little Yorkshire Headmistress, Dr Anderson.

Aged seven, I did not share my mother's optimism. My Hampstead school was run by a woman who controlled it with the tenacity and venom of a spider in her web. If that sounds harsh, it is because my memories of her sadism are still fresh in my mind. We knew that if we were summoned to her study, she would only let us go after we had burst into tears. We passed on the advice to each other, as little girls do: 'The sooner you cry, the faster you'll get out.' Once when I was laying the table for school dinner, I placed the knives and forks the wrong way round (I am left-handed). I was summoned to the Head's study but stubbornly refused to cry for twenty minutes. She broke me in the end, but I reached a definite conclusion in my mind. I decided that bullies were bad, and headmistresses were the worst bullies of all.

It was, however, her anti-Semitism that caused my parents to remove me from her school. An unwise prejudice to voice in North West London, it was the deciding factor for my family — and off I went for the entrance exam to the enormous school in its glorious grounds. The exam over, I waited for my interview with the Headmistress. I was of course expecting sarcasm, sternness and ritualised humiliation. I couldn't have been more wrong.

Dr Anderson greeted me with a smile. That in itself was unprecedented in my experience. What's more, she had teeth like mine. That cheered me up too. I read to her, and then we had a conversation together. I was hugely impressed by the magnificent cedar I'd seen in the grounds, so she took me by the hand and led me to a window from which I could see a second cedar tree. As we talked, I forgot she was a headmistress. This kindly little woman, full of laughter, gave me more confidence than I knew I could possess.

Many years later, when I was in the Upper Sixth, I remember waiting with the rest of my class outside her room. When eventually she let us in, she apologized for the delay. 'I was interviewing a seven year-old for the Junior School who was so shy it took twenty minutes before she relaxed enough to talk to me,' she told us. She looked reflectively at the huge school block and said, 'I sometimes wonder whether it is too crushing for a little girl like that to be part of a community this big. There really should be different sizes and types of school for every different kind of child.' Now, with children of my own, I appreciate her wisdom.

Dame Kitty taught me at various stages of my school career. One Founder's Day she masterminded the building of a model Tudor street, the highlight of our class exhibition. In the Sixth Form she taught us the value of democracy, urging us not to waste our Vote which had been so hard won. In contrast, she read us Hitler's recipe for effective propaganda, which was never to appeal to the crowd's intellect, always to aim for the lowest common denominator. Today, whenever I see xenophobic newspaper headlines, I remember that lesson.

I wonder how many head teachers these days have the time or the inclination to carry on teaching — I believe this was one of the secrets of Dame Kitty's inspired leadership. Another was her incredible memory, not only for present pupils and Old North Londoners, but for their parents and boyfriends. She was no snob — not even an intellectual one. When I was preparing for the Oxbridge entrance exams, she was just as enthusiastic about my ability to bake a fruit cake as to translate Virgil, and where other members of staff made it clear they disapproved of my extra-curricular activities, Dame Kitty egged me on. In that final, fraught term while we were desperately preparing for Oxbridge interviews, I wrote a pantomime, *Cinderfella;* I'm told it pioneered the scurrilous tradition of *The Canons Follies*. Dame Kitty, who hated exams and encouraged us to take as few as possible, loved the irreverence of creating a daft pantomime to take our minds off our anxiety.

Dame Kitty was of course a serious academic. She loved History and communicated that passion. She ardently believed that women could and should fulfil their ambitions no matter how unprecedented and pioneering these might be. But she was never earnest or pompous. In one lesson she described to us her own interview for the job at NLCS, how she had bought a smart new hat for the occasion, and carefully wound her chignon over the back of the brim to hold it in place. At the end of her interview she was dismayed to be asked: 'We wondered whether you would be so kind as to remove your hat so that we may see your face more clearly.' She described desperately unwinding her hair and trying to find ways of surreptitiously re-pinning it so as to remain tidy, as befits a headmistress.

I bless the Governors who had the intelligence and foresight to appoint the little Yorkshire woman with buck teeth. She created a caring, happy community in the school without piling on pressure. (The School Inspectors in my time remarked on the fact that NLCS had a shorter working day than any other equivalent school.) She applauded innovation but as a historian always did so within the context of the School's heritage. And above all, for me, she laid to rest the ghost of that sadistic, intimidating headmistress I had known.

Esther Rantzen 1947-59

2

'Seventeen is much too young': Kitty Anderson, student of history

CAROLINE M. BARRON

In September 1920 I was fortunate enough to be awarded a North Riding scholarship. I was still at school (a small maintained girls' grammar school) and had made no university applications. My Head Mistress was a former student of Royal Holloway College — so my parents, after consulting with her, wrote to the Principal of the College asking whether I might become a student. I well remember the Saturday at the end of September when I had a telegram offering me a place and inviting me to go up to the College as a student the following Thursday. I was a schoolgirl on the Saturday and a student the following week — no entrance examination, no interview and for me my first visit to London! There followed for me four wonderful years; a new and exciting world such as I had never believed possible was opened up.[1]

This is how Kitty Anderson wrote of the start of her University career forty-three years later when she gave the Fawcett Lecture at Bedford College in 1963. The arrival of the telegram and her precipitate departure for Royal Holloway were events of immense significance to Kitty. Until the end of her life she preserved the telegram and the letters that were exchanged between her father (clearly a very strong influence in her life) and Miss Higgins, the Principal of Royal Holloway.[2] In fact the story was slightly different in that Kitty's father, on learning, early in September, that

---

[1] Kitty Anderson, *Women and the Universities: A Changing Pattern*, Fawcett Lecture, Bedford College, 1963, p 13.
[2] N[orth} L[ondon] C[ollegiate] S[chool] Archives, Anderson File marked 'First Degree'.

Scholarship girl

she had been awarded a scholarship wrote at once to Miss Higgins (with whom he had earlier been in correspondence about a place for Kitty at Royal Holloway) who replied in her own hand that it would be unlikely that they would have a place that September and that there was a waiting list. She asked Kitty to wait a year, and in any case she added, 'seventeen is *much* too young to come to a residential college'. Fifteen days later a place materialised, Miss Higgins overcame her scruples, and the telegram was sent. On 28 September Mr Anderson accepted the place for his daughter and she arrived at the College on Thursday 30 September, brought by her father.[3]

When I was at NLCS in the 1950s we knew the outline of this story, if not the details. We knew that 'DA' was the first member of her family to go to University and that this had only been made possible by the award of a scholarship. At Royal Holloway College she read history and then went on to study for a doctorate in history: as our headmistress she was 'Dr Anderson', and on Founder's Day she wore the claret-coloured robes of a doctor of the University of London. We knew, also, that she had carried out her doctoral research on the administration of the poor law in Elizabethan

---

[3] NLCS Archives, Anderson File marked 'First Degree'. On 1 October 1920, Miss Higgins wrote to Mr Anderson to say: 'I forgot to tell you yesterday' about how he should pay the additional £20 in fees.

London, for the history of London crept often into our lessons and discussions with her.

The story was unique for us because it was Kitty Anderson's story: but how did her university career — and her later teaching career — compare with those of her contemporaries? Where did she fit into the patterns of women's education in the years following the Great War? What made her stand out and at what point did her career accelerate so that she came to hold such important positions later in her life? Was it possible to go back beyond the distinguished headmistress to catch sight of the eager young Yorkshire woman in 1920? What did she do in those 'four wonderful years' at university? How did she come to study for a doctorate? It is possible to attempt to answer some of these questions because the surviving records of Royal Holloway (now Royal Holloway and Bedford New College), University of London, are unusually rich and complete. There are remarkably detailed admissions registers listing all the girls who entered the College, with information about their parents and their occupations, their home addresses, educational qualifications, scholarships, courses and achievements. In addition there is a single sheet for almost every student that provides similar material but is more informal: recorded are details about 'Health and Games' and 'Social Life' and, of particular interest, a list of the friends of that student. Then there are minute books of student societies and volumes of photographs. Finally, the printed College calendars record details of the subsequent careers of the students, or at least some of them.[4]

Putting all this material together it begins to be possible to get Kitty Anderson into focus and to see her through the eyes, and in the context of her contemporaries.

Kitty Anderson came from the small town of Saltburn-by-the-Sea in the North Riding of Yorkshire where she attended the Girls' High School, a small maintained girls' grammar school. She was one of only seven pupils in the sixth form. Kitty was not unusual in coming to Royal Holloway from such a school: almost all the girls who entered Holloway in the 1920s came from the urban girls' day schools which had been founded at the end of the nineteenth century, schools such as those of the Girls' Public Day School

---

[4] Archives, Royal Holloway, University of London. I am extremely grateful to the archivist, Mrs Nicky Sugar, and to her assistant, Ms Heather Wardle, for their help in providing information for this essay.

Trust or the Frances Mary Buss Foundation. Very few of Kitty's contemporaries had been to girls' boarding schools, or had been educated at home, and in this respect they seem to have been rather different from the girls who went to the women's colleges at Oxford and Cambridge. Again, like most of her contemporaries, Kitty had gained her Higher School Certificate before coming up to College.

The scholarship from the North Riding of Yorkshire awarded to Kitty was worth £100 a year for at least three, and possibly five years. In 1920, Royal Holloway charged fees of £120 a year that covered all expenses except laundry, medical attendance (although there was a College nurse) and fees to enter University examinations. Special subjects such as music, painting and laboratory materials cost additional sums. Many of the students were at College on scholarships, provided either by their local education authorities or by the College. In Kitty's year, twenty-nine (56%) of the girls had scholarships of some kind: some held several.[5] The College awarded eighteen entrance scholarships or bursaries worth £30 to £60, and Kitty and fifteen others held scholarships from their local education authorities. Kitty's award, of £100 for a possible five years, was one of the more generous. Some girls had awards from city livery companies or other charitable trusts, or leaving scholarships from their schools. Clearly, Kitty's father would have had to make some contribution to the cost of sending her to College: there were the fares between Yorkshire and London, her clothing and pocket money, and, of course, the £20 difference between her scholarship and the fee to be paid each year. Kitty, moreover, had two younger brothers who were still at school. But Mr Anderson was evidently a successful chartered accountant; although the family was not wealthy, they were careful and comfortable. The award of the county scholarship made it possible for Kitty to attend Royal Holloway, which would have been more expensive than a local, non-residential university. However, judging by Mr Anderson's intense interest in his daughter's education, he would certainly have ensured that she received some further training after leaving school.

Kitty's year at Royal Holloway — those who entered in 1920 — was very small (which may explain why they accepted her so easily without an interview and so late). There were only fifty-two students in all, whereas in

---

[5] In 1919-1920, 30 (46%) girls had scholarships, 18 from the College, 16 from Local Education Authorities and 7 girls held other awards.

most years the numbers were somewhere in the sixties. It is possible to analyse the social backgrounds of most of the girls who came to Holloway when Kitty did. Two others had fathers who were accountants, and overall, 57% of the fathers were in 'the professions'; 33% were in 'trade', and there were also a railway worker, two farmers and two widows. Obviously these classifications are very imprecise, not least because they depend upon the descriptions of their fathers provided by the girls themselves (or possibly their parents). These percentages remained roughly consistent between 1918 and 1923, and again between 1929 and 1933.[6] The number of girls with working-class backgrounds was very small: never more than one or two a year in the earlier period (and in some years there were none at all). In the later period there were about three a year. As might be expected in the aftermath of the Great War, there were more widows listed in the earlier period. So Kitty's social and economic background was very comparable with that of the other girls who came to study at Holloway in the 1920s.

Again, Kitty was not so exceptional in coming from Yorkshire: there were five other girls from Yorkshire in her 'class'; overall, 19% of the girls came from the northern counties, 19% from the Midlands, 56% from the South-East (which included Surrey itself, London and Middlesex). Only a very few girls came from the South-West and from Scotland, Ireland and Wales. As before, these proportions remained roughly consistent in both the earlier and later periods. It is perhaps interesting that Yorkshire and Lancashire almost always produced more girls for Royal Holloway than the equally populous Midland counties. There were plenty of good girls' schools in the Midland counties, but they must have been choosing other London colleges or, perhaps, their home universities at Birmingham or Nottingham. So Kitty's Yorkshire accent would not have made her feel out of place or uncomfortable.

Kitty's particular friends well exemplify the College community in the early 1920s.[7] Winifred Reeve came from Essex where she had attended Romford High School. Her father was a solicitor. Agnes Selman had

---

[6] These figures are based on an analysis of the entries in the Royal Holloway College registers for 1918-1924 and 1928-1933: these two periods were chosen to cover the two periods when Kitty Anderson was a student at Royal Holloway. In the earlier period the percentage of professional fathers ranged from 45% to 62% (average 57%), and in the later period the range was 51% to 69% (average 58%). Those in trade ranged from 26% to 38% (average 33%) and, in the later period, from 21% to 35% (average 31%).

[7] RHUL, Archives. Single sheets of information about each student, RHC AR/201/3.

attended Mary Datchelor School; her father was an outfitter in Denmark Hill, south London. Freda Winter lived in Highgate and attended Kentish Town County Secondary School. Her father was a commercial traveller. Maisie Thomson lived in Dulwich; her father was a chartered accountant. She had attended James Allen's Girls' School. Zadie Craggs went to Sheffield High School; her mother was a widow. Sarah Sissmore's father was an Anglican priest and she had been to Bath High School. The only one of Kitty's friends who had been to a 'private' school was Marjorie Strong, whose father was a solicitor in Highgate where she had attended a school called Southwood Hall. Of these seven friends, four read English, two read History, like Kitty, and one read French. Of the seven, only one, Zadie Craggs, is recorded as having been married by 1947, and she is also the only one who appears not to have had a job. The other six had a variety of careers. Only one, Agnes Selman, became a teacher. Thus Kitty's friends at Holloway came from a range of backgrounds and schools: only one of them, as it happens, Zadie Craggs, came from the north of England.[8]

In entering Royal Holloway at the tender age of seventeen, Kitty was rather younger than most of the other women, as Miss Higgins had pointed out to her father. She was enrolled for the Intermediate Arts course, which involved the study of Latin, English, French and History. At the end of her first year Kitty failed Latin and French (this did not form part of the NLCS myth!) and had to retake the course, which she passed in 1922. The intermediate History course had consisted of two lectures a week on 'English History generally' with a prescribed book which in 1920-21 was Isobel Thornley's *England Under the Yorkists* (published in 1920). Once Kitty had surmounted the Intermediate hurdle, in 1922 she moved on to the two-year Honours course. She studied a broad sweep of English History (political and constitutional), European History and the History of Political Ideas. She then chose to study British Colonial History since 1783 and a special subject. A choice of only two special subjects was offered at Royal Holloway: The Minority and Personal Government of Henry III (1216-1258) or the Unification of South Africa. Perhaps her trouble with Latin had discouraged Kitty from the study of medieval history. In any case she chose the South African papers. It was a very staid and traditional history syllabus, laid down by the University of London. The constituent colleges of the University prepared students for the degree examinations conducted by

---

[8] Information derived from the College Register, collated with the later printed annual calendars of Royal Holloway College.

The class of 1921 at Royal Holloway College — * identifies Kitty's particular friends

From left to right
Far Back row   R.E.A. Stuart S.M..Sissmore* K.Selman* W.Reeve* M.E.Browne R.Cary A.E.W.Davies
Back row   M.A.Beggs M.Thompson* F.Winter* E.Cox K.Anderson R.Lees M.Pyke G.Patten A.W.Duncan W.Savill M.Strong* P.Hunt
Middle row   D.Carter D.E.Gillett D.King M.A.White M.P.Ferguson S.Willis D.Dews B.Waddington
Seated (half row) W.M.Pope B.Bartlett V.Barton D.Putnam
Seated (front) B.Rutherford F.W.Margerison W.Hartwell W.Easom E.Fletcher E.M.Clegg Z.Craggs* G.Dyson H.Kayser D.Goyer M.Balch

23

the University, not the Colleges. Kitty would have attended at least six lectures a week in College as well as essay and tutorial classes. But the history students of Royal Holloway were exposed also to other influences; every week they attended the intercollegiate history lectures held in central London. We know that Kitty attended these lectures, since in 1923 she seconded a motion in the College students' meeting to ask Miss Dolling (the immensely imposing secretary to the Governors and, in effect, the business manager of the College)[9] 'why the allowance made for dinner to students who attended lectures in town was only 1/6d while 2/3d was charged for visitors' dinners in College'.[10] The motion was carried, but Miss Dolling's response is not recorded. One day a week the Holloway history students took the train from Egham up to London where they met other students at the Intercollegiate Lectures and 'for other activities'.[11]

Fire practice in the RH quad, 1921

Helen Cam, head of the History department when Kitty arrived at Royal Holloway, left in 1921 to take up a Fellowship at Girton College.[12] It seems to have been her successor, Professor Hilda Johnstone, who played the major part in forming Kitty Anderson as a mature historian. Professor

---

[9] see Caroline Bingham, *The History of Royal Holloway College 1886-1986* (London, 1987), pp 132-4.
[10] RHUL Archives, 8 September 1923, Minute Book of Student meetings, AS/125/10.
[11] Fawcett Lecture, p 13 (see note 1).
[12] see Janet Sondheimer, 'Helen Maud Cam, 1885-1968', Edward Shils and Carmen Blacker, eds., *Cambridge Women: Twelve Portraits* (Cambridge, 1996), pp 93-112.

24

Johnstone's influence must have been considerable since Kitty was to go on (albeit not immediately) to study history at doctoral level. It would be interesting to know what Kitty thought about her teacher and supervisor, but there is no record of this. Hilda Johnstone came to the chair at Royal Holloway from Manchester University via King's College, London. During the Great War she had worked in the War Trade Intelligence Department and she had a wide circle of friends both at home and overseas. At her house in Englefield Green on Sunday afternoons she entertained any students who wished to come along, and was remembered as a warm and friendly hostess, with a wide interest in travel, literature and art. But she was an austere person, with a dominating personality and very high standards: she expected complete commitment to the work in hand. Her own scholarly output was impressive and her teaching lively and demanding. The History results at Royal Holloway improved dramatically after her arrival.[13] There can be no doubt that her scholarship and personality must have had a very considerable influence on Kitty Anderson in her formative years.

Something of the social life of students at Royal Holloway in the twenties is revealed by the minute books of the College meetings (chaired by the Principal, Miss Higgins) and of the Student meetings (chaired by the Senior Student), as well as by reminiscences of former students.[14] Kitty herself described the daily life of a student at Royal Holloway in a letter dated 4 May 1921, which she wrote for the magazine of her old school.[15] The account is a very impersonal one, describing the times of bells, attendance at chapel and lectures, and meals. Kitty noted that at 4pm the students had tea in their studies 'and at this time we visit or entertain one another'. She mentions the Saturday games (hockey, tennis, netball, lacrosse), the two chapel services on Sundays and the music concert at 8pm on Sundays in the College museum. The letter ends 'I remain, yours sincerely, Kitty Anderson': a certain formality which would always be a characteristic of her written, though not her spoken style. The minutes of the Student meetings, however, provide a rather different picture: there is much debate about the

---

[13] The material in this paragraph is based upon a letter, and account of Professor Hilda Johnstone, written by her ex-student from Royal Holloway, Babette Evans (née Roberts) who taught History at the University of Leicester, RHC RF/132/5.
[14] RHUL, Archives, Minute Book of College meetings, AS/100/5; Minute Book of Student meetings, AS/125/10; reminiscences of old students collected by Caroline Bingham in 1986, RHC RF/132/5.
[15] NLCS Archives, Anderson File marked 'First Degree'.

dances, whether men should be invited, and about the excessive number of suet puddings served in the dining hall. There were problems about the use of the sewing machines; in 1921 the departing third-year students gave a foot pump for the bicycle room and a wringer for the laundry room. When the secretary of Ruskin College invited Royal Holloway to send representatives to a conference on 'Higher Education for Working Women' there were no volunteers. There were complaints about those who 'bagged' a bathroom and then did not use it promptly, and protests when Miss Higgins forbade bicycling on Sundays. It appears to have been possible to order breakfast in bed three times a term. The presence of young women servants is an essential part of the picture. In January 1922 the Principal urged the students not to waste food 'especially as it set such a bad example for the maids'. These maids brought hot water to the students' rooms before 7am and then, while the students were in chapel, tidied their studies, cleaned the grates and filled the coal-scuttles.[16] It was a close, secure, regulated world in which the students occasionally protested about the rules. There is very little evidence of concern for issues beyond the college boundary, although there was discussion whether to affiliate to the National Union of Students and the University of London Students' Union.

Kitty does not seem to have been a high profile student. Her first appearance in the minute books comes in the summer of her second year when she was elected one of the six girls to help with the flowers in the Dining Room at Whitsun, and she and her friend Zadie Craggs were elected to the Albums committee, which compiled and wrote the annual student album. A year later, in the summer of 1923, she was proposed as a committee member of the College Union Society, but was not elected. Kitty never held office of any kind during her college career. My guess is that she may have been not only very young but also, perhaps, quite homesick in her first year. She was not particularly musical, nor sporty:[17] she may even have been quite shy. Perhaps she had quite a bit of growing up to do, and the failure in the intermediate exams at the end of her first year must have been a shock to a young woman who had hitherto been successful. It seems that her College career may have got off to a slow start. By her fourth year, however, even though she was not elected to the Student Committee, she

---

[16] RHUL, Archives, copy of letter from Mrs Jean Hope (née Beharell) who was at RHC in 1929-32. See Royal Holloway, *Alumni News, Spring/Summer 2003* (Issue 19).
[17] RHUL, Archives, Kitty Anderson's College record notes under 'Health and Games' that she played hockey and was efficient at sculling.

begins to voice her opinions quite frequently in student meetings. She was elected to the dance committee and was vociferous in proposing that the College should buy a gramophone for use at the dances held in the Picture Gallery: she assured the doubtful that the type of gramophone which they proposed to buy 'was made with a sound box so that it was suitable for a large hall'. When some of the students demurred at the cost, Kitty explained that to purchase such a gramophone would, in the long run, be cheaper than buying printed sheets of dance music since 'a double-sided record could be bought for 3/- while dance music was 2/-'. Perhaps we glimpse already the shrewd business woman who put the finances of NLCS onto a sound basis twenty years later?

Kitty Anderson Ph D
Was this the most prized of all her hats?

In the summer of 1924 Kitty left Royal Holloway with a second-class degree in History: the 'four wonderful years' had come to an end. That year 111 students graduated from the University of London with Honours degrees in History.[18] Of these eight had firsts, sixty-eight had seconds and thirty-five had thirds. Each of the eleven Royal Holloway candidates secured seconds. Bedford College for Women had twenty-seven candidates of whom one secured a first, although seventeen got thirds. But the most striking aspect of this 1924 pass list is the preponderance of female graduates: 77% of the History candidates were women. This imbalance was certainly not to be found later. It may reflect the lingering impact of the losses of the 1914-18 war.

---

[18] NLCS Archives, University of London BA examination pass list 1924, preserved in Anderson File marked 'First Degree'.

After graduating Kitty appears to have spent a year at home 'doing social work in the North Riding, also helping with an election campaign in the same area'.[19] In 1925 she enrolled at the London Day Training College in Southampton Row (the forerunner of the Institute of Education) where she studied full-time for a year for her Teacher's Diploma. The fees were £20 a year, plus a further six guineas payable to the University of London for the examination. Here again it would appear that Mr Anderson paid for his daughter's further training. Teaching posts were scarce and the diploma would considerably improve Kitty's chance of securing one.

In the course she studied teaching methods, especially related to History, Psychology and Hygiene, the Principles and History of Education and the English Educational System.[20] Kitty later recalled this period at the Day Training College when she was taught by 'the great lecturers Dover Wilson, Margaret Punnett, Cyril Burt and Percy Nunn'.[21] Students also undertook teaching practice: three weeks before the course began and then regular teaching days throughout the course, numbering sixty days of teaching practice in all. Kitty did her practice at the Hornsey County Secondary School, where she taught History and English. She seems also to have had some training in Geography. In her final report (signed by Margaret Punnett and Percy Nunn) her teaching was assessed as 'very good' (there were five grades, and this was the second). They reported that she was a student of 'attractive personality, full of enthusiasm which she succeeds in imparting to most of her classes ... Her manner with her classes is bright and alert; her pupils like her and work happily with her'. They also noted that she had taken part in the play produced by the College Dramatic Society.[22] Thus armed, Kitty secured her first post as an assistant mistress at the Craven Secondary School in Hull, a co-educational maintained school.

Kitty Anderson's four years teaching in Hull had an important bearing on her development as a historian. It must have been during this time that she began her work in the archives there. The sixteenth-century judicial and financial records of the city were kept in the Guildhall; it seems likely that

---

[19] NLCS Archives, Dame Kitty Profile: 26 Years as Headmistress by Elizabeth Willatts in *The Time Educational Supplement*, 5 May 1957.
[20] For details of the course at the London Day Training College, I am indebted to Ms Sarah Aitchison, archivist at the Institute of Education. Kitty preserved the exam papers that she took in July 1926: see NLCS Archive, Anderson File marked 'First Degree'.
[21] Profile by Elizabeth Willatts, note 19.
[22] NLCS Archive, Final Training College report, Anderson File marked 'First Degree'.

Kitty read through them during the holidays, collecting the original and interesting material that would form the basis of her later PhD. Who encouraged her in this work is not known: perhaps Professor Johnstone had realised that Kitty could move beyond the BA and undertake research. Or it may have been Harry Shoosmith, Headmaster at the Craven Street School, who advised her to take this step. A further influence may have come from her friend Margaret Yates who had followed Kitty from Saltburn High School to Royal Holloway to read History. She had gained a second-class degree in History in 1926 and had gone straight on to read for a doctorate. After two years, however, she left Royal Holloway to take up a number of interesting jobs and did not complete her doctorate until 1935.[23] Whatever the influences, it seems that the desire to pursue this research triumphed over the desire to teach: in 1930 Kitty returned to Royal Holloway as a graduate student. It is not clear how this first year of research was funded; the College charged resident postgraduates £112 a year, but there was a reduction for graduates of the College, who were charged only £105. Perhaps Kitty had been able to save money from her teacher's salary to pay for this year of research; possibly her family once more came to her help.

In 1930 Kitty successfully completed her preliminary research and competed successfully for one of the two Christie Scholarships in History awarded by Royal Holloway. There were three candidates: the other two each took three written examinations, but Kitty wrote a report on her research for which she was awarded a mark of A-. The Christie Scholarship was worth £60 a year over two years, so this must have helped to fund Kitty's research for a doctorate, although clearly it did not cover all her expenses.

The doctorate was a degree comparatively new to British universities. It was to be awarded after a period of at least two years of full-time work

---

[23] RHUL, Archives, information on Margaret Yates derived from the College Entrance Register, her student record sheet and the published College calendars. At College she had a much more glittering career than Kitty: she played many sports, was involved in numerous activities and became the Senior Student, 1926-27. On her record sheet it is noted that she was 'most able, speaks well at meetings, good looking'. Margaret Yates became the private secretary to the British Minister in Cuba, assistant mistress at the North London Collegiate School and at Bromley High School, lecturer at the Lincoln Training College, all before 1934, when she was appointed Headmistress of Newcastle Church High School. It is not surprising that she did not have time to finish her thesis. During the war she was the Chief Staff Training Officer at the Ministry of Labour. After the war she was appointed Headmistress of the New Grammar School at Gateshead.

devoted to advanced study or research. The University of London first awarded doctoral degrees in 1921 to sixteen candidates, only one of them an historian. By 1933 two hundred doctorates were being awarded each year.[24] Out of Kitty's year of fifty-one students at Royal Holloway, six came back to do graduate work (two in History, two in English, one in Physics and one in Chemistry). Although the numbers of History PhDs at London University rose in the next thirty years, between 1921 and 1965 Royal Holloway produced only three successful History doctoral students, so Kitty Anderson and Margaret Yates must have appeared exceptional.[25] During the 1930s there were probably six to ten graduate students living at Royal Holloway in any one year. It may seem strange that a woman in her late twenties, who had lived the independent life of a teacher for four years, should have chosen to return to the enclosed world of the Royal Holloway College community. The issues that concerned the students were much as before: problems about the bathrooms and the food, the desire for a cigarette machine in College, and a petition to Miss Higgins to be allowed not to wear stockings in the College grounds. The departing students gave sewing machines and drying racks and wringers to the College.[26] Yet it is clear that Kitty was both happy and successful. Another graduate student at the time remembers her 'gusty zest and confidence. She enjoyed everything, but always with a sense of proportion and a hearty north-country commonsense'. This friend remembered also her hospitality and her 'sense of fitness': both characteristics that would be much in evidence when she became a headmistress.[27]

It is possible to recreate something of the lifestyle of a postgraduate student in History in the 1930s. Kitty had chosen to study the treatment of vagrancy and the relief of poverty in the Tudor period in Hull and also in London. Much of her time must have been spent travelling up to the City where she made extensive use of the Record Office of the Corporation of London at the Guildhall. In a new search room opened in 1929, she was recorded as a reader throughout 1930–34. Here she had access to the

---

[24] Negley Harte, *The University of London 1836-1986* (London, 1986), p 200.
[25] see Irena Nicoll, 'A Statistical Profile of the London PhD in History 1921-90', *Oxford Review of Education* (1996), p 22, pp 273-94, esp. pp 278-79. Bedford College and Westfield College produced 4 PhDs each, but 36 women completed PhDs at the four larger mixed colleges in this period.
[26] RHUL, Archives, Student meeting book 1929-35, AS 125/13.
[27] NLCS School magazine, 1965. Special number, supplement on Dame Kitty, p 2.

detailed records of the government of London in the sixteenth century. It was very much a man's world, presided over by the learned Deputy Keeper, A.H.Thomas.[28]

In addition to long hours in the Record Office, Kitty attended seminars at the Institute of Historical Research, set up in 1921 to facilitate and, perhaps, professionalise, historical research in London University. It was to be a 'workshop' or a 'laboratory' for historical research, albeit housed in a makeshift hut for the first fifteen years of its life.[29] Seminars which, in the words of A.F. Pollard, were to achieve 'cooperation and discussion' among the students themselves,[30] were held every evening between four and six. Kitty, in her first year, attended a seminar run by Hilary Jenkinson on 'Practical Work in Archives' on Monday evenings; a seminar run by Dr Eliza Jeffries Davies on London History on Wednesdays; and two seminars on Thursdays — Professor Johnstone's English Medieval History, followed by Canon Claude Jenkins's seminar on Latin palaeography. Over the next two years she attended only the seminars of Dr Jeffries Davies and Professor Johnstone. The attendance registers reveal that the numbers at these seminars were small: only four to six at Professor Johnstone's seminar that Kitty rarely missed. Her attendance at the London History seminars was not so faithful: she might miss a quarter to a third of these in a year. At these London seminars several post-graduate students were to become very well-known historians: Marjorie Honeybourne, the learned topographer of medieval London; Sylvia Thrupp, whose book, *The Merchant Class of Medieval London*, published in 1948, is still an invaluable paperback; the American scholar, W.K. Jordan, who wrote seminal books on the practice of philanthropy in Tudor and Stuart London; and N.G. Brett James, who wrote on the expansion and topography of seventeenth-century London.[31] So Kitty could rely on the community at Royal Holloway, and the smaller, more focussed community of history scholars at the Institute, to provide her with companionship and support. In June 1933, the College was allowed a limited number of tickets for students to attend the ceremony for the laying

---

[28] I am very grateful to the City Archivist, James R. Sewell, for help in tracking Kitty Anderson down in the Corporation of London Records Office in the 1930s.
[29] Debra Birch and Joyce M.Horn, comps, *The History Laboratory: the Institute of Historical Research 1921-1996* (University of London, Institute of Historical Research, 1996), esp. chap 4.
[30] *Ibid*, p 129.
[31] Institute of Historical Research, Seminar Registers (University College, London; King's College and Royal Holloway College) kept at the Institute.

of the foundation stone of the new University building (the later Senate House) and Kitty was one of the three elected to attend.[32] She belonged both to Egham and to Bloomsbury. She possessed the maturity that derived from working to the demanding timetable of a teacher, the enthusiasm inherent in her nature, and the determination to achieve the doctorate and move on to the next stage of her teaching career. It is not surprising, in the circumstances, that she completed the thesis by the summer of 1933. Hilda Johnstone wrote of her in January 1933: 'As a graduate student, she has done more than merely work hard and with enthusiasm. She has shewn real ability in hunting out and weighing evidence.' Miss Higgins wrote: 'She appears to have original power, and also the patience and industry required for research.'[33]

What was the product of this patience and industry? Kitty Anderson's thesis is an impressive piece of work. It does indeed show originality and very considerable industry. The copy deposited in the Institute of Historical Research is still being consulted: there have been seven readers since 1976.[34] In 1973 the Centre for Research Libraries at Chicago made a microfilm that has doubtless been much used in the United States.[35] The reason the thesis remains of use and interest some seventy years after its completion is because Kitty systematically read through the sixteenth-century administrative records in Hull and in the Corporation of London Record Office, extracting material relevant to the problems of controlling vagrancy and relieving the poor. She looked back to the fourteenth century and traced the development of the policy of the city of London from the aftermath of the Black Death of 1348-49. Here we may detect the influence

---

[32] RHUL, Archives, 23 May 1933. Student meetings minute book 1929-35, AS 125/13.
[33] NLCS Archives: copies of testimonial letters written in January 1933 when Kitty must have been applying for teaching posts, kept in Anderson File marked 'First Degree'.
[34] Listed readers are: 1976 Janice Galletly (Florida University); 1977 J.J.Goring (Goldsmiths' College, London); 1979 G.L.Gronquist (Cambridge University); 1982 Ian Archer (Oxford University); 1983 Gervase Rosser (Bedford College, London); 1991 Johannes Fabricius (Copenhagen); 1992 Mary Erler (Fordham University, NYC). The pages that would have recorded the names of readers before 1976 have, unfortunately, been removed.
[35] The correspondence relating to this was inserted inside Kitty Anderson's own copy of the thesis, given to me after her death. When Dame Kitty granted permission for the microfilm to be made, characteristically she took care to specify that she retained the copyright in the work and also that the cost was to be met by the Centre for Research Libraries, not by herself. She also said: 'I intend to publish my work now that I have some leisure.' Unfortunately, this did not happen.

of Hilda Johnstone, who had herself written about the administration of poor relief in the royal households in the medieval period.[36] The thesis is certainly factual, but it also draws out the distinction (not always clearly perceived at the time) between vagrancy, or voluntary poverty, and poverty which was the result of illness or misfortune. Kitty also demonstrates the way in which Tudor politicians and civic governors gradually came to realise that many men and women were not work-shy, but, rather, work-hungry, and that the real problem lay not in human sin but in the shortage of work. In the only reference to contemporary society in the thesis Kitty wrote that 'in the present age of economic depression when urgent problems of unemployment and poverty are engaging the attention of economists, politicians and all interested in the welfare of society, an age of commissions and reports, it is interesting to look back to the sixteenth century when a very similar situation stimulated general interest and resulted in the rapid development of poor law policy in municipality and state'.[37] For Kitty Anderson the study of the past was a means to understanding the present. The solution, first tried in towns such as London and later in Hull, was to set the poor to work by providing capital for pin-making or knitting, or by setting up workhouses, the first of which was London's Bridewell.

The chronicle of civic ordinances, royal proclamations and Parliamentary statutes does not make light reading: most theses contain a fair amount of tedious material. Indeed, in some ways, that is their value. But Kitty lightens the tale by reference to individual cases she has found in the London records and by an unusual and impressive use of contemporary ballads, printed tracts, sermons and chronicles. In this way she brings the intellectual concerns of the time to bear upon the actual solutions proposed and executed. She gives due weight to external factors which aggravated the problems such as foreign wars, outbreaks of plague, harvest failures and the dissolution of the monasteries. Her analysis of the causes of increased poverty differs from those of contemporary historians in laying very little emphasis upon the massive rise in population which converted an acute labour shortage into a labour glut. The population of London, about 50,000

---

[36] Hilda Johnstone, ' Poor Relief in the Royal Households of Thirteenth-century England', *Speculum* 4 (1929), pp 149-167.
[37] Kitty Anderson, 'The Treatment of vagrancy and the relief of the poor and destitute in the Tudor period, based upon the local records of London to 1552 and Hull to 1576' (London University PhD, 1933), 1-2.

in 1500, rose to 200,000 by 1600. But she is ahead of her time in choosing to focus her attention upon 'social history', and in considering the ways in which the local government in towns attempted to tackle the serious problems they faced.

In form the thesis looks and feels much more like my own thesis of 1970, than those presented for examination in the University of London today. The paper is the old quarto size, it is typed and the duplicate copies are carbon ones. Kitty's thesis is a far cry from the modern word-processed volumes. But it is by no means a casual or sloppy piece of work. The typist appears never to have made any mistakes and there are only a couple of places where Kitty has forgotten to add in the page references. It is a highly-polished professional job, and a real credit to Kitty herself and to her supervisor, Hilda Johnstone, who was noted for her ferocious concern for accuracy. In some ways this thesis has some of the characteristics of a continental thesis (on which English doctorates were originally modelled): there are ninety pages of transcribed documents to demonstrate the candidate's mastery of palaeography and to substantiate the arguments. Moreover, the bibliography is divided into different kinds of material, rather in the style of the annotated French bibliographies. London history theses have now shed these continental practices!

The examiners for the thesis appear to have been Eliza Jeffries Davies, the Reader in London History at University College and Conrad Gill, an economic historian and Professor at the University of Hull.[38] The copy of the thesis that was returned to Kitty has a few pencil markings made by an examiner: mostly trivial points, but the examiner was concerned that Kitty did not always date the contemporary ballads that she cited. But in a thesis of some 500 pages, this examiner pencilled in only six comments.[39] Overall the thesis is a thoroughly sturdy piece of work, and bears considerable

---

[38] The examiners were appointed on 5 May 1933 and the successful outcome of the examination was reported to the Senate on 19 July 1933; see University of London Archive, Minutes of the Board of Studies in History, AC 8/27/1/9 and Senate Minutes, ST 2/2/49. The Revd Dr H. Salter from Oxford University was named as an alternative external examiner. I am grateful to the University Archivist, Mrs Judith Etherton, for her help in providing this information. A friend who was a graduate student at the same time recounted how Kitty had come up to her in the British Museum to say that she had spotted the external examiner reading her thesis in the Round Room. See NLCS School magazine, Dame Kitty supplement, p 2 (see note 27).

[39] Copy of the thesis in the possession of the author, see pages 70, 150, 155, 252, 291 and 492. The examiners also wanted the title changed to refer not to 'local records' but to 'municipal records'.

testimony to Kitty's industry, for it was completed and examined within three years. There are few flights of fancy, and it is written in a straightforward way, without literary embellishments. The material is well organised and the structure clear — if, sometimes, a bit pedantic. There is little sense of Kitty's own personality breaking through the text. In her rather formal written style, evident also in her letters, one feels Kitty may have been influenced by her father. But there is no doubt that the thesis was a piece of enduring scholarship of which Kitty was justifiably proud.

Not surprisingly, Kitty secured a job teaching History at the Burlington School for Girls in Boyle Street, near Piccadilly and within six years she was appointed Headmistress of Kings Norton School for Girls, Birmingham. She always hoped to find her way back to historical research, and to publish her earlier work, and it is interesting to observe that while she was teaching in London she made time to attend Professor Johnstone's seminars at the Institute of Historical Research.[40] In the end, however, her demanding and absorbing career led her in other directions.

Many of her contemporaries also became teachers. Among those who graduated from Royal Holloway in the 1920s teaching was far and away the dominant profession, accounting for 75% of those whose careers are known. If we look at those who graduated in the 1930s, the percentage drops to 60%: it is clear that a wider range of jobs was beginning to open up for women. The 1939-45 war further developed the possible careers available. The College calendars, which record the married names of Holloway graduates, suggest that few of Kitty's contemporaries married. Of those who came up between 1918 and 1923 only 34% are recorded as having married, and for those who came up between 1929 and 1933 the figure is 28%. Moreover, none of those who married are recorded as having had a career. It seems clear that in the 1920s and 1930s a university-educated woman had either a career or a marriage, but not both. Kitty Anderson made a brilliant success of her career.

The young Kitty was not an outstanding student as an undergraduate either academically or socially. Miss Higgins may have been right when she said

---

[40] Institute of Historical Research, Seminar Register (Royal Holloway). Kitty attended three seminars in 1936-37, and five in 1938-39.

that seventeen was too young to leave home for College. Yet Royal Holloway did give Kitty the chance to grow up, independently of her close family. She was just beginning to get into her stride in her final year at College and she may then have begun to nurture intellectual ambitions. Here her determination and character came into play. When she secured her first teaching job in Hull she spent her spare time during her four years there in the archives working on the material that was later to form part of her thesis, and thus made possible her return to Royal Holloway to take her historical studies further. Guided by Professor Johnstone, she wrote an efficient and scholarly doctoral dissertation that has stood the test of time.[41] In the thesis she hints at her concern about contemporary social problems, and it may have been this that drew her out of the ivory tower and back into the classroom. Yet her enthusiasm for history was infectious and enduring, and the rigour of her historical training underpinned her later achievements. Throughout her life she remained an enthusiastic historian.

Caroline Barron (Hogarth) was at NLCS 1947-58. Dame Kitty's teaching in the Lower Fourth, and later in the Upper Sixth, was one of the formative influences that led to her reading History at Somerville College, Oxford. She specialised in medieval English history and went on to write her PhD thesis on Medieval London (again perhaps influenced by Dame Kitty's research on Tudor London). Since 1964 she has taught history at Bedford College (now Royal Holloway and Bedford New College) and is currently Professor of the History of London and Dean of the Graduate School. She is married to John Barron (Master of St Peter's College, Oxford). Their daughters, Catherine and Helen, both went to NLCS.

∾

A great persuader all her life

When Dame Kitty arrived at Canons in the autumn of 1944, I was in the Upper Sixth and entering the final year of preparation for the Higher School Certificate. Nowadays the approach of A-levels seems to blight the lives of

---

[41] Babette Evans records that although Professor Johnstone provided excellent training in historical methods, once the research student was launched, she was left to sink or swim: Professor Johnstone was not inclined to nurse the infant thesis — see note 13.

most pupils from September onwards, but we had never been encouraged to think solely in terms of examinations, and our new Headmistress held to that tradition.

In fact, Dr Anderson seemed to be constantly enlisting our time and energies for projects that had nothing to do with 'the syllabus' and everything to do with our development as responsible, aware, outgoing and useful members of the school and the wider community: we were to be feeling and thinking beings. She set us a good example by her boundless energy and enthusiasm and her passionate belief in her ideals. She was a small, not so dormant volcano that was liable to erupt suddenly in the Entrance Hall just as you were relaxing after a class; she'd whisk you off to her room, or engage you there and then in a breathless conversation designed to elicit your reaction to her latest idea and secure your support — which of course she did, every time. You felt privileged to be enlisted; I think none of us realized how well she made use of the prefects and other senior girls. She was a first-class manager, before the word had ever been applied in an educational context. Whenever her name is mentioned, I see a huge smile, a brisk trot (she never seemed merely to walk) and a warm, friendly presence impossible to resist.

Less obvious was her capacity for mastering detail and her decisiveness (not the same thing as enthusiasm). No project was proposed, no idea mooted, I am convinced, without long and careful consideration of the possible implications. Once, when I was in her room, she opened the door of what I had thought was a cupboard, but which proved to be more like a walk-in recess, and showed me a large sheet of paper pinned to the back of the door. It was the school's teaching timetable. I looked at it with deep respect: it resembled a map of the railway system of a major industrial nation, or the battle plan for a particularly involved campaign — which I suppose it was, in its way. It made me realise that there was more to Dame Kitty's success than charm and energy. She had, and gracefully concealed it from us most of the time, a formidable intellect.

If I relate an incident that concerned me personally, it is because I know that it was not unique. Dame Kitty was determined her girls should realize their potential to the full, and she cared equally for every girl's talents, whatever they were. There were problems for some of the most academic of us, however, because many parents did not view university education as the normal route for women. My own parents were divided. My father wanted his daughters to have the university education his own parents had not been able to give him; my mother took the view that education beyond the Sixth Form was unnecessary — if not rather dangerous — for girls.

Dame Kitty summoned them to a meeting, along with my desperate self. She told my mother that I *ought* to go on to university. She made it sound like a moral imperative. My mother finally said that she supposed it might be possible for me to attend London University and live at home. Dame Kitty seemed to grow about twelve inches taller; she shook her head sorrowfully at my mother. 'This girl *must* go to Cambridge', she said. That was the end of the argument, and it taught me that one should never give up one's reasonable goals without a fight. But what was most remarkable was that my mother did not in the least feel that she had been coerced — which taught me that persuasion is the most effective kind of fighting. Dame Kitty was a great persuader all her life.

Norma Rinsler (Lee) 1940-46

~

'On no account should this girl enter university'

I knew from the age of ten that I wanted to spend my life working with books, a decision I came to one day during the London Blitz, when I accompanied my father on a visit to his publishers, Chapman & Hall, not far from the Strand. Somehow I fell in love with the atmosphere of those dusty old offices that Charles Dickens had once visited, where clerks still perched on high stools as they wrote in their huge ledgers. Yes! One day I too would work in a publishing house ... and I would also become a writer myself.

I was always writing: stories, plays, poems. In the Upper Third, one of my stories was accepted for the School Magazine: I awaited the printed copy with desperate impatience. Finally it arrived. My first published work! Eagerly I turned the pages until I found *my story,* a lurid tale about smugglers inspired by one of Robert Louis Stevenson's poems. But as I read it, I became uneasy: surely some of the words were spelled wrong — and wasn't the punctuation all awry? Then I realised that as other people read it, they were laughing ... laughing at *my story!* The Editor, that lofty Prefect, had included it with all my mistakes! She *meant* readers to laugh at it.

'I say, did you *mean* your story to be funny?' my Best Friend asked. She knew I took my writing very seriously. — I lifted my chin. 'Of course I did!', I told her ... and then I went down to the cloakroom in the dungeons to sob my disappointment into my red shoebag. Next day, the Editor approached me and said she should have let me know that she intended to include my story warts and all. It was a sort of apology.

That wound, so deeply felt, proved a useful extra-curriculum lesson. A few years went by, and I became a Prefect, and Editor of the Magazine in my turn. I was very careful to treat every contribution with respect. Over the years this has also applied to the innumerable unsolicited manuscripts that have come to me as a publisher: in today's jargon they are often referred to as 'the slush pile', but I have always regarded them as potential treasure trove.

I enjoyed my decade at school, but I worked only at things that interested me and neglected the hard slog that got you through exams. However, when I reached the Upper Sixth, Dame Kitty thought I should attempt Oxbridge entrance. I especially enjoyed my tutoring sessions with Miss Scrimgeour, who introduced me properly to Jane Austen — reading *Pride and Prejudice* at snail pace in the Lower Fourth didn't really count. (In 1980, my novel *Jane Austen In Australia* was published by Secker & Warburg, an end product of those sessions.) But as usual I slacked off in other subjects. Dame Kitty was disappointed when I failed to gain university entrance, but she was determined to persevere with me. She arranged an informal interview at St Hilda's College, Oxford, with Dr (later Dame) Helen Gardner, the distinguished academic and Old North Londoner, who gave me a thimbleful of sherry in her room and engaged me in conversation. She then reported our meeting to Dame Kitty: '...*on no account should this girl enter a university*', she wrote, a message DK duly passed on to me. At the time I felt somewhat miffed: but in fact, as I soon acknowledged to myself, Dr Gardner was quite right. I was a 'hands-on' person: I needed to become part of the wide world of work to show what I was made of.

Dame Kitty did not give up. She arranged another meeting for me, this time with the legendary editor and publisher Grace Hogarth, whose daughter Caroline was at school. (The same Professor Caroline Barron who has contributed the piece about Kitty Anderson, Student of History, for this book.) It was Grace Hogarth who really introduced me to publishing when I worked for her in her home office at Hampstead for a short while as an inexpert secretary, taking away with me each day the spoiled letters I had mistyped and crumpled up. After completing a secretarial course I gained entrance to Oxford University Press, where I received a thorough grounding in all aspects of publishing — I even became expert at arithmetic and algebraic equations when I was given book estimates to work out in the Production Department, engaged on a task involving real pounds, shillings and pence instead of working out how long it would take X, Y and Z to fill a mythical swimming pool! Finally I graduated as a junior editor.

As Dame Kitty had divined, Real Life was the right course for me. I wrote in my spare time, and as I turned twenty-four, OUP published my first book, *Scottish Folk Tales & Legends,* and then I had my first teenage historical novels published. — And yes, it was Dame Kitty who had fired my enthusiasm for History, both ancient and modern. It was only later that I realised the vital role my Headmistress played in my life. She did not abandon me as an academic failure but set me on track for a wonderful working life.

Barbara Ker Wilson, 1938-48

Crunch Time

'What's this all about?' My father had received the letter from Dame Kitty requesting a meeting to discuss my future. Art had always been my natural expression — my destiny — but for the parents of a wayward seventeen-year-old beatnik folk-singer, Art school was definitely NOT on the agenda. Instead they proposed secretarial college, which they hoped might lead to marriage to a successful professional boss! Anathema!

It was only through Dame Kitty's persuasive powers that I was still at school to take A-levels, having intended to leave after O-levels to escape from the uniform and the discipline. I did so well in the exams she flattered me into staying on 'to consolidate your success'. Now it was crunch time. I could NOT face the envisaged future. Did she think I could apply for University? Maybe read French? She wrote in my testimonial: 'Susan seems to have identified herself with things French!' I'd fallen in love with a French boy when I was fifteen. The infatuation coloured my existence. She never missed a thing. I told her my parents had never thought of me going to University (nor had I hitherto) and they might prove difficult to persuade. Hence the letter. In 1961, parents held teachers, particularly Dame Kitty, in high esteem. It was devious of me to go behind their backs but I knew she could prevail where I would fail.

I sat outside her office while discussions took place. Finally, beaming, with a wonderful twinkle in her eye she beckoned me in. I entered, not daring to look at my parents. Instead I studied the flowers of the lovely handwoven rug on the floor. 'Well, Susan, we have reached a compromise — your parents will agree to your attending University on condition that you take a secretarial course first.' I felt a great sense of relief but no great triumph. Art was still my dream, reluctantly abandoned. I dropped out of the secretarial course after two terms preferring to busk in Paris and pursue the bohemian life of a (pseudo) artist.

In 1962, I took up the place offered following an interview at the new University of Sussex. I threw myself into student life. I ran the Folk Club, designed posters, organised pottery classes, acted in plays, performed in revues — and true to form I dropped out — twice. On the second and final occasion the Vice-Chancellor, Sir John Fulton, who was a friend of Dame Kitty's, called me into his office. 'What went wrong?', he asked sadly. 'You were one of our brightest hopes.'

I think Dame Kitty would have understood. Her underlying confidence in me gave me courage and eventually, under my own steam, I found my way home to Art. In 1983, established as a potter, self-sufficient and finally fulfilled, I was invited by Mrs Keightley to teach pottery part-time at NLCS for six weeks at the end of the summer term 'to help out in an emergency'. Petrified, I agreed. I left in the year 2000, having taught under three headmistresses.

I learned, I hope, how to become a good teacher. I treated my students with respect, fired them with enthusiasm, encouraged them to be true to themselves but always with consideration for others and ultimately to give to society at large.

Recently, looking through a magazine from my schooldays, I came across one of Dame Kitty's Founder's Day addresses. Years of Founder's Days (I entered NLCS in Form I) had left me jaded. I'd stare out at the pond while the songs were sung and the addresses read – in a world of my own, or so I thought! The philosophy and principles that have guided and illuminated my life and become 'My own' were all there — HER words. What a wonderful gift. I thank and bless her.

Susan Bennett (Rose) 1950–61 and 1983 – 2000

3

Craven Street, Burlington, King's Norton — Kitty Anderson's teaching career before she arrived at the North London Collegiate School

KATHARINE McMAHON

In 1926, when Kitty Anderson applied for her first job, teaching was an overcrowded profession. Fortunately her only criterion in choosing a school was that it should be co-educational: in this respect at least the Craven Street Higher Grade School, Hull, fitted the bill.

'When she arrived and saw the old unprepossessing building she went on to the interview with mixed feelings. On meeting Mr Shoosmith [the Head Teacher] and Archdeacon Lambert [Chairman of the Board] she decided that human beings were more important than buildings. Accepting the post, she began ... her life's work.'[1]

Craven Street School was situated in a damp street of terraced houses and the school buildings were excessively inconvenient. To reach the Cookery room or Science labs, pupils and teachers had to cross a wet and windy yard. If anyone was foolhardy enough to switch on the light in the bicycle shed they were likely to receive an electric shock. There was a thin partition between the hall, where music lessons took place, and neighbouring classrooms, which led to a degree of conflict between exuberant music teachers and those trying to teach English grammar next door. The playing fields, between the Crematorium and the Isolation Hospital, were a tram ride away.

Only the school uniform sounds truly robust, with the girls sporting pork-pie hats in winter and straw 'bangers' in summer, box-pleated gymslips and black stockings. The boys, of course, wore the school cap, of which they were extremely proud.

---

[1] Professor F.W. Land, citation for the presentation of Dame Kitty Anderson at the University of Hull, 8 July 1967.

The Craven Street School had been established in 1893 to provide education for children above the normal school leaving age (eleven when the school opened). The education was not free — parents paid a guinea a term — but there were scholarships. As a result there was a truly eclectic mix of pupils, 'some from appalling circumstances [as we would consider today]; fathers with large families who didn't work because the dole was greater than any wage they could earn ... '[2]

The school was divided into two sections: boys upstairs, girls downstairs, each with a Head master or mistress. In the Fifth Form boys and girls shared strictly segregated classrooms, boys on one side, girls on the other.

Kitty starts work!

At the time of Miss Anderson's appointment there were great changes afoot. She seemed to have the knack of joining schools when they were in the throes of upheaval. The Head Teacher, Mr Shoosmith, had realized that the buildings could no longer accommodate the needs of a modern school and had found a new site on parkland. Like so many school building projects, the work took far longer than expected and past pupils wistfully remember having to buy penny bricks for the much anticipated move to the new site, which never happened for them during their school careers. The new school, with its south-facing rooms and view of park and lake, finally opened in 1932, two years after Kitty Anderson's departure. Perhaps, when she first saw the North London Collegiate School at Canons she was reminded of Mr Shoosmith's wonderful vision.

Harry Shoosmith, appointed Head in 1922, was an inspiring and dynamic character. He and the young Miss Anderson took to each other

[2] Frank Moss, pupil at Craven Street School 1927-34.

immediately. During her interview Shoosmith asked her if she could manage boys. — 'Well, sir, I've no sisters, only brothers and I manage them ... ' she replied.[3]

Kitty's niece, Mary Anderson, remembers that in the same interview she was informed that swimming lessons were part of the job description: '"But I can't do that, I can't swim", Kitty said in horror. [Evidently living beside the sea had not included venturing into the water to swim.] — "Nonsense — you're a teacher, aren't you?", Shoosmith demanded. After her appointment she went to the library, found a book on learning to swim, and successfully taught her classes from the side of the pool, shouting out instructions.'[4]

Typically, young Miss Anderson not only taught swimming, she turned a potential weakness into a triumph. Years later, in the reference he provided for her application to NLCS, Shoosmith observed: 'her work in connection with the Voluntary Girls' Swimming Club was invaluable ...'

Kitty's rapport with Shoosmith had a far-reaching effect on her career in education, and in those first years as a young teacher she formed her fundamental ideas about how a good school should be run. 'These four years helped to mould my life and establish my philosophy of education,' she wrote later.

'In Hull she learned the importance of the influence of the Head, the value of Staff cooperation, the enjoyment of teaching.'[5]

Shoosmith wanted to make higher education accessible to more pupils, and fought to have the number of university scholarships in Hull increased from two to twelve. He was not afraid to speak his mind. One former pupil, Edith Metcalf, remembers him saying that it is better to know five or six books thoroughly from cover to cover, than to read hundreds in a superficial way.

Like his new teacher, Miss Anderson, Shoosmith was not one to rest on his dignity. At a school Sketch Club meeting he was quite happy to don a kimono.

There are few personal memories of Kitty at this time, but according to

---

[3] Dame Kitty Anderson, in a speech made to Kings Norton Boys' School, c 1944.
[4] Mary Anderson, 'Accounts of Aunt Kitty', 8 November 2001.
[5] Supplement to *Dialogue*, Schools Council Newsletter.

one 'old boy'[6] the young blonde teacher caused hearts to flutter when she taught the Sixth Form boys. There is an appealing photograph showing her curled up and looking confident in the front row of a staff group. She sports a cloche hat with a floral pattern round the band and a fashionable coat with a fur collar.

The testimony of past pupils speaks of a happy and well-run school, though it contained the usual selection of eccentric teachers, including a Mr Batty who was very free with the cane. There was a full range of extra-curricular activities, sport and drama being especially popular.

Kitty's success in her new career is best summed up by Shoosmith's reference dated 1 February 1944 for her application to NLCS: 'I can say without hesitation that Dr Anderson's work gave complete satisfaction in every detail. As form mistress her influence was admirable. Her discipline was excellent and easily maintained, her classes were stimulated by her refreshing personality, her work was most carefully prepared, whilst her successes in the School Certificate Examination were highly gratifying.'

Harry Shoosmith sent Kitty a letter of congratulation on her appointment to her first headship at Kings Norton School. It is a measure of their relaxed and friendly relationship: 'Dear Doc,' he begins, 'Very hearty congratulations indeed, especially to Kings Norton school ... '

Life outside school seems to have been just as lively for Kitty, especially during the holidays. Her old bedroom in Saltburn where she still kept many of her books was always ready for her and she would often make up a foursome with her parents and brother Walter on the golf course. 'We were none of us any good', Walter remembered ruefully. He added: 'Until shortly before the war the family always went together for their annual holiday. Frequently these would be to resorts in Scotland where there was an opportunity to play golf. On several occasions Kitty's friend Ingrid Fernyhough joined us on these holidays.' In 1928 the family cruised to the Canaries, in 1929 to Morocco. Given the woefully low salaries of classroom teachers (at Craven Street Kitty earned £210 a year) it is likely that such holidays were subsidised by her parents.

Although Kitty enjoyed her years at Craven Street, which undoubtedly provided an excellent training ground, she stayed at the school only four

---

[6] Albert Royle, cited in a letter from Geoff Bell, 18 December 2001.

years. Perhaps, inspired by Shoosmith and her love of teaching, she had already set her mind on becoming a headmistress and knew that she could not afford to stay too long in her first post.

Perhaps, too, she was influenced by another powerful Hull personality, Archdeacon Joseph Malet Lambert, a prominent clergyman and leader of social reform in the city … though by the time Kitty knew him he had apparently become 'ultra-reactionary and a great snob'.[7] In his heyday, however, Malet Lambert was a benefactor and social reformer, as well as an enthusiastic educationalist. Above all he was concerned for the plight of the poor in Hull and the conditions in which they lived. He worked on improving sanitation and hospitals. It may have been in part due to his influence that Kitty was inspired to write her PhD thesis.

A second, more modest benefactor, T.R. Ferens, a Member of Parliament, gave large sums of money for the building of the Art Gallery, and to Hull University College. These elderly men were quite distant figures to the young teacher at Craven Street, but they were very prominent examples of those who are not afraid to seek change and try to make a difference within the community. The Craven Street School seems to have been steeped in an awareness of Hull's past. Mr Sheppard, son of a former Headmaster, was the curator of the Hull Museums and probably keen to share his knowledge of local history with the enthusiastic young History teacher.

So Kitty decided to move on and take the unusual step — especially for one so practical and skilled at teaching — of returning to full-time study. Shoosmith, ever the optimist and encourager, wrote in the reference he supplied for her NLCS application: '… although I greatly deplored her loss to the school, I could not but approve the step she was taking.'

After she completed her PhD, Kitty Anderson was again on the hunt for a teaching position. This time she was appointed Head of History at London's Burlington School, in Boyle Street, Piccadilly. Her letter of appointment, dated May 1933, states that she was to teach History throughout the school, be form mistress of the Upper Fifth and give classes in Geography to the Third and Lower Fourth Forms.

Burlington was an old-established girls' charity school with a very different ethos to the hurly burly of Craven Street, Hull. Although it was

---

[7] Gillet, Edward, *A History of Hull*.

situated in central London there was a healthy mix of nationalities. The Head Teacher was Miss Marion Burgess. Certainly Dr Kitty Anderson's enthusiasm and vivacity made an extraordinary impression on pupils and staff, although a colleague describes the humorous, urbane atmosphere of the staff room as 'stemming partly from Miss Burgess's inimitable courtesy and gracious sophistication'. Kitty was probably bursting with energy after spending three years in academia, which may have seemed rather dull compared to the cut and thrust of the classroom. The words 'inspirational', 'fun', 'lively' recur time after time in recollections of her. Any teacher of our twenty-first century would be proud to receive the kind of accolades showered on Kitty Anderson for her skills in the classroom. Her exuberance must have been all the more exciting for pupils accustomed to rote learning and copying out exercises. She was also famous for her tea-parties, and for being the driving force behind a staff drama production of *Arms and the Man*.

Meanwhile, in the frightening world beyond the microcosm of school, Italy invaded Abyssinia. Kitty Anderson didn't flinch from encouraging the girls to discuss international issues: '... she made everyone feel involved and responsible', May Eppel, a former pupil, observes. Dr Anderson also ran the Current Affairs Society, in which Communism and Fascism were explored.

Kitty Anderson's rise through the school hierarchy was meteoric. By 1936, when the school moved from Piccadilly to Wood Lane, Shepherd's Bush, she was Second Mistress. In a reference dated January 1938 the Headmistress, Miss Burgess, wrote: 'Miss Anderson ... has had valuable experience in what has practically been the creation of a new school, and the organization necessary to meet new conditions and a sudden increase in numbers ... I have left the conduct of the School to a great extent in her hands, with perfect confidence.' After just six years' experience in the classroom, Kitty was capable of running a bustling girls' grammar school.

Burlington was a good training ground for a future headmistress. Kitty had to help manage a school under pressure from great changes, both international and domestic, and she was able to put into practice lessons learned at Craven Street: the value of good leadership, and the need to treat pupils as individuals. There is a touch of Harry Shoosmith in some of her tenets. One former pupil remembers her telling her class not to accept what they were told in lessons, but to go and find out the truth for themselves.

Her last days as a subject teacher were spent at Burlington, and it is always her ability to communicate and inspire her pupils about History which receives the most glowing praise. Ennis Brandenburger recalls that as a pupil at NLCS, she has vivid recollections of a first 'lively and imaginative' lesson on Ancient Greece. 'I see her sparkling with some exciting story ... Really she is the strongest evidence I know of the timelessness and changelessness of certain values, such as spontaneity, respect for creativeness and for people, and sensitivity in all things.'[8]

Dame Kitty's ability to live on in memory is a testament to her vivid personality. Irene Diederichsen recalls that 'to put it simply, she was a treasure ... a breath of fresh air. Dr Anderson put us at our ease, and she was so helpful. She supplied notes for us, gave encouragement, even to slow starters. ... She brought History to life, taking us to Windsor and similar venues. We all loved her ... she created a happy atmosphere wherever she was, she laughed a lot. Although brilliant, she was so modest, homely and comfortable to be with ... Dr Anderson was wonderful, a brilliant teacher'.

With such affirmation of her skills, it is small wonder that Kitty Anderson was soon applying for a headship. By now the country was on the very brink of war and once again she took a post in a school in the process of upheaval, this time due to wartime evacuation.

Kings Norton School for Girls, in Birmingham, was a large four form entry selective State Grammar School. It represented a quite ambitious move for a youngish teacher. (Kitty was now thirty-six.) Harrison Barrow, in his reference dated February 1944 for her application to the NLCS headship, provides a glimpse of the Kings Norton School: 'This grammar school, at that time, was in some difficulties, and the atmosphere of the school and the curriculum were not all that could be desired.'

The previous Head Teacher, Mrs Sant, had been at Kings Norton for twenty-eight years, so perhaps the school had become somewhat staid and elitist. Judging by Mary Anderson's account of her aunt's interview, she seems to have been undaunted by the challenge:

'She went into the waiting room, which was rather dull, and occupied by the other candidates, all of whom were older than her and very serious of expression. In the corner of the room was an old-fashioned weighing

---

[8] May Eppel, *Kitty Anderson 1944-1965*, Supplement to NLCS Magazine.

machine — the sort you had to balance up. So she hopped onto the machine and weighed herself. After her interview she weighed herself again to see if she had lost any weight due to stress. The other ladies looked at her askance. When the interviewing panel came out at the end of the interviews, and asked her to step forward she sneaked a look at the rival candidates, who to a woman looked most put out.'

Kitty Anderson's first weeks at Kings Norton were hectic. By the end of August 1939, pupils and teachers had been recalled from their summer holidays to begin the process of evacuation to Gloucester. The girls were excitable and frightened and the international news was catastrophic: war was declared on 3 September. In notes she made for a speech years later, Dame Kitty jotted down some tantalizingly brief reminiscences: *'station, lost child, and billeting, holidays, blankets, illness, nativity play, blitz.'*

In Gloucester, Kings Norton shared buildings with another school that worked there in the mornings while Kings Norton used the playing fields and a church hall. In the afternoon Kings Norton piled in and had lessons from 1 to 5pm. The girls soon grew fed up and bored; there seemed to be no danger after all from falling bombs. While many pupils remained in Gloucester, others drifted home to work on assignments set and marked by teachers they rarely saw. When air-raid shelters were finally built at Kings Norton, Dr Anderson had to share her time between the two schools, spending a fortnight in each.

Miss Tebbutt, a former staff member, writes in *A History of Kings Norton Girls' School:* 'For those of us in Gloucester, the pace of life slackened when she was absent, and speeded up briskly again with increasing interest when she returned. Her joyful vigour was infectious.'

This 'joyful vigour' must have been hard to maintain under the circumstances. Prize Days were interrupted by repeated air-raid warnings, girls came to school exhausted, in need of hot baths and breakfast after nights spent in cold shelters: 'School was an emergency feeding centre ... Staff undertook fire-watching duties and took turns at sleeping in the building ...' Sometimes the pupils had to be sent home because there was no coke for the boilers. In 1944 there was an influx of London evacuees fleeing the flying bombs.

Through all this turmoil the Headmistress did not lose sight of the need to improve the girls' education. The pressure she felt is reflected in a hurried letter dated 8 June 1943 which she wrote to Royal Holloway about her 'war work': 'I continue to be very busy — especially as my school grows larger and larger. We are 600 now and shall be 630 in September! Really too big I think; sometimes I feel rather like mass production, but it is all very interesting. In haste ...'

She broadened the curriculum to include non-academic pupils and encouraged shared events with boys. In a later speech to Kings Norton Boys' School, she spoke of how the Headmaster there had been her 'guide, philosopher and friend', but also how she had once noticed some Sixth Form boys showing surprise at the girls' curriculum, which included Pure and Applied Maths and Physics. 'I rather wondered what they were expecting to see — perhaps plain sewing and knitting predominating', she commented dryly.

The girls were expected to participate in harvest camps, a Gardening Guild and a School Council, started by their Headmistress to encourage the girls to feel part of the school community. She found time for a bit of frivolity, too, writing an end-of-term report for Orlando, the School cat, in which she urged him to learn 'not to distract others'.

Once again, it is a reference which provides a clue to the quality of Kitty Anderson's leadership:

'She has a most sympathetic understanding of the interests of those pupils who are less successful in the more formal subjects of the curriculum, with the result that she has welded her whole school into a most happy community with both a vigorous and varied life of its own, and a proper sense of its relationship to the outside world.'[9]

It's hardly surprising that there's no record of Kitty Anderson enjoying a social life at this time. For five years she must have been completely immersed in keeping the school on its feet, something she achieved with spectacular success. Her decision to apply for another headship came as a real blow to the school. After all, there would doubtless have been a general expectation of long service in such a prestigious and expanding school as Kings Norton.

'... if we had been spared the worst of the blackness of the war days, we felt things were very grim when we heard that Dame Kitty was to leave us in 1944 to go to NLCS', writes one former member of Kings Norton.

---

[9] Martineau, W., Chairman of the Education Committee.

'However, we had learnt a great deal as a school; we had become a community ... we were beginning to learn to live within a bigger community, and I believe, despite those war days, we had begun to know something of the meaning of women's education.'

Katharine McMahon was a pupil at NLCS 1968-75. She is the author of four novels published by Flamingo (HarperCollins). It was the twenty-year reunion at Canons of the leavers of 1975 that gave her the idea for her novel 'Confinement', the study of life in a school for girls. She is currently the Royal Literary Fund Fellow at the University of Hertfordshire.

Acknowledgements

Mary Anderson, Accounts of Auntie Kitty, 8 November 2001
Geoff Bell, Archivist, Malet Lambert High School, Birmingham
Jenny Fern, Archivist, Kings Norton School, Birmingham
Joan Hunt, Burlington School (later Burlington Danes)

Bibliography

Bell, Geoff, *Malet Lambert High School,* Hull,1982
Bell, Geoff, Benfell, Roy, John, Noel, Maw, Ivor, Royal, Albert, *The Magpie. Malet Lambert High School 1932-1982* (including recollections of the Craven Street School)
Kings Norton Girls' School, 1994

A Shock for the Sixth Formers!

Kitty Anderson was universally recognised as a dynamic and inspiring headmistress, whose contribution to girls' education was enormous. Perhaps not so widely recognised was the fact that she was an equally inspiring and uncompromising teacher, as I was fortunate enough to discover.

Dr Anderson arrived at North London when I was twelve, in the Lower Fourth form. I had been at the school for a year and was able to recognise the contrast between her personality and that of our former Head, Miss Harold. My friends and I were impressed with Dr Anderson's bubbly, friendly and enthusiastic manner. The fact that she was 'Dr' Anderson also impressed us.

We respected her greatly. I think we all viewed her as a dedicated Headmistress who jealously guarded the traditions of the school and its reputation for excellence, always reminding us about how much we owed to the pioneering vision of Frances Mary Buss. Yet to me she almost came over as a 'soft touch' because she was always full of encouragement, always congratulating those who had achieved successes, academic or otherwise; one never seemed to hear any serious criticism from her. We did not think of her as a teacher in conventional terms.

Over the years my personal encounters with her were of a general nature (asking permission to leave early for a dental appointment, for example). This entailed standing in line to see her as she came out of Prayers. She always seemed sympathetic and there was never a problem about such requests.

In 1950, I was in the Upper Sixth. Matric had gone well for me and I was in my second year as a prefect; all in all I felt — as I think all of us in that situation did — that I was a rather superior being. One of my Higher School Certificate subjects was History. Unfortunately, the mistress who was to teach us one topic, 'England in the seventeenth century', had a breakdown. For once, the school failed to secure a replacement, and Dr Anderson came to teach us instead. She set an essay topic and we all duly wrote our essays. When she returned them to us, we were expecting congratulations on our erudition and brilliance. No such thing! Before handing back any of the essays, she explained to us at some length, pleasantly but firmly, that none of us had approached the task in the proper manner and our work was just not of a high enough standard. The outcome was that she opened our eyes as to how to structure, think through and present an essay. What a shock for the arrogant and complacent Sixth Formers! She proved a hard taskmistress, but it was enormously good for us and we thoroughly enjoyed being taught by her; we owed a great debt to her for opening the door to the pursuit of excellence.

Margaret Wicks (Bruce) 1943–50

From orange-peel teeth to Senior Prefect

When I joined the school in September 1946, the country was still suffering from the aftermath of the war. Many things were in short supply and we were unable to obtain a brown uniform tunic, so I started in the Upper Third wearing a rather dreary brownish frock that my mother thought 'suitable'. Several food items were still rationed and school dinners reflected this, but it was possible to wangle a second helping, especially if you sat at a table with a few Jewish girls on the days when sausages were on the menu.

I had no idea of the school's recent history, of its move from Sandall Road to Canons or the fact that DA had been appointed Headmistress only two years previously. There was little reverence for authority; orange-peel teeth, mimicking DA's somewhat distinctive dentition, was about the level of our mockery.

The years sped by and I became Senior Prefect. Like many Senior Prefects before and after me, the highlight of each day was my session with Dr Anderson in her room after morning Assembly. The content of these discussions included such serious topics as disciplining girls for failing to wear their berets and such frivolous items as a prefects' party (with boyfriends) to be held in the Old House. I recall on these occasions sitting on a low chair to the right of the fireplace, well below her eye-level but never patronised by her, no matter how foolish or arrogant my opinions may have been.

1953 was the year of the Coronation of Elizabeth II. NLCS, together with all other London schools, was allocated a number of places along the route to Westminster Abbey. I was delighted when Dr Anderson overruled the more democratic members of the Sixth Form who wanted a ballot for all the places; she insisted that her School Captain and Senior Prefect should be included *ex officio*. She herself was actually seated in the Abbey; next day she regaled the whole school with detailed descriptions of the Service and of course the robes and coronets, the length of the Queen's train, the Orb and Sceptre and the Imperial Crown.

Sometimes, during our times together, we discussed personal matters. I was hoping to gain a place at a London medical school and when I failed to do so, DA was very keen that I should apply to Royal Holloway, regardless of the fact that Medicine was not on offer there. (The nearest we could get to Medicine was Tree Science!) When it became evident that I would not take that option, even to please her, she suggested I should stay on and take the Oxford Entrance examination.

During my third Sixth Form year, spent preparing for that exam, general lessons with DA were a stimulating experience. We read Plato and Racine, we talked politics and philosophy and we wrote an essay each week which she read and marked with all the commitment of a young teacher.

The first day of those Oxford exams lives on in my memory, probably not for the right reasons. I was by then a habitual cigarette smoker and to calm my nerves I tripped off to the dungeons to indulge my habit. The member of staff who caught me felt obliged to report me: sure enough I had to present myself to DA. She herself was a smoker; in those days schools were not bound by published statements of policy on such matters. Her response to my offence was: 'My dear Joan, if you feel the need to do this again, come to my room.' It was a splendid example of her understanding and her sense of proportion, and I went into the examination room with a lightened heart.

The 1950s were not very liberated times. When I went up to Oxford I thought myself quite familiar with the ways of the world but I was somewhat surprised by the goings-on with regard to men and alcohol at my college. These observations I related to DA over a dinner during the Christmas vacation, and the following spring my tales were relayed to the Headmistresses' Conference. I think uppermost in DA's mind was the need to warn her sister Heads about some of the behaviour their students might encounter on going up to university. However, she was not as discreet as I would have wished; on returning to Oxford I found myself explaining to the Principal how the gossip about her college had been spread abroad!

I gave up Medicine after leaving Oxford, marrying and becoming pregnant. I was not as fearful of telling DA as I was of breaking this news to my immediate family. Somehow I knew that she would continue to support me. She never undervalued the role of the wife and the mother, even when encouraging her students to have a career and never give up on their education. In 1960 she invited me to teach Biology at NLCS, to cover for Mrs Gagarin's Grace term. I had a degree in Physiology but no professional teacher training, but she allowed herself to be led by her own instincts — and so I made my first step on the teaching ladder. In 1964, when an emergency arose in the Science department, she asked me to join the part-time staff … and so began a teaching career at School which lasted over thirty years and brought me immense satisfaction and happiness. How blessed I was to have been so close to such a great Headmistress.

Joan Lundie 1946-54, Staff 1966-96

She respected us

My clearest memories are of Dr Anderson's lessons. She taught us Medieval History when we were in the Lower Fourth. She always arrived on time, set and marked our exams and more importantly inspired us with her own enthusiasm for History. She astonished us with her revelation that History was not merely a neat chapter in a book — she showed us documents and various sources of evidence for us to consider. Typically, she welcomed individual interpretations but encouraged and expected a spirited and intelligent justification for our conclusions. I think she missed regular classroom teaching and the chance to communicate her subject, as well as the very personal working relationship with a class.

Of course I can describe her physical appearance — small and stout and so on — but what I really saw was a lively, attractive woman with very blue eyes and an infectious smile (or sometimes a fierce gaze). She had enormous presence. This was evident in Assembly where she effortlessly commanded total attention the minute she bustled in, ascended the platform and surveyed us all before she began to speak. We respected her totally, but then she respected us, too.

I feel privileged to have been at North London during Dame Kitty's era. It was immensely civilised, intellectually stimulating and great fun.

Mary Wilson (Buss) 1951-58

Bright powder paint in baking tins for buns

For those who joined the school immediately after World War 2, childhood had been marked by shortages of paper, paint and pencils and a careful use of what prewar resources remained. The London streets were drab and art galleries had not reopened. As a result, not surprisingly, my early memories of Art at NLCS are of vibrant colour: the abundant bright powder paint piled up in baking tins for six or eight buns: lemon yellow, yellow ochre, two blues and two reds, from which we made all other colours, although some tins had black and white as well. We lay on the floor with our paints, jam-jars of water and large sheets of wall lining paper or grey sugar paper and painted thickly with long, rough hog's-hair brushes.

The Art room was almost a separate domain, situated on the top floor of the new building at the farthest end of the corridor, which was decorated with constantly changing and exciting works produced by the pupils. In her deep croaky Scottish voice, Mrs Richards (Peggy Angus) would give us a choice of titles to paint, usually including a quotation to fire our imaginations. I remember painting 'Breathless she flung herself on the windy hill'.

Mrs Richards was usually encouraging about our work but could be fierce and downright rude at times, calling us 'spoilt brats' … but soon she would be cracking a joke and laughing raucously. I thought she was marvellously Bohemian and uninhibited; everything An Artist was supposed to be. She sang a lot of Scottish Socialist songs which I already knew.

There was also a massive still life cupboard, its shelves arrayed with all sorts of exciting things to draw. Apart from the joy of colour there was the joy of choice: in most other lessons we were told exactly what to do, but not in Art. We were guided instead, but only if we hit a problem. We also made designs, working on tiles and plates, and made lino cuts for the School Magazine.

We did pottery with Mrs Cowles in a small room in the Old House, which was fun but the space was so cramped that you rarely got a chance to use the wheel. I don't remember any other Art teachers until I was about fifteen, by which time Mrs Margaret Brown and Miss Moy Keightley had arrived. When I was in the Sixth Form, Mrs Richards invited us in ones or twos for weekends at Furlongs, her tiny, primitive cottage in the midst of the

Their turn on the wheel at last!

South Downs, a mile away from the road. We foraged for firewood, fetched water, lit paraffin lamps and sang 'Rock of Ages' which she played lustily on her harmonium. In the uninhabited cottage next door were piles of drawings by well-known English artists who were her friends.

At NLCS there was absolutely no atmosphere of Art being for the less bright children, as in so many other schools. For example, I took Latin, English, French and Art at A-level, then, undecided whether to study English or Art, was offered university places for both subjects. To me that, more than anything else, sums up the ability Dr Anderson had to see life in the round — she knew that Art, Music and Drama were important forces for social change as well as contributing factors to general happiness and culture. We were all trying to build a new and better world in those days.

Margaret Glover (McKechnie) 1946-53

4

'I have at least got a hat' —
Dr Kitty Anderson and the North London Collegiate School 1944 - 1955

ANN THOMAS

The appointment of Dr Kitty Anderson to the Headship of the North London Collegiate School in September 1944 began a new era in both her own history and that of the school.

In 1944 she was forty-one years old. Behind her was a distinguished academic career and teaching experience in three schools, the last one as Headmistress. The testimonials and references she presented on her application to the Governors in February 1944 included those from the Principal of the Royal Holloway College, her former Professor of History at the University of London, two influential members of the City of Birmingham Education Committee and both the Head teachers under whom she had taught. All were unstinting in their praise. She was described as 'a brilliant teacher' an 'inspiring colleague' and 'an outstanding success as Head teacher', and all stressed her enthusiasm, energy, vitality and personal charm.

The North London Collegiate School was established on 4 April 1850 at Camden Town, in North London. Its founder, Frances Mary Buss, was the great pioneer of girls' education who in 1874 had set up the Association of Headmistresses. Her successor, Sophie Bryant, was the first woman to be awarded the degree of Doctor of Science and had been prominent in the promoting of women's Suffrage as well as Irish Independence. It was Isabella Drummond, the third Headmistress, who inspired the school's move in the 1930s from Sandall Road, Camden Town, to Canons Park at the end of the Northern Underground Line in Middlesex. The new school was on the site of the great palace of Canons built in the early eighteenth century by Robert Bridges, first Duke of Chandos, patron of George Frideric Handel. At the heart of the school was a later, much less palatial mansion built in 1767, on to which had been grafted, by the eminent architect Professor (later

The staff 1949

From left to right

Back row   Misses Clay Marshall Hogg Raeburn Hall Macqueen Pusey Bolton Kitching Worthington Ellis Jewsbury

3rd row   Misses Webster Parkins Ridgley Mrs Kirkham Miss Gare Mrs Harris
Misses Molony Lambert Mrs Brown Mrs Richards Miss Shillito Mrs Hodkin
Misses Cawley Atkinson Turpin Lindsay

2nd row   Misses Harker Nicholson Mrs Cowles Misses Senator Gossip DrAnderson
Misses Parks Hawley Mlle Woodward Misses Hill Scrimgeour

Front row Misses Beaumont Birch Henderson Foster Bartlett Lewis Westlake Dickenson

Sir) Albert Richardson, a series of new buildings surrounded by terraces and gardens. The school was completed soon after the outbreak of war in 1939.

Kitty Anderson knew of the school's reputation and was anxious to gain the position of Headmistress. Writing to her father on her decision to apply she stated: 'North London is one of the few schools in the country I would be proud to command.' The day before her interview she described to both parents in glowing terms the beauty of the school and its grounds. In the same, often quoted letter she told them that the previous day she had visited the department store Bourne and Hollingsworth and had bought 'a very smart model hat which should give me great courage', adding philosophically that even if she was not successful 'I have at least got a new hat'. Later she used to tell the girls how, at the interview, the Governors had asked her to remove the new hat in order to see her face more clearly, and how she had feared her hairpins would fall out and her carefully arranged hair collapse around her. She was delighted when she was offered the Headship, generously telling her mother and father: 'this very great honour is yours rather than mine' — because it was the result of — 'your personal sacrifice.'

In spite of the new Headmistress's pleasure at her appointment it was by no means the easiest of tasks she faced in the autumn of 1944. Britain was still at war, already facing the horrors of flying bombs and about to confront the V1 and V2 rocket attacks. The new school buildings were not fully complete or properly finished. Peace, when it came, was to be followed by a period of austerity and shortages. Moreover the resignation of Eileen Harold in 1944, after only four years as Headmistress, had caused unease and uncertainty among many staff and pupils. That the Governors had made the right choice in Kitty Anderson was, however, soon apparent. Her careful judgement and tact, her warmth and friendliness were quickly appreciated. It was also clear that her values, especially her respect for the individual, and for independence of mind were in close harmony with the school and her distinguished predecessors.

One of the first undertakings faced by Kitty Anderson when the war ended was the restoration of the decoration and furnishings of the school buildings. She was greatly helped in this by having an experienced Chairman of Governors in Dr Clegg, a hard-working Secretary and Clerk to the Governors in Edith Hill, an extremely capable Domestic Bursar in Winifred Turpin, and by her self-effacing but immensely competent Second Mistress, Miss Gossip.

Between October and November 1945, the wartime air-raid shelters were dismantled and the cloakrooms, with large glass windows, completed. In June 1946 Miss Drummond's clock was installed. The clock, designed by Professor Richardson, had been presented to Miss Drummond by the school as a parting gift for the new building. It was placed, with her name, at the front of the Organ Gallery and became a symbol of the new postwar school. The following year the hockey and rounders pitches and tennis courts, neglected for so long, were renewed and re-surfaced and a tractor was bought to help maintain the large playing fields. Because of continued restriction it was not until 1950 that the cloakrooms could be re-decorated. It was characteristic of Kitty Anderson's approach that staff and girls were involved in deciding the colours. This was not achieved without some controversy. Peggy Richards [Angus] collected colour charts and displayed exhibitions in the staff room to illustrate that there were alternatives to the tendency to choose green and cream. They opted for diversity rather than uniformity and each form room had its own colour scheme. Peggy's scheme for the Art department had been glowing Indian red to support the bright children's paintings. However, after the summer holidays she found that her scheme had been reversed. 'We felt sure you had made a mistake', Peggy was told. She was furious and immediately tendered her resignation — 'Not because you have no faith in me as an art teacher but because I have no faith in you as a headmistress', she told Dr Anderson. The colours were altered the very next week. Peggy Richards stayed on at NLCS.

In 1951 the school organ was installed. It had been bought some years previously by the Governors after the organ at Sandall Road was destroyed in an air-raid. Government restrictions meant that it had been in storage for some years, but it now came joyously into its own as it accompanied school assemblies and concerts. Slowly but surely, inspired by the energy and enthusiasm of Kitty Anderson, the beauty of the school at Canons re-emerged.

Although the Headmistress's ideas were to develop more fully over the next ten years, from the beginning she had decided views on the education of girls. She had welcomed the radical Butler Education Act of 1944, especially when it was confirmed that the North London Collegiate would continue as a Direct Grant Grammar school. As she later explained in a film made in 1965, a Direct Grant School is a 'state school but fee-paying': at least 25% of the pupils must have free places given either by the local authorities or the Governors. About half the pupils at NLCS had free places. When asked how the candidates were selected she explained that everyone applying for a free place (including the members of the Junior School) had to take an entrance exam as well as the eleven-plus examination. A very large number of aspiring pupils, many more than there were places for, were interviewed by the Headmistress herself. She believed that the combination of free places with fee payment based on parental income gave such schools a unique position between the independent and state systems, providing stability and encouraging innovation.

Although numbers had inevitably dropped during the war, in 1945 the school had 645 pupils, with some 23% of girls going on to university. Kitty Anderson, who saw the North London Collegiate as an academic school, believed that many more girls were capable of gaining university awards and she was determined to ensure this. One immediate problem, however, was the Government's decision that 90% of university places should be given to ex-servicemen. Kitty Anderson, like many other headmistresses, accepted this but thought it unfair that the remaining 10% would, in the main, also go to male applicants. She encouraged the senior girls to write in protest to Members of Parliament and other leading political figures. The school archives record these letters of protest and replies from a number of MPs — most, but not all, supporting the girls' position. Eventually, much to the relief of all concerned, it was decided by the government that there was to be no discrimination in the final 10% of places. In 1946, North London Collegiate gained seven open awards to universities.

Kitty Anderson's educational aims were explained more fully in an address she was invited to give in 1951 to the Annual Inspectors of Schools. Entitled 'The Education of Girls' it was later published in pamphlet form. In this address she stressed the need to develop the aesthetic taste of girls who, she believed, were greatly influenced by the appearance of a school — its furniture, decoration and colour. She acknowledged that her school was exceptionally fortunate in this respect but thought that more could be achieved simply by 'avoiding the drab, the dull green and the muddy chocolate'. Books, she believed, were essential and should be readily available both in the library and in classrooms. They should be as diverse and catholic as possible. 'A magazine table or stand is essential', she stated, 'even the most academic of girls eagerly await the new copy of *Vogue*.' The curriculum should be as wide as possible. Girls should be encouraged to think for themselves. 'We all tend to teach too much and do not give our pupils enough time to think for themselves', she stated. The tendency to over-examine and test should be avoided. Although she accepted that co-education represented more nearly a normal society she believed that girls flourished best if taught separately from boys. There should, however, be as much contact as possible in clubs, societies, parties and dances. She accepted that the number of girls staying on at school would increase only if the girls and their parents acknowledged the value of education, yet she considered that more could be achieved through better staffing and improved maintenance grants.

Although almost all the ideas put forward in 'The Education of Girls' are now taken for granted, back in the late 1940s and early 1950s many were new. At the North London Collegiate School most had already been introduced. The curriculum was wide, covering a range of academic, cultural and practical subjects. A system of voluntary subjects existed; girls could study a range of creative subjects such as pottery, bookbinding, dance and art or music appreciation. As well as examination subjects there were, for older girls, non-examination topics such as politics, philosophy and comparative religion. In 1951 the School Certificate and Higher School Certificate were replaced by Ordinary and Advanced Levels. Kitty Anderson and her staff decided that only five subjects should be examined at O-level (with mathematics compulsory for those studying Arts subjects). This meant that A-levels were not examined at O-level. Overt competition between girls was frowned upon at all levels. Class lists were not published and a girl's grades were available only to herself, never in public.

With her belief in independent thinking Kitty Anderson was almost always sympathetic to new ideas put forward by the girls. One such idea was proposed in 1944, soon after she became Headmistress: the setting-up of a School Council. This had been discussed under the previous Headmistress, Miss Harold, and a similar idea had been suggested at Kings Norton School. The new Headmistress was receptive to the request, although she made it clear that she saw such a Council as advisory — 'not in the making of school laws but in providing justification for them in discussion and in ventilating criticism and discontent'. After discussion with staff, prefects and senior girls a committee was set up to investigate in more detail how the Council would be established. Reports in the school archives show what an encouraging and constructive role the Headmistress played in the decisions. It was decided that the Council would be under the chairmanship of the Senior Prefect but would include representatives of each form from the Second Year upwards. The prefect body numbered only twenty-four and Kitty Anderson was anxious that as many girls as possible, especially those in the senior forms, should be involved. The School Advisory Council eventually came into existence in March 1945. Among its earliest proposals was a change in the length of the school dinner hour and the abolition of the compulsory wearing of hats in summer. In a somewhat different and continually evolving form the School Advisory Council still exists at NLCS today.

One year after that setting up of the SAC, Kitty Anderson agreed to a Sixth Form request to hold a school dance with the boys of Aldenham and Mill Hill schools. Although she believed in single-sex schools she had taught in a mixed boys' secondary school in Hull, had two younger brothers and enjoyed the company of young men. Her easy conversation and vivacious laugh put them at their ease and she was always ready to dance if asked. She loved shopping and clothes and was always interested in the girls' party dresses. In a later Founder's Day speech she was to quote Miss Buss's comment to Dr Bryant concerning the latter's niece: 'There are such pretty shoes now-a-days for girls. I hope you have got her something pretty. A girl's first dance comes only once.' The Sixth Form dance was a great success and became a yearly fixture in the school calendar … until the era of a more permissive society that offered many more opportunities for socialising outside the world of school. Meanwhile, in 1953, the then Senior Prefect persuaded Dr Anderson to hold a prefects' party to which boyfriends were invited. This too was enjoyed by the girls and their partners — and, apparently, by the Headmistress.

A more serious aspect of the life of the school that Kitty Anderson was determined to retain was the school's commitment to charity and social service. After she graduated from university she had spent a year carrying out social work in Yorkshire and had helped with a parliamentary election campaign in a mining constituency. She believed that social service benefited not only those who were helped but also the social and personal development of the benefactors, in this case the girls themselves. In the ten years after the war the school's activities centred round the Frances Mary Buss House. Mainly inspired and planned by Isabella Drummond, in 1927 NLCS established a settlement home at Bromley–by–Bow in London's East End. Under a paid warden, the Frances Mary Buss House ran a number of clubs for girls and boys. Parents who lived in the Bromley area were also involved. Kitty Anderson played an active role in the running of the organisation, chairing both the ordinary meetings of the FMB House as well as its Annual General Meeting. She visited it often, especially when NLCS girls and staff were involved. She attended the first Christmas party held at the school in 1946 when over a hundred children from the Aldenham Street School were taken in a fleet of buses from St. Pancras to Canons. She supported the summer camps held under canvas which were revived after the war in 1946 and the Thrift Club re-established for the Bromley mothers in 1947. The distance from Canons Park to Bromley and changes over the years in the needs and outlook of both communities meant that eventually links weakened, but certainly during the ten years following Kitty Anderson's appointment in 1944, the Frances Mary Buss House remained the dominant focus of the school's charity and community service, including parents and Old North Londoners.

Another postwar venture to which Kitty Anderson gave enthusiastic support began in October 1949, with the first exchange visit between NLCS and the girls of the Goethe Gymnasium (then the Goethe Realschule) at Ludwigsburg, Stuttgart. NLCS was not the first after the war to link with a German school, but this exchange became one of the strongest and most enduring. It was inspired by two other remarkable women — Caroline Senator, in charge of Modern Languages at NLCS, and Jenny Heymann who taught at the Goethe Gymnasium. Like Caroline Senator, Jenny Heymann, was Jewish. She had lost her position in the school when the Nazis came to power, and both she and Dr Elizabeth Kranz, the former Headmistress of the school, were forced into exile. After the war Jenny Heymann returned to her old school and her former friendship with Caroline Senator was renewed. Together, they planned and set up the exchange. Kitty Anderson played an active role in the link between the two schools, especially in its early days. She was at the station to meet the German girls and their teacher on the first day of their visit and took part in their lessons and entertainment. In 1950, she went with the exchange party from NLCS to Ludwigsburg. Writing a year later, a German pupil described how Kitty Anderson took them to St Paul's and Westminster Abbey and then on a river launch down the Thames, describing 'with great enthusiasm the palaces and churches on either side'.

1950 was the year of the NLCS Centenary and its celebrations. Kitty Anderson had looked forward and anticipated this even before she was appointed as Headmistress. Well in advance it was decided that a book about the first century of the school was to be written under the general editorship of Ruby Scrimgeour, the head of English. Kitty Anderson, who over the years had developed a great admiration for the school's first headmistress, agreed to write the chapter on 'Frances Mary Buss, the Founder as Headmistress 1850 – 1894'. Preparations for the Centenary were already under way when in May 1949 the school heard of the death of Isabella Drummond, Headmistress from 1918 to 1940. Kitty Anderson was deeply saddened by the loss; she had appreciated the wise and honest advice Miss Drummond had given her on her appointment in 1944, and had relied on Miss Drummond's help with the Centenary celebrations. She wrote immediately to the Vicar of St Martin-in-the-Fields and asked that a memorial service be held for Miss Drummond in the same church as the service for Dr Bryant had taken place. This was held in June 1949, the Address being given by Dr Clegg, who as a Governor from 1928, had known and admired Miss Drummond for many years.

The Centenary celebrations began on 30 March when the whole school gathered in the afternoon in the Assembly Hall. The girls were impressed to see that a Press table had been set up at the back of the Hall. Messages of congratulation were read from the Queen, who as Duchess of York had been the school's Patron until the accession of her husband in 1937 as King George VI, from the Duchess of Gloucester, the current Patron, and from Mr George Tomlinson, the Minister of Education. The Queen's message read: 'Her Majesty, the Queen, conveys her good wishes to you and your governors and to every one of your students who are following in the footsteps of that great pioneer, your Founder.'

Kitty Anderson had been anxious that the Centenary should be seen not solely as marking the hundred years of the school itself but as a thanksgiving for a century of progress in the education of girls. This was reflected in her choice of speakers at the opening ceremony, who were all associated with Miss Buss's inspiration and girls' educational progress. They included the Principal of Queen's College, Harley Street, the Mistress of Girton College, Cambridge, the Director of Women's Studies at Hughes Hall, Cambridge and the current President of the Headmistresses' Association. Kitty Anderson made the speech of thanks, stating simply: 'It is the birthright of every child to have a good education.'

The following day, girls, staff (including many Old North Londoners) and parents attended a special Service of Commemoration in Westminster Abbey. The sermon was preached by the Archbishop of Canterbury, and the Dean of Westminister, the Bishop of Willesden and the Archdeacon of London also conducted the service. On 1 April a dinner was held at London's Waldorf Hotel by the Old North Londoners' Association, which had been set up by Frances Mary Buss in 1874.

'An Old North Londoners' meeting' — one of the many *tableaux vivants* presented for the Centenary celebrations in 1950

The celebrations concluded with Founder's Day on 4 April, exactly one hundred years from the day the Founder had opened her school in the family home at Number 46, Camden Street. After the traditional psalms, hymns and prayers and the Daffodil Procession, which had been introduced in 1896, there came a series of *tableaux vivants* depicting Frances Mary Buss and the school from its earliest days. Finally, a series of gifts were presented to the school. An eighteenth-century table from the Governors, an 1810 centre light for the hall of the Old House from the staff, specially commissioned lights for the Assembly Hall from the pupils, a cheque for new school gates from past and present parents and a cheque for a new organ from the Old Girls.

The Centenary celebrations were judged a great success and were widely reported in the local and national press. Kitty Anderson must undoubtedly have been delighted that the school she had guided for the last five years was so greatly admired and its history and reputation so clearly recognised.

A footnote to the celebrations came with the first visit of the Duchess of Gloucester to the school. She had been on an official visit to Kenya at the time of the Centenary but came to Canons in November 1950. She met the assembled school, was presented with a copy of the centenary book, had coffee with the Governors and then toured the form rooms and buildings. Kitty Anderson was resplendent in her red doctoral gown. She did not, on this occasion, wear a hat but photographs show her accompanying the Duchess wearing the most elegant of black lace-up shoes.

After the Centenary celebrations were over Kitty Anderson continued to work immensely hard, with little time for leisure and recreation. When she first came to NLCS she had taken a flat in Stonegrove, Edgware. She walked to school each day and found it an excellent way to get to know her pupils, most of whom took the same route, along Canons Drive. Later she moved even nearer to the school, buying a house in Lake View, off Canons Drive. Her new home gave her more space to entertain, which she always enjoyed. For some years her nephew, who was studying in London, shared her house and this gave her great pleasure. She remained devoted to her parents and went on holiday with friends but her main relaxation was reading. Friends described the rooms in her house as filled with books, many of which she generously lent or made available to her students. She used to tell the girls at NLCS how she had spent the whole of her first dress allowance on books, unhesitating in her choice despite her love of clothes, hats and shoes.

By the mid-1950s, Kitty Anderson's reputation as a forward-looking educationalist was already well established. In 1946 she had become a member of the Carr Saunders Committee on Education for Commerce. In 1953 she was appointed to the National Advisory Committee on the Training and Supply of Teachers, a position she held until 1960. Since her appointment to NLCS she had taken an active role in the Association of Headmistresses at Independent and Direct Grant Schools. She was Secretary from 1946-49, became a member of the Executive Committee in 1950 and Chairman of the influential London and Middlesex branch in 1953. At the Centenary the then President of the Association described her as 'one of its leading and most valued members'. Her appointment as President in 1954 was both expected and warmly welcomed. As President (from 1954 to 1956) she attended numerous meetings and was involved in arduous committee work. She had, however, a great capacity for hard work and needed, as she always maintained, very little sleep.

In a Presidential address to the Headmistresses' Association she returned to many of the themes she had developed at the North London Collegiate School. She warned again of the dangers of too many examinations, referring to them as 'the bogey of the educational world'. To replace the stress they caused she argued for more oral testing and written examinations using 'open books'. She made a strong plea for the reduction of class sizes, especially at the primary stage, where she believed the foundations of later development were laid. Heads of departments should work closely together so that syllabuses could be pruned and links and overlaps between different subjects put to good use. In particular, the connection between the arts and sciences should not be lost if a fully rounded education was to be achieved. She concluded by reiterating her belief that 'whatever needs our schools may be called upon to fulfil the most important is the need of each girl to find the sphere in which her own particular talent may develop and feel fulfilled. The attempt to hone people into one mould is both perilous and unsound'.

Kitty Anderson was once asked what she thought made a successful and happy school. She singled out the 'availability of the Head and good communication'. She loved talking to the girls, sometimes formally after assemblies but often informally in corridors and outside the libraries. She chatted about major events — the wedding of Princess Elizabeth, the Coronation, Royal Garden Parties, all of which she attended, but also about less important events, perhaps a conversation with an Old North Londoner she had met or the planting of a new tree in the grounds at Canons. It was not only the older girls she communicated with; she loved talking to members of the Junior Department, the 7-11 year-olds who occupied four large classrooms on the lowest level of the school near the gymnasiums. She especially enjoyed her visits there on Founder's Day; with a child clasped in each hand she would go from room to room praising the exhibits, especially the woollen blankets traditionally knitted for charity. She thought it essential that a Head should teach as many layers as possible. Acknowledged as a brilliant teacher, this gave her great pleasure, and as she said, 'how else would I know all their names?' Whether or not Kitty Anderson did know the names of every girl in the school is perhaps debatable, but they thought she did and this gave them pleasure. Always respectfully addressed as 'Dr Anderson', she was not unaware that she was referred to, at least by the senior girls, as 'DA'.

Inevitably there was occasional criticism of Kitty Anderson. A few parents felt that the academic success encouraged by the Headmistress was too stressful for some girls, especially those competing for places at Oxford and Cambridge. Conversely, other girls felt they were undervalued and not encouraged to seek ambitious jobs if they were not academically gifted. It is certainly true to say, however, that the majority of girls and parents admired the Headmistress, especially for her approachability and perceptive recognition of both groups.

One of the frequent comments made by those who supported Kitty Anderson's application for the Headship in 1944 referred to her success in establishing good relations with her staff and her ability to encourage and motivate them. In 1944 the school already had many highly qualified and experienced teachers, some of great quality and character. She was anxious to retain them, but equally pleased when they were promoted, as was Miss Raeburn to the headship of Westcliff High School and Miss Marshall, who became one of HM Inspectors of Schools. Dr Anderson took great care with her appointment of new staff and at least one reported that she had accepted the post because of the warmth and friendliness of the Headmistress at her interview. She always showed great respect for the senior staff but also encouraged the younger staff to take part freely in staff meetings and discussions. In the Education Act of 1944, for the first time married women were allowed to teach and Kitty Anderson was anxious to see them in the profession. She later stated: 'The reform I would most like to see is married women coming back into school – full-time or part-time.' During the first ten years of her Headship most of the staff at North London remained unmarried and few stayed in teaching if they did marry, but this was not for lack of encouragement by the Headmistress.

By the mid-1950s, Kitty Anderson had guided the school for more than a decade. Ten years of considerable change but also much continuity. There had been great success and the occasional disappointment and frustration. The buildings and furnishings of the school had continued to develop and improve. In 1952, the Centenary gates were opened, providing an impressive entry to the Old House. In the following year, which saw the Coronation of Queen Elizabeth II, the school grounds were re-landscaped and restocked. Many Old North Londoners and parents had contributed

What pleasure the new swimming pool gave everyone!

generously to a memorial in Isabella Drummond's name. As a result the library was refurbished and many new books added. It was re-named the Drummond Library. There was as yet no Sixth Form block or common room, but the fact that their classrooms were grouped together in the Old House gave the Sixth Form a sense of identity and their own space. The only new building undertaken in this decade was the result of a generous gift from John and Mary Done whose daughter had died in 1943 just before entering the Sixth Form. They enabled the school to build an outdoor swimming pool, which, after an unavoidable delay of twelve years due to current building restrictions, was dedicated by the Duchess of Gloucester in 1955. Because of the vagaries of the English weather it was used only in the Summer term. Surrounded by bushes and rose trees it was a place of great pleasure and relaxation and in time came to rival the popularity of Lime Avenue and the great cedar trees in the school's affection.

By this time the school had over eight hundred pupils and more buildings were clearly needed. Direct Grant status meant that the school was responsible for its capital building, and as the Ministry of Education kept a tight grip on fees little extra money was available. Facilities for art, craft and music were especially cramped; more science laboratories were needed. It was clear that Kitty Anderson and her Governors would have to address the problem in the near future.

By the end of her first decade Dr Kitty Anderson had established a position as an outstanding Headmistress, an excellent committee woman and a teacher in the forefront of educational reform. Those who prophesied that she and her school were destined for even greater prestige in the future were not to be disappointed.

Ann Thomas read History at the University of Bristol and later took an MPhil in psychology and the teaching of history at the London Institute of Education. She came to NLCS in 1966, was appointed Deputy Headmistress in 1980 and served as such under three Heads: Madeline McLauchlan, Joan Clanchy and Bernice McCabe. She is delighted that her great-niece is now at NLCS and will share in the traditions that Dame Kitty did so much to foster and preserve.

'I delegated everything except knowing people'

Dr Anderson took over as Headmistress in September, 1944, as I became a Sixth Former and returned to a form room in the Old Building, where I had begun my school life in 1935. She was embarking on a new phase in her life and the life of the school, and appeared to enter into it enthusiastically. However, as she confided to me years later, after I had taken part in her Retirement Presentation in 1965, in reality she was not so confident. She wrote: ' ... my mind went back to 1944 and my first days at Canons. When one is a new and raw Headmistress one feels very much an outsider. The help and friendship all you who were in the sixth and upper sixth gave me, helped me to start off on the right foot. I shall always be grateful to you all.' As usual, she gave the credit to others.

By Autumn 1945, with the war over at last, there was a new impetus to school life, stimulated by Dr Anderson. The School Advisory Council was an example of education in citizenship and committee procedure. Out-of-school activities flourished, we went to theatres and held the first School Dance.

At our weekly Civics lesson, I remember Dr Anderson stressing the importance of reading a 'sane' newspaper, and she introduced me to the (Manchester) *Guardian,* which I have continued to read (mostly) for over fifty years.

In 1946, in order to cope with the flood of ex-Service applicants only 10% of university places could be offered to school leavers. Dr Anderson suggested we should write to our MPs asking if some priority might be given in 1947 to those who had not been offered a place. It was a very useful 'hands-on' exercise and we were thrilled to receive replies from our Members of the House of Commons, where questions were asked and noted in Hansard. Some assurance was given. In the event, I believe all thirty of us gained places. (Some of us even eventually married the dreaded ex-Service men.)

Dr Anderson got to know us all very quickly. Her warmth and friendliness gave a new dimension to the school. I had viewed our previous two Headmistresses with respect and some awe; it was a new experience to find the Head could also be a friend. Years later, my husband once asked her how she managed to cope with such a large school, with all her other activities. She replied: 'I delegated everything except knowing people.' Dame Kitty remained accessible to all her ex-students and always delighted in their progress, whether academic or not.

After her retirement to Northallerton, I was able to visit Dame Kitty on several occasions and she also stayed with us at our Victorian vicarage near Doncaster. She entertained us with stories of her adventures, including her visit to Russia. On one occasion, attending a meeting at the London School of Economics, there was a very hostile student demonstration outside. Dame Kitty told us: 'I put on my little old lady act, tucked my papers under my arm, and they escorted me through.'

The bungalow at Northallerton was a great joy to her, and she soon endeared herself to her neighbours. In her garden she had devised a system for dealing with weeds. She methodically collected a daily bag of weeds. Whenever she had to be away, she would increase the number of bags to make up. In retirement, the exuberance that was so much a part of Dame Kitty's life continued. After a serious bout of illness, she told me with great glee on one of my visits that she had made Medical History. She also occupies a significant place in the History of Education, and in the hearts of all whose lives she touched.

Mavis Greathead (Cosgrove) Senior Prefect 1945-46

~

Short, rather plump, with a ready smile

At first sight our new Headmistress seemed rather unprepossessing. She was less stern than my first Head, Miss Drummond, and very different to Miss Harold, with her aesthetic appearance and distant manner. Dr Anderson was short, rather plump, with a ready smile. Her manner was informal and friendly, even on solemn occasions, such as Founder's Day.

About twenty years after I had left school and become a doctor, Dame Kitty addressed a meeting entitled 'How to bring up our Daughters'. She said that as a headmistress, she always made a point of being visible and accessible. I realised then that the way she would pop out of her room when the bell rang between lessons, as we were all going up and downstairs and along the corridor to different rooms was a deliberate act and not sheer chance.

I knew about her accessibility. Anyone could wait outside the Hall after morning Assembly if they wished to speak to her. In the Fifth Form we had a form mistress who was new to the school and we all thoroughly disliked her. Towards the end of the Autumn term two or three of us, with me as spokesman, waited to see Dr Anderson with our complaints, which she listened to. The following term that teacher had disappeared from school and our well-liked games teacher, Miss Lewis, became our form mistress for the next two terms.

I regret that Dr Anderson never taught me. I am sure her lessons must have been magical.

Anne Holmes (Robinson) 1938-49

Things were going to be different

It was the first Assembly of the new school year. I was now in the Upper Fourth and feeling relatively grown-up. I sat with my friends and awaited the arrival of our new Headmistress with interest and some trepidation. What a surprise when Dr Anderson walked in. Instead of the tall, remote Miss Harold, her predecessor, here was a small, round lady who bustled up to the Hall platform and stood there looking at us all with a smile and very sharp eyes. You could feel her energy as she talked to us. Things were going to be different.

During that term Dr Anderson took us for Current Affairs lessons, no doubt in order to get to know us. As a somewhat diffident teenager, my main concern was to keep my head below the parapet in class: no chance with this teacher, however! She stood in front of us and saw us all. Her finger pointed round the room as she waited for answers to her questions and we all had to speak up when called upon. Those lessons introduced me to the world around me in a way I never forgot.

When the time came for me to think about a career path, I met a quite different person. At first, I only knew very definitely what I did not want to do with my life, but I was lazy about the way to achieve my preferred lifestyle. Dr Anderson could not have been more patient and helpful in clarifying my ideas and guiding me towards the degree in Horticulture that I subsequently obtained. This was a somewhat unusual choice for a girl in those days, as I discovered when I got to University, but it was the right one for me, even though I later slid sideways into teaching.

I have the feeling that Dr Anderson remembered every one of the hundreds of girls that she met; I wonder what she remembered about me?

Margaret Keeble (Jones) 1941–48

∼

'Scintillating'

My first impression of Dr Anderson, our new Headmistress, was how different she was from her predecessor. In the eyes of an eleven-year-old, Miss Harold had seemed quite formidable. Dr Anderson's eyes danced, her face was quicksilver. Defining the word 'scintillating' for us, one of our teachers said: 'Dr Anderson is scintillating.' We could only agree.

Her general approachability led me to ask her to read a lurid historical drama I had written, about a medieval girl who is forced into a nunnery and starves herself to death. I cannot recall Dr Anderson's comments on this grim work, but I do remember that she was tactful.

In later years, I came to marvel at Dame Kitty's memory, not only for faces, but also biographical details. She might, for example, meet me at a School open day and say something like ' — was in your year, wasn't she? She's living in Rhodesia now, married to a missionary and she teaches English to disabled children and has three children of her own.' I feel sure all these details were correct.

It was Dame Kitty who launched me as a public speaker. She invited me to speak about my career as a reporter on the *Jewish Chronicle* at a meeting of the Parent-Teacher Association. My first impulse was to refuse; the prospect was terrifying, but my mother said: 'You can't refuse Dame Kitty,' so I accepted. One of the other speakers was Esther Rantzen, who at that time worked behind the scenes on the BBC tv program *That Was the Week That Was*. Finding myself sitting on the platform in the Hall, with Dame Kitty alongside me and some of my former teachers in the audience was terrifying; what made it worse was that Esther, the first to speak, was so brilliant. She held the audience in the palm of her hand; I could see their eyes shining, and I secretly prayed that I would not be chosen to follow her. Dame Kitty must have divined my thoughts, for she chose me to be the third speaker, and my talk went down quite well. After that I was invited to address many meetings over many years; I have to thank Dame Kitty for giving me that initial courage.

The next time I spoke publicly in Dame Kitty's presence was at a meeting of a Jewish women's group where Dame Kitty was the speaker and I proposed the vote of thanks. In a 'thank you for your vote of thanks' postscript, Dame Kitty's famous memory for once deserted her; she recalled that I had always been 'a very naughty little girl', whereas in fact I had always been depressingly good.

The last time I ever saw Dame Kitty was at my wedding. A student friend of my brother was asked to pick her up, escort her to the synagogue and the reception hall, then take her home again. This young man later admitted to me that he had been frightened at the prospect of escorting an elderly lady of such eminence. However, like all who met her, he was charmed by her and much enjoyed her company. Indeed, my final memory of Dame Kitty is of her sitting between the Editor and Managing Director of my newspaper at the wedding dinner; it was plain from their expressions that they were equally charmed. Above all, I remember her own expression, with those dancing eyes — she was indeed 'scintillating' as one of my teachers had so aptly described her.

Pamela Melnikoff 1942-49

5

Everyone Matters — A Decade of Change 1955-65

OLIVE MELLOR

Remarkable changes in the life of the country characterised the second decade of Kitty Anderson's tenure as Headmistress at North London, from 1955 to 1965. By the mid-1950s the postwar era of austerity was over, symbolised by the abolition of rationing in 1954. The claim of Prime Minister Harold Macmillan in 1957 that Britain had 'never had it so good' was possibly an exaggeration but these years did see a booming economy and virtually full employment.

The early 1960s were to see the greatest social change. It was the age of the Beatles, of Flower Power, of Carnaby Street and the concept of a swinging London. Women's lives were transformed by improved contraception, provided free on the National Health after 1961 and culminating in the invention of the Pill in 1963. Such changes inevitably affected the life and development of the school at Canons. Most of the changes were welcome but there was a need for leadership in tolerance and adaptation to change. The North London Collegiate School was fortunate that in Kitty Anderson it had a Headmistress who possessed both qualities as well as considerable experience and much wisdom.

Within Dame Kitty's own life and the life of the school three major issues became apparent. The first was the enhancement of the school's facilities by the development of the site, and she was encouraged by the Governors to set about exploring possibilities. She saw this as a prerequisite of her second goal, that of sustaining the increasing academic success of her pupils. Thirdly, she had to effect a satisfactory synthesis of her own growing involvement in the national education scene with her role within the school if these external affairs were not to be (or considered to be) to the disadvantage of the school.

During this decade increasing prosperity, as the country emerged from the Austerity Years, made addressing the problems of overcrowding and limited facilities easier. The twelve years that had unavoidably elapsed between the Done bequest and the delayed completion of the swimming pool due to building restrictions had become a thing of the past. All over the country, schools like the North London Collegiate were busy trying to raise funds for new or at least separate accommodation for their Sixth Forms. The potential for growth in this area of education was great and the provision of more space was a means of encouraging students to stay on in the Sixth Form, a goal of prime importance to Kitty Anderson. In the autumn term of 1956 she told the Governors that the school 'is bursting at the seams. There are 116 girls in the Lower school and 697 in the Upper school of whom 188 are in the Sixth and Upper Sixth Forms, making a total of 813 girls. One difficulty of course is dining-room space and one table of "cold lunch girls" has to be in the Entrance Hall lobby at Senior dinner time!' The pressures on space were readily identifiable: the occupation of a room in the Old House by the Art department for craft and pottery which could be well used to house the growing number of Sixth Formers; the occupation of the room at the north end of the science corridor on the top floor as a second teaching room for Art — a room which more rationally could be used as a laboratory, thereby improving facilities for the teaching of Science; and the need to find an alternative home for teaching Art if those two steps were implemented. It is difficult to imagine that such a vigorous and volatile head of the Art department as Peggy Richards (better known later as Peggy Angus) would relinquish her empire without seeing that adequate new provision was made for it.

The Industrial Fund for the Advancement of Science in Schools had been set up by the Government in 1955 and the Governors were strongly in favour of applying to this fund for financial assistance. In July that same year, Mr D.B. Briggs, one of the assessors for the Industrial Fund, visited the school and was shown the ongoing work in Science and the accommodation available. Although he was very pleased with what he saw, he strongly recommended that the school should, as soon as possible, obtain the use of the second Art room for a Junior Physics laboratory. He thought the Fund would give sympathetic consideration to the application for a grant towards the installation of electric power in the laboratories and the modification of the water pressure — at a cost of £1,000, plus the equipment of a Middle school laboratory in the existing Art room at a further cost of £1,250. He advised that an application should also be made for a grant towards the cost of freeing the Art Room for the proposed laboratory. The estimated cost of furnishing such a laboratory would be £4,000. He knew that the Governors had planned to build a separate Art block, but in view of the heavy expenditure entailed and the additional maintenance costs, he suggested that the Art extension should be on the flat roof of the north wing of the two-storey 1939 building, which had provision for the foundations of a third storey. This would involve less capital expenditure as well as lower maintenance costs. In that way the school would gain an urgently needed laboratory and free the craft room in the Old House to become an additional Sixth Form room. This shrewd suggestion was not followed, however, perhaps because the plan to build a completely separate Art block was always present in Dr Anderson's mind, no doubt encouraged by Peggy. Plans for the construction of a new Art block were actually under consideration at an estimated cost of about £20,000 (£300,000 in today's money).

The Industrial Fund promised to make a grant of £4,200 towards the provision of electric power and adequate water pressure to all the laboratories and the conversion of an Art room into an elementary Physics laboratory; in addition a further grant of £1,100 was to be made available to provide more scientific apparatus for the Physics and Chemistry laboratories. However, the money would not be forthcoming until the work was completed. This plan would not fund any substantial provision for Art. Dr Anderson then proposed a School Building and Endowment Appeal addressed to parents and Old Girls, to be launched the following year. Typically democratic, to assist her in this appeal she proposed to set up a committee of parents and Old North Londoners. Money thus raised, plus a small sum from the Industrial Fund (justified by the freeing of space for the sixth laboratory), allowed the Governors to set in motion a program for the building of the Drawing School.

Naturally, Peggy Angus was very enthusiastic about such a scheme and keen to be involved in decisions about the design. Carolyn Trant, an Old North Londoner and a distinguished artist, who is presently researching biographical material about Peggy, describes what happened: 'A previous pupil of [Peggy's] had recently become a qualified architect working on the Board of Education, and on the principle that North London should be encouraging professional women, Peggy worked with her on designs for the new building that incorporated all the young woman's ideas. A scale model was made and exhibited on Founder's Day. Unfortunately for Peggy, the school was already committed to Professor Richardson, who had designed the existing new part of the school. She insisted on trying to modify his ideas; she did succeed in making sure that every unglazed surface was lined with soft board to enable exhibitions to be put up and taken down easily.'

Dr Anderson laid the foundation stone for the new Drawing School in May 1958 and by the Autumn term the building was in full use. Meanwhile, the new Physics laboratory was proving most valuable and the release of the room in the Old House had considerably eased the crowding there, while the Art room over the Main Hall had been converted to a Music room — 'to everyone's delight'. But Carolyn Trant observes that 'Peggy Angus didn't relinquish her influence in the main school, where she continued to maintain an artistic presence whenever possible — for example at Christmas the long windows in the Hall were turned into "stained glass" using solid black and transparent coloured paper (as they still are!)'

Dr Anderson's annual reports to the Governors trace, as she had hoped, a gradual rise in both the student numbers at NLCS and the academic achievements of its leavers. That 'bursting presence' of 813 in the 1955 academic year indicated an increasing popularity; soon there were four applications at the eleven-plus exams for every place. By autumn 1962 there were 885 pupils. Over the same seven years the Sixth Form numbers rose from 188 to 223. These totals were higher than most Direct Grant girls' schools elsewhere. They yielded a correspondingly larger number of both state and university awards, to Dr Anderson's immense pleasure.

The class of '58 gained a record eight State Scholarships and went on to garner eighteen Oxbridge places the following December after their time in the Remove; but all the A-level cohorts in this period gratified their teachers by their fine results and were commended warmly by Dr Anderson to the Governors. Her regime ended with a flourish in '63 and '64: the first layer gained thirty-four distinctions at A-level and seventeen Oxbridge places, while the second took fourteen Oxbridge places, including five Open Scholarships. Sixty-three university places were gained in all. When she had reported forty-two university places in 1957 *that* had been 'something of a record'. Her belief that girls would take up more and more places in Higher Education was vindicated by such students, whose hard-working teachers were a source of great delight to her. Meanwhile, these successes were being reflected in the increasingly higher profile of women in the outside world. Dr Anderson did not, of course, wish schools to be 'apart from life'. In his Sesquicentennial history, *And Their Works Do Follow Them*,

Nigel Watson records that 'more than 50% of working women were married by 1961 thanks to a booming economy and plenty of jobs.'

In 1958, with a lack of pother and anxiety that seems remarkable today, the school got ready for a four-day visit from Her Majesty's Inspectors of Schools. When they arrived they found a community bustling, like so many schools all over the country, with a building and improvement program in these more affluent years, and they also noted with surprise and enthusiasm that same community several times humming with the sounds of discussion and thinking aloud. Dr Anderson's girls were not just high achievers academically, with more of them going to university and getting State Scholarships than comparable Direct Grant schools: HM Inspectors observed that they nearly all 'exhibited independence of mind and judgment to a remarkable degree' and 'their oral work, particularly in discussion, [was] outstanding.' Their self-reliance was developed by the unusual ratio of lessons to private study periods. 'Over teaching is to be avoided'; 'girls are expected to learn as much as possible on their own'; 'substantial homework assignments are the natural complement of short hours in the classroom', the report declared. Dr Anderson's ideas are recognisable in the Inspectors' plaudit: 'the climate of the school is so stimulating and the range of interests it offers so wide that the girls are encouraged to make the very most of their abilities.'

They also reported: 'some special features of a carefully thought-out, very flexible organisation are these: a second foreign language — Latin or German — in addition to French (which is studied by all girls from the beginning of the Upper Thirds) may be undertaken in the second or fourth year; Greek is a possibility in the fourth year and Spanish in the sixth form. Options in the fourth year also include alternative courses in Science and Additional Mathematics. Certain voluntary subjects (cookery, craft, dancing, drama, dressmaking, musical appreciation) are all available to each "layer". All girls from the Fifth Form and above must take the cookery course at some stage. Normally girls offer 5 subjects at the Ordinary Level in the external examination, working directly towards the Advanced Level in some subjects and taking non-examination courses in others. In the Sixth Form girls virtually have their own timetables.'

It is worth commenting here that this focus in the Upper Fifth on non-A-level subjects and the school's ability to shape the course of the A-level study for several years beforehand not only suited Dr Anderson's belief in a broad flexible curriculum but was how the system was intended to be used when it was set up in 1951. Ironically, it was the very universities called into being by the Robbins Committee whose increasingly complex admission policy found five O-Level grades unhelpful and who put pressure on schools like NLCS to show what they could do in their 'relevant' subjects. (By 1970 this pressure had become irresistible and the school's policy had to be changed, with subsequent loss of freedom.)

Overall the Inspectors were lavish in their praise: 'The work of the school as a whole is very good indeed; in every department of learning there is some distinction to show. Particularly outstanding are the achievements in Art, English, Mathematics and Science and in the Sixth Form Classics, History and Modern Languages.' They spoke warmly of the teachers, describing many as 'outstandingly able', and noting that 'many of the experienced teachers have kept their vigour and freshness to a remarkable degree'. (All Dr Anderson's former students will think they know who those 'many' were!') The Inspectors made a point of commenting on the approaching retirement of the school Secretary, Miss Edith Hill, who had been appointed in 1915. Her forty-three years service reflected the stability and in turn the contentment of the school's staff and the happy, mutually supportive atmosphere of the Staff room. It was clear that Dr Anderson ran a happy ship, even if it was no longer so entirely democratic in decision-making as in previous epochs — 'Heads of departments are a relatively recent institution', the report commented. Of the thirty-six full-time staff, they noted, four were married, and of the nine part-timers (in Art and Music) three were married.

Yet this established scenario was on the cusp of change: as Nigel Watson records in his Sesquicentennial history *And Their Works Do Follow Them*, the school fees were halfway through a series of small increments (1956-61) to implement the new mandatory equal pay for women teachers. That it was done so gradually shows that Dr Anderson and the Governors were aware of the need to keep costs down for many of the girls' parents: after all, 50% of the pupils were on full scholarships from Local Authorities. Perhaps it was a reluctance to spend money or allow fees to rise that was the cause of some of the Inspectors' guarded criticisms. Their suggestion 'A second film projector ... in the Geography rooms would be useful' seems astonishingly modest from today's perspective; in the Domestic Arts room they recommended that 'more up to date equipment and some re-planning of the room is needed'. Similarly, with reference to English they point out that 'not all [girls] come from homes where there are many books and it might be possible to develop the book provision in the lower part of the school.' The abundance of story-telling, debates and drama in English teaching perhaps helped to remedy the shortage — one Old North Londoner says she was so enchanted by Miss Clay's Greek stories, which she told perched on her desk, that she pursued a further degree in 'Story' later on.

In the Classics department the perceived weakness was bound up with its scholarly strengths: 'much is done to widen the study of Latin beyond the essential grammar and syntax' but 'how much the least able set gains from a four-year course of Latin at this (very ambitious) pace ... is open to question'.

The sheer lack of space which Dr Anderson was aware of was picked up: facilities for indoor physical recreation were pronounced 'inadequate', and the Inspectors' reservations about music were hardly surprising when, for lack of space, the department had to teach class music on the Hall stage and instrumental lessons in the tiny rooms in the wings.

The new Drawing School

Still, by the Autumn term when the report was published, the Drawing School was built and Music had moved into the large room over the Hall which Art had vacated. The site was improving!

And there were no reservations from the Inspectors about the Headmistress: 'As a distinguished teacher she contributes personally to the high standard of scholarship developed in the sixth form — not only in her own subject, History — and her stimulating influence is felt in every aspect of the school's life. She is a very well known figure in the educational world and her public work and many outside contacts have enriched her own school also. The manifold calls on her time and energies do not prevent her from having an intimate and detailed knowledge of all that goes on in the school and she is never too busy to welcome visitors, to be accessible to every member of the community and to plan, with vision and practical realism, for its present and future welfare. In everything she has the help and support of an exceptionally able and versatile staff.'

Plenty of light and room for display — the interior of the South Studio of the Drawing School opened in 1959

Dr Anderson wrote to the Governors: 'I hope you are pleased with the report on the school.' Her strengths as a leader are revealed in her following words: 'I have read to the staff the general comments — and each department has had its own section. My own pleasure lies in the richly deserved tributes to the staff and in particular to the senior members of staff. I am glad that all they do for the school has been recognised.' She realised and publicly acknowledged that her frequent absences imposed great responsibility on those who ran the school when she was away, without parade or complaint.

During the second half of her Headship, Kitty Anderson held key positions in the world of education. The end of her Presidency of the Headmistresses' Association was marked by her attendance at a conference in Istanbul as its representative. Her vivid account of that trip was recorded in the school magazine for 1956:

> I must confess that ... my first thoughts were of my miraculous good fortune that the conference should be held in an historian's paradise! I decided to make the journey across Europe to Greece by train ... It was a marathon journey, starting on Saturday from London and ending in Athens on

Tuesday midday ... The route was through Belgium, Germany, Austria, Yugoslavia and Greece. At each frontier there was a change of dining car and so one had the excitement of a variety of meals. ... The most interesting part of the journey for me was that through Yugoslavia ... especially was I fascinated by the journey from Belgrade to the Greek frontier. The railway follows the valleys of the Moravia and the Vardar rivers and there is a pervading and growing sense of isolation. ... The valleys form a natural route into Europe and have been traversed by many invaders in past centuries; the mountains are well wooded and have made guerrilla warfare possible. Agriculture is in many ways primitive, farmsteads small with few cattle. I saw threshing done by a pony and donkey harnessed together in the care of a little boy, beating out the grain with their feet. For one whole day, although the road ran alongside the railway, I saw no motor car, only barefoot peasants travelling on foot or with donkeys or small pony carts. Gradually the Turkish influence became obvious, for once the great Turkish empire included this area. The mosque often replaced the church and some of the peasant women were wearing the baggy Turkish trousers which, incidentally, I have never seen worn in Turkey. The peasant craft for which Yugoslavia is famed was seen in the gaily coloured patterns of the hand woven aprons worn by many of the women. The vivid impressions left with me were of the vastness of the country, the remoteness, the beauty of the valleys and poverty.

From Athens I flew to Istanbul, arriving about 10pm and was met at the airport by my Turkish host. From the airport ... I was driven over incredibly rough roads into Istanbul and down to the ferry across the Bosphorus because my host's house was on the Asiatic shore. ... As we sailed away from the quay I had my first glimpse of Istanbul at night. Against a dark velvety sky I could see the lights of the town, which is built on a hill so that there seemed to be tier after tier of twinkling stars and the dark outline of domes and minarets. The passengers were many and varied — business men with opulent cars, peasants, farmers and as I stood on the deck looking at the incredible beauty of the night and the town in silhouette, my attention was drawn to the fact that a sheep was nibbling my coat. There behind me was a freshly washed very woolly sheep ... We landed in Asia at Uskudar (Scutari) where the fruit traders with stalls piled high with melons and peaches were doing business by the light of flares. We went on by road past the site of Florence Nightingale's hospital where today a modern hospital stands, to ... my new home on the shores of the Bosphorus. The conference meetings were held in the Lycée Galatasaray, one of the oldest and most famous of the Turkish boys' schools. Each day I made the journey by passenger ferry across the Bosphorus to the Galata quay.

The city of Istanbul is cut in two by the Golden Horn ... the two parts are linked by the Ataturk and Galata bridges. To the north lies the newer town, Beyoglu, with its modern shops, hotels, schools and Embassy buildings. To the south lies the old town bounded by its city walls and here are the Bazaars, the University, the ancient Hippodrome, the great mosques, Saint Sophia and the Seraglio palace ... One might almost say the present is in Beyoglu and the past in Stamboul but of course, this could only be a loose distinction. The cosmopolitanism of the city is most striking, with contrasts on every side. One sees enormous cars, men and women well dressed by any Western standards and then the peasants and the poor, some of the women covering part of their faces, and small horse-drawn carts with a string of blue beads over the horse's ear to keep away evil spirits. There is much human porterage; I saw one man carrying on his back a plate-glass window, another bent double under an enormous crate filled with live hens. There are wonderful restaurants ... and there are water sellers in the streets. There are great stone houses and small squalid wooden structures. The Mohammedan mosque and the Christian church — contrasts are everywhere.

Of all that happened during my stay, the Conference where teachers from twenty-three different countries gathered to discuss educational matters ... the visits with my hosts to a well-known Turkish girls' school housed in a former palace and to the home of a distinguished Turkish family — a wonderful country estate with its vineyards and marble swimming pool ... I think most of all my visits in the old city stand out as the high spots.

Two buildings especially gave me an unforgettable experience. The first was Saint Sophia, the early Christian church later transformed into a Mohammedan mosque ... The whole interior gives the immediate feeling of quiet grandeur and peaceful worship. Recent work of restoration has revealed early mosaics dating from the sixth century that were plastered over when the Turks made the church into a mosque. All the symbols of a mosque are still there superimposed on the original church and at the same time there is evidence of Christian worship. The beauty and simplicity of the mosaics high on the walls are striking ... one could imagine the joyful colour and glory of the original interior when all the walls were adorned in this way.

But I was to know more of this for I was given the rare opportunity of a visit to the Kahriye Djami mosque, also formerly a Christian church, Saint Sauveur, in Chora ... Today it is no longer used for religious services and for some years American scholars from the Byzantine institute of Boston have been working on the restoration of its superb Christian mosaics ... When the church became a mosque after the Turkish conquest, once again the decorations were plastered over in order to remove all traces of Christianity. ... A maze of scaffolding supported platforms high up in the roof where by the light of arc lamps the skilled work was going on. I was allowed to go to the scaffolding and up to the mosaics and examine them closely. This series of mosaics tells the story of the Virgin Mary. The delicacy of design and composition, the sincerity, the rich exuberant colours and the sparkling shining quality of the mosaic work, each piece looking as though just painted because of the clear glass-like surface, were enthralling. ...

All that I saw and did in my short visit to Turkey whetted my appetite; here I found untold wealth of interest and so much that was fascinating to explore. Do you collect 'musts'? One of my pre-eminent ones is now to study more of Byzantine history, art and architecture and then one day to be again a passenger to Istanbul.

This account amply reveals Kitty Anderson's wonderful ability to set her experience in a historical context, her eye for detail and her boundless enthusiasm.

Following her retirement from the Headmistresses' Association she remained a member of the National Advisory Council for the Training and Supply of Teachers, and then in February 1959 the Chairman of the Governors announced the appointment of Dr Anderson to the University Grants Committee — the first woman to achieve such distinction. An appointment, he said, which showed the high esteem in which she was held in the field of education generally. It was a great honour, and he added that the school would benefit from Dr Anderson's close contact with the Universities. Clearly he had confidence in her ability to combine public service with her duties as Headmistress!

Kitty Anderson DBE outside Buckingham Palace with her Senior Prefect Jane Kenyon, the School Captain Brenda Barrett and the Chairman of the Governors, Canon Carpenter

When, only two years later, Prime Minister Harold Macmillan invited her to serve on the Robbins Committee on Higher Education, she had perforce to leave the UGC, and her presence on it was 'sorely missed'. During these years, in spite of the great demands made on her time and energy, she also served on the Governing bodies of Royal Holloway College, Bedford College, the London School of Economics and Furzedown, Maria Grey and Dartford Training Colleges, giving invaluable help to them with her experience and wisdom and sharing her delightful, friendly personality. One cannot but wonder how she found time for it all.

For her dedication and invaluable service to education, in the 1961 New Years Honours List Dr Anderson was awarded the DBE and became Dame Kitty. We were so proud of her! She was only the third Headmistress to have been made a Dame. Her photograph accompanied a lengthy article in the *Manchester Guardian* for 16 January. It began: 'The appearance in the New Years Honours List of Dr Kitty Anderson, Headmistress of the North London Collegiate School, would have pleased the school's first Headmistress, Miss Buss.' (Or perhaps not: — 'I don't know what she'd say about the North London becoming a Dame's school,' Dr Anderson quipped.) After giving details of her education and teaching career, the article continues: 'Dr Anderson still teaches at her school. "I think every headmistress should," she said, "one advantage is that I get to know the girls. Fortunately I have a good memory for names and you cannot fail to get to know people when you live with them, can you?" Any girl who wants to talk to her can make an appointment to do so either through one of her secretaries, or "sometimes they stop me in the corridor and arrange to come," she added.'

The article continues: 'Outside school (and her other educational commitments) Dr Anderson finds time to do her own gardening at her house five minutes walk from the school and to be a very enthusiastic cook. In *The Canons Cookery Book* is her mother's recipe for Hot-pot.

'The outside of a headmistress's room can be more alarming than the inside,' avers the *Guardian* journalist, 'but this one is saved by the Headmistress's personal bookcase, kept unlocked just outside the door. It is there so that any girl can borrow any one of the recently published books (biography, novel or poetry) which the Headmistress has bought for herself, and the borrowing book is well-thumbed and at present three-quarters full. "I sometimes fall over one of them sitting there browsing," Dr Anderson said. ... I noticed as I took a short cut with Dr Anderson through the kitchens where the mince tart was being prepared that no dreadful hush fell on the place at her unexpected arrival, only cheerful "good mornings" on all sides. That is the kind of headmistress this distinguished woman is," the *Guardian* article concluded.

The investiture of Dr Anderson as a Dame of the British Empire took place at Buckingham Palace on 7 February 1961, a memorable day for her. Typically she chose family, staff members and her Senior Prefect and School Captain to accompany her. The vast numbers of letters of congratulations in the school archives from friends, headmistresses, former colleagues and pupils show what pride and pleasure the award gave to all who knew her. On 27 May the Association of Headmistresses gave a luncheon in her honour.

In 1962 Dame Kitty went to the USA and the USSR to make a study of Higher Education as part of her work for the Robbins Committee. She gave a report to the Governors in July: 'I had a most interesting and stimulating time in America. I had talks with those concerned with planning for higher education and teaching in this field. Then in Russia, in Moscow and Leningrad, I took part in similar discussions. There is so much to remember besides these exchanges: I shall never forget California, the Pacific, the skyscrapers of Chicago and New York, the historic buildings of Boston — and, in Moscow, the Kremlin and the Bolshoi Ballet, in Leningrad the Hermitage and its priceless treasures. During my visits I learnt much of educational value, but, important as this was for my work on the Robbins Committee, for me personally the complete break from school was more refreshing than I could have possibly believed. I am very grateful indeed to you for allowing me the opportunity for such a truly rewarding experience and to my deputy, Miss Gossip, and all the staff for all they have done to ensure that I should have no school worry and anxiety. Since my return I have been talking to the girls in groups about my visits and sharing with them my slides and adventures. I expect I shall go on talking about it for a long time.'

Dame Kitty spoke about these visits in her 1963 Founder's Day address:

'Conversations I had during those foreign tours and the institutions I visited opened my eyes, widened my horizons, giving me new ideas. Windows were opened. The result was that personally I found myself with a fuller appreciation of all that is good in our own educational system but also with a desire to make what is good even better, perhaps by applying to it some of the ideas culled from others. Barriers disappear in the field of education because learning knows no artificial frontiers: scholarship and knowledge carry an international passport.'

(On a personal note, I myself did an exchange with an American teacher and spent the year 1962-63 teaching in a Junior High School in New Jersey, near New York City. I recall that when I tentatively broached the subject of an exchange with Dame Kitty she immediately and enthusiastically agreed I should apply. Her own experience from those visits to the USA and the USSR had made her fully aware of the benefits and the interest to be gained from such an exchange.)

During her last year at NLCS, Dame Kitty became a member of the Council for Academic Awards. She was also elected to the Council of the Girls' Public Day School Trust and was soon to become actively involved in every aspect of its work.

Her national reputation by now was such that she and her school were considered interesting enough for the mass media; in the spring of 1965 Stephen Hearst, a BBC producer whose daughter, Daniela, was at NLCS, descended upon us with his camera crew to make a film about life at Canons. This caused great excitement amongst the pupils; amongst the staff whose lessons were to be filmed there was perhaps more apprehension than pleasure. The star of the film was inevitably Dame Kitty, who remarks at the beginning: 'A school is a place for learning to live life fully and to enjoy learning. It is a community: a community of people in which each one, from the youngest girl to the Headmistress, has something to give to the whole. Everyone matters.' These last two words were adopted as the title of the film.

In the opening scene the Assembly Hall is filled with pupils and staff. Dame Kitty, having already taken prayers, is solemnly reading the notices — mostly about lost property. Suddenly the customary silence gives way to laughter. A bird is fluttering about the stage. Immediately Dame Kitty responds by telling the girls that she had seen that same bird in the Hall the previous evening, at a parents' meeting. She copes with the situation with her usual good humour, eventually asking the girls to be very quiet lest the little thing should become even more frightened.

Later in the film we see her interviewing prospective candidates for entry into the Upper Thirds. These eleven-plus girls are obviously nervous but Dame Kitty puts them at their ease by talking to them, first asking about their favourite books, their pastimes and their pets before asking them to read a passage from the adventures of Gulliver in the Land of the Giants — less familiar to young readers than Defoe's account of his visit to Lilliput and therefore likely to be more testing. Even in 1965 students entering NLCS were expected to show a high degree of literacy.

Dame Kitty also appears conducting lessons for different age groups — with the Upper Fourths she is teaching about the development of world trade in the seventeenth century; with the Lower Fourths it is Greek history and the construction of the Parthenon: no notes and much interaction. In her Philosophy class with the Sixth Form she is clearly interested in the girls' contributions to a discussion about citizenship. In all of these lessons she appears relaxed and full of enthusiasm for her subject. Dame Kitty's very real interest in all things historical is demonstrated later in the film when she is addressing the Current Affairs Society on 'Down and Outs in the Sixteenth Century' (the subject of her doctoral thesis). It probably came as a surprise to her listeners that she had grown up in the North of England and had witnessed the ravages of poverty there in the Depression.

One television critic said of the film *Everyone Matters* that Dame Kitty's girls 'worked and argued and sang and sewed and laughed and ate with a tremendous zest which made one feel that the future is going to be better than anyone dared to hope'.

In 1964, before the film was made, Dame Kitty had already informed the Governors about her intention to retire in 1965 and had written to the Duchess of Gloucester to tell her of the appointment of her successor, Miss Madeline McLauchlan.

To mark her retirement the Old North Londoners held a dinner for her at the Criterion Hotel on 6 April 1965. Over 360 former pupils were present; the oldest had left school in 1897. Predictably, the evening was a cheerful and celebratory occasion. Several lively speeches of appreciation were given by former pupils: one mentioned Dame Kitty's innovations, such as the School Advisory Council and the School Dance, and her inciting of senior girls to write to members of parliament about women's places at the universities after the Second World War. Another speaker told how Dame Kitty's charm always got her breakfast in bed in Moscow when the Robbins Committee were there — a privilege enjoyed by *no one else!*

The NLCS staff held a farewell dinner for her at Canons on Saturday, 24 July. She received warm tributes of thanks and praise for all that she had done for the school, its pupils and its staff over twenty-one years.

The national press reported on her retirement; in an article in the *Daily Telegraph* headed *Retirement means more work,* Dame Kitty is quoted as saying: 'I think people should finish their professional careers when they still have the energy and interest to make a new career out of retirement. One shouldn't sit back and feel neglected and unhappy because life is suddenly empty — intelligent people can always find a place in community life and often renewed education is the key to the door!'

Olive Mellor, appointed by Dr Anderson, joined the staff at NLCS in 1955 as an assistant teacher of French and Latin. She became Head of Modern Languages in 1971. She served as Chairman of the Staff Committee and also as Senior Mistress, and was Staff Representative on the ONLA Committee for sixteen years. She retired in 1988.

'She was actually in tears ...'

I entered the Junior School at the age of nine in 1945, and remember Dr Anderson as a comforting and kindly mother figure. I recall seeing her on a train during my first half-term holidays, when she addressed me by name. Most impressive. Although she was warm and sympathetic, I remember feeling that her Room was a 'hallowed sanctuary' and entering it something very special. However, Dr Anderson always made me feel that she had all the time in the world to discuss my problems and to help with sorting them out.

One memory remains firmly fixed in my mind. Someone had scribbled some anti-Semitic comments in one of the library books. Dr Anderson called a meeting in her study of all the senior Jewish girls. She was actually in tears and told us how distressed she was that such a thing should have happened in her school. She asked us to tell her how we thought she ought to deal with such a happening. I remember being incredibly moved at her distress.

She was a warm and caring Headmistress with an amazing sense of fun and as much time and concern for the less academic as for the 'bright sparks'.

When I left NLCS in 1954 I felt that I was saying farewell to a great lady who played a major role in preparing me for the outside world. I also felt that if, at any time, I had a problem I would be able to return to Dr Anderson for advice. It was the custom to give a gift to the school before leaving. I racked my brains for something appropriate and came up with the idea of a china tea-set for the Headmistress's Room. Dr Anderson was really delighted and I'm sure it was put to good use.

Adele Beverley (Selby) 1945-54

∼

'Hello, hello!'

A couple of years after I left school I was walking through the University cloisters one dark, misty November evening when I heard a voice calling 'Hello, hello!' I turned to see a distant figure: on closer inspection this turned out to be Dame Kitty. She was at the University to attend a conference. How she recognised me in the dark and mist I shall never know, but it was typical of her genuine interest in all her pupils, past and present. The next day a group of us Old North Londoners had tea with her. I wonder how many people from other schools could genuinely say that tea with their former Headmistress was an enjoyable experience. I can.

Margaret Bates (Cooper) 1948–57

∼

'Her enthusiasm was infectious'

As I approach retirement, I look forward to writing as much as possible of my father's life from transcriptions of his diaries — 'very useful historical documents', as Dr Anderson would have said. It was my good fortune to have her as my History teacher in the Lower Fourth, and I remember so much about medieval London thanks to the work we did and the model we made of Cheapside. I think she would have been pleased to know that her own enthusiasm for historical documents had been passed on to me.

Enthusiasm is the word that I think best describes Kitty Anderson's personality. She was enthusiastic about anything and everything that pupils at NLCS did. Her enthusiasm was infectious and encouraging whether it was related to the hockey field, the Art room or Science labs, the Library or Domestic Arts room. She also rejoiced in every girl's and every staff member's success whatever it was — she showed great generosity of spirit.

She supported everything that was done in those days for 'Bromley' — the Frances Mary Buss Foundation Settlement in Bromley-by-Bow, East London, where NLCS girls were introduced to another part of London and provided clubs and support for local people. I find it curious that one of my

Dame Kitty presents a trophy at the FMB House
(The Frances Mary Buss house was subsequently used for different social causes during the 1970s and 80s. It was administered by the NLCS Trustees but the school itself lost contact with it. In 1995 the Trustees surrendered the building and its assets to 'Mind in Tower Hamlets' which is part of the well-acclaimed Bromley-by-Bow social enterprise. The 'old Dairy' is now a well appointed 'drop-in'centre.)

last jobs has taken me back to Bromley-by-Bow, to work with Home Carers obtaining their National Vocational Qualification in Care, in almost the same streets through which we walked in the 1950s to visit the Frances Mary Buss House. Nor was Dame Kitty a one-way thinker. The girls from Bow came out to weekend camps at Canons (we slept on the floor of a junior school room). I wonder what those girls' memories of the North London Collegiate School are today?

The room she occupied as Headmistress was, to my childish eyes, huge! But it was always friendly. At my interview as a nervous eleven year-old, I read a book and we talked happily about an unusual way of describing stairs as 'risers'. Part of the remembering is thanks to Kitty Anderson's ability to put everyone at ease and make everyone feel important — pupils, teachers or parents. I think my father was her greatest fan! She used to gather groups of Sixth Form girls in her room. We sat on a richly coloured Turkish carpet while one of us led a discussion on a topic chosen from a list. I recall one of my choices: 'If each before his own door swept, the village would be clean.' Later we would realise the importance of such discussions as an introduction to university tutorials and seminars.

These are my youthful memories of 'DA'. However, in retrospect the profundity of her approach to education influenced all my work as a teacher, especially with those who were less able pupils. When teaching adults, I was often saddened to discover the paucity of other people's educational experiences and was frequently reminded of the richness of my own. I believe we have a duty to remember Dame Kitty Anderson's precepts and her example for future generations of teachers and students.

Janet Wells 1951-58

~

The first role model in my life

'Hello, Ann' — this was Dame Kitty's unhesitating greeting as we found ourselves face to face in the London Underground. Nothing surprising about this, one might think ... except that our chance meeting took place long after I had left school, completed my three university years and then married. The fact that Dame Kitty knew us all by name when we were under her care at NLCS was a familiar comfort during our school years. What amazed me was that her knowledge, covering an ever increasing number of people, stayed with her so that she could recognise one of us immediately years later. The awareness that the Headmistress knew not only your name but who you were and what you were trying to achieve gave a very positive and supportive atmosphere to the school. During Dame Kitty's era, which to my great personal benefit covered the whole of my school career, we all knew there was someone rooting for us and actively seeking to ensure we realised our potential. Dame Kitty was the first role model in my life. Contact with other Old North Londoners over the years makes me realise that my warm gratitude to her is shared by many others.

To start at the beginning: my interview for the school took place on a February day of sleet and winds. My mother and I had to walk up Canons Drive and in marked contrast to others who came by car or taxi, we arrived in a very bedraggled state. My mother lost heart and was convinced I had no chance of obtaining a place. But this Headmistress was never one to judge by appearances. Hers was a hands-on Headship, which involved her in interviewing not only the girls but also our mothers in order to form her own judgement of the applicants. I was not the only one to arrive on foot that day who would be offered a place.

In the early days one had few direct conversations with Dame Kitty, but as we approached GCE exams, she discussed with each of us in turn which subjects we would take. The choices we made would set the pattern for the rest of our school careers. — 'Ah yes, Ann — now you are one of our Oxbridge candidates, aren't you?' she asked me. I had to confess I did not know what 'Oxbridge', meant. This was how Dame Kitty set me on my path.

I was clearly a linguist, and when the detailed A-level syllabus was being worked out for pupils and staff, I found myself unable to decide whether to focus on Ancient or Modern Languages. Finally I was sent off to see Dame Kitty. After discussing the problem a little, she said I should 'hitch my wagon to a star' — take five A-level courses in the first year of the Sixth Form and then decide which to drop. The relief after weeks of fretting was immense! By the following summer the final decision was easy.

Preparation of the complex timetables for each Sixth and Upper Sixth Form pupil and member of staff was taken on by Dame Kitty herself — a weekend job, she explained, done by spreading large sheets of paper all over her floor. No computer spreadsheets in those days!

Towards the end of my first term in the Sixth Form, Dame Kitty told me that the school wished to nominate a few girls, including me, for a course in Paris in the Easter holidays. The cost of the course would normally be met by the girls' parents. However, she suspected (quite rightly) that mine would be unable to pay. So she offered to send me at the school's expense. This quiet help was typical of Dame Kitty's careful observation of her pupils and their real needs.

When I was at school I did not realise how unusual a person Dame Kitty was. As an unmarried woman of her generation she was exceptionally broad-minded. She could and did deal sympathetically with her pupils' emotional problems. I was the one who was shocked when she gave those of us heading for Oxbridge a little pep talk on the need to avoid unwanted pregnancy. She was realistically aware of what we might face in those days when boys at university outnumbered girls by eight to one.

NLCS was essentially a Christian establishment. However, the school had some 10% of Jewish pupils (of whom I was one). For Dame Kitty this provided an opportunity to demonstrate what Christianity meant to her and the importance of unity within the school. Four days in the week we had our own Jewish prayer meetings, but on Mondays Dame Kitty kept us all together and conducted an ecumenical service in which we could all join. The day before each principal Jewish holiday she never forgot to wish those of us who would be absent next day a Happy New Year or whatever else was appropriate. For her the vital goal was to give us a sense of school as an entity to which we could all feel allegiance. In this I believe she succeeded wonderfully. My greatest tribute to her has to be the smile with which I always respond to her memory.

Ann Beaton 1952-59

'For me, NLCS and Dame Kitty are one'

I attended NLCS from 1953-57 and 1960-64, having spent the intervening years in Canada. Dame Kitty was Headmistress throughout my time at

School, very much a part of my memories of those years. My first meeting with her took place when I attended an interview for entry into the Junior School. Although this was quite a daunting experience, I can remember being very much at ease and able to talk to her comfortably.

I enjoyed my time at NLCS and I think this was partly due to Dame Kitty's view of education — although we were encouraged to do well academically, she wanted us to be educated in the broadest sense, including Art and Sport. This view of all-round education made such an impression on me that I looked for a school with a similar philosophy for my own sons.

I remember Dame Kitty for her enthusiasm — for education generally, for the school, for sharing her experiences, particularly her pleasure at hearing from and meeting 'Old Girls' at any opportunity. I remember her support for us as individuals, being prepared to give time to her students when we needed her help.

One enduring memory reflects the interest she took in all her girls. When I returned from Canada on holiday, I asked if I could visit the school to see her. She not only found time to meet me, but also took the trouble to find out who my friends had been in the Junior School, and arranged for me to spend time with them during my visit. When it became apparent that we would not be returning to Canada, Dame Kitty agreed that I could take up my previous place in the school. I shall always be grateful to her for that; I was able to complete my education where I had started it, and also resume friendships that still last today. For me, NLCS and Dame Kitty are one.

Carolyn Spittle (Wiggins) 1953-57 and 1960-64

A dance dress with detachable sleeves

I first met Dr Anderson in 1955 when she interviewed me for a place in the Second Form. We spent some time discussing the delights of going up and down in the glass lift at Heal's London store (clearly this had some academic relevance) and I was struck by her sense of fun and her toothy laugh. She seemed to symbolise both God and the Queen (albeit with a Yorkshire accent). This was especially true on Founder's Day, when she led the long service, resplendent in her red PhD gown, while we trembled with nerves and excitement at the formality of it all.

Dame Kitty always maintained that everyone mattered; achievements, however humble, were noticed. I was once summoned to her room when I was still in the Junior School; I went filled with trepidation ... to be warmly congratulated on a much better term report.

Later I took Social History — Dame Kitty's own subject — and she herself did much of the O-level teaching. She brought her lessons to life with such clarity (and often hilarity or pathos) that I got an 'A' — I remember her vivid examples still.

Slow, slow, quick, quick, slow - a couple enjoy the School dance in the 1960's

She was ahead of her time in trying to understand the generation gap. Once, during a Sixth Form discussion, she referred to a struggle she had with her parents when she was a student at university. It was about her declared intention to go to a dance wearing a sleeveless frock — this was considered unsuitable, even immoral by her parents. She neatly got round the problem by making, unbeknown to them, a dance frock with detachable sleeves. They never found out.

I saw Dame Kitty for the last time in 1978, when I went with a friend to Founder's Day. She remembered our names instantly and embraced us both warmly, exclaiming: 'Oh, I *am* glad to see you.' The feeling was entirely mutual.

Laura Fransella (Propper) 1955-66

6

Ideals and Practice —
Some postwar limitations and stresses during the time Dame Kitty Anderson was Headmistress

ERICA BROSTOFF

The overall purposes of this book are to record and pay tribute to Dame Kitty's achievements, to understand how she came to be so prominent in her field and to command such a loyal following among many parents and pupils. As a pupil in her time I admired many aspects of the school, but I was puzzled by apparent contradictions. Belatedly, I turned to Dame Kitty's PhD thesis, as a piece of original work in her own words, to seek possible insight into her personality and beliefs. In a roundabout way this led to the present chapter.

In view of the enormous contribution that Dame Kitty made to NLCS and girls' education in general, it may seem ungracious or inaccurate to point to possible shortcomings. Some of these may be understood as the result of the specific stresses of running a large girls' day school immediately after World War II, as chronicled by Nigel Watson in his Sesquicentennial history *And Their Works Do Follow Them*. In Dame Kitty's own talk to Inspectors of Schools in 1951 entitled 'Education for Girls', she refers to 'school life which moves at a breathless pace'. She uses the metaphor of a 'whirlpool' of information that could be overwhelming. In addition to specific stresses of the time, it is hypothesized in this chapter that some of the problems pupils experienced were the consequence and downside of Dame Kitty's extroverted personality, and her strong underlying emphasis on academic concerns that led her to inherit the mantle of Frances Mary Buss. Despite personal regrets, it is still a joy and privilege to visit the school she nurtured. This chapter is offered as a pragmatic account that touches only lightly on formal theories.

As Dame Kitty was a historian of the Tudor period, it is satisfying to start with a reference to Tudor times. A writer in 1897 on girls' education states: 'The destruction of the monasteries found women quite unprepared and dealt their education such a severe blow that it passed under a cloud for three hundred years.' As this early education was mostly convent-based it grew more and more isolated from mainstream life as Catholicism became a minority religion. In *The Best Type of Girl: a history of girls' independent schools*, Gillian Avery notes that some boys' independent public schools had foundations and endowments going back to medieval times, or other long-standing income. Hand in hand with other problems in establishing themselves, virtually all independent girls' schools have suffered periods of financial insecurity because they lack such endowments, a challenge and stress to which this chapter later returns.

At the level of personal conflict, it is interesting to note certain problems in the time of Frances Mary Buss. Lilian Murray (1837-1901) is mentioned in *The Macmillan Dictionary of Women's Biography* as follows: 'she defied the insistence of her teacher Frances Mary Buss that she should become a teacher of the deaf and dumb. Miss Buss apparently threatened to stop her entering any other profession; to which she replied "you cannot stop me from becoming a dentist".' Lilian Murray became the first woman President of the British Dental Association. Avery quotes another pupil as saying: 'one heard tales of poor girls reduced to sobs and almost hysterics as girls bent under a storm that went on and on and on' — as Frances Mary Buss harangued pupils for breaking one of the many school rules. Since NLCS was the first girls' day school that was not a religious or charitable institution, Miss Buss must have been especially aware of the need for the girls to show decorum and to lean towards service rather than self-promotion. Dame Kitty could be brusque over minor infringement, too.

In his Sesquicentennial history, Nigel Watson mentions that there was some criticism that the 'school neglected those who were less academically inclined'. Separately, he refers several times to Dame Kitty's reputation for awareness of the needs of individual girls. As mentioned above, Dame Kitty gave her own assessment of the girls' needs in 1951 in her talk on 'Education for Girls'. This is compared in this chapter with reports from some former pupils. The way in which these reports were collected is explained in an endnote. All pupils quoted are now professionals in their own right. Their recollections are likely to be reliable, though their perceptions were influenced by feelings they held at the time.

One former pupil (later a magistrate) recalls quite a general view in the lower stream that left in the early 1950s that there was no incentive to do better, unless you were going to University. Despite the increased numbers going to University in successive years, this was still the view in the reminiscences of *The Class of 71: Twenty Years On* produced after Dame Kitty retired in 1965. A former member of staff (Modern Languages) feels that this was an unfair assessment, since the school ran special courses for girls going on to be teachers or nurses; however, this was many a girl's perception. In fact, one of the questions from the audience after her 1951 talk was: 'Does the grammar school do enough for girls of good ability not seeking entrance to University?'

We learn from the chapter herein, 'Kitty Anderson: student of History' that she failed her first year at university, being a young entrant at the age of seventeen. For this reason she may have felt ambivalent about how much to expect of girls at a relatively young age. One girl (later a solicitor) remembers Dame Kitty being very helpful when she decided to read Law rather than History at university. On the other hand, two pupils (later doctors) had angry confrontations with her, in one case about dropping a Science subject and in the other case about sitting a Science subject, both at GCE A-level for entrance to medical school. Hallam Tennyson, a parent whose daughter while at NLCS had leading parts in Benjamin Britten productions, felt everything was judged on academic lines, as his daughter had great difficulty in obtaining any time away from school for rehearsals. The personal communication between his daughter and Dame Kitty left much to be desired.

In her 1951 talk, Dame Kitty expressed her views about the educational needs of girls. She divided problems into two categories, 'social' and 'educational', but noted that this was not entirely satisfactory as they overlapped. Discussing 'social problems' she mentions that 'frequently the high cost of living has been met by mothers becoming wage earners as well as fathers ... the conditions of life today impose great physical and emotional strain on the girls. Their responsibilities at home are often great and they tend to share in adult problems more than in the past, which often gives them an apparent maturity, which is misleading.' She does not suggest how this might be dealt with, but goes on to say: 'frequently it is difficult for them ... to have quiet and leisure for private study. This calls for understanding and sympathy on the part of the school.'

This chapter goes on to focus on the pastoral side of school life, and on occasions when educational needs overlapped with social needs of specific pupils. Undoubtedly Dame Kitty was sensitive to the needs of specific girls, and two examples are given here. A former pupil (later a physiotherapist) reports that as a twelve-year-old, after a bout of illness she felt unable to go to school, but for no obvious reason. Dame Kitty's kindly manner and practical wisdom in suggesting that the girl should come only when she felt able to do so seem to have contributed to these symptoms subsiding within a term. A physical cause was identified, which the pupil feels was possibly triggered by her anxiety about her parents' high expectations for her school achievement. Dame Kitty also offered the part-time post of laboratory assistant to enable a girl with financial problems to stay in the Sixth Form. This was after consulting the girl's close friend, 'with the utmost tact and concern'.

However, Dame Kitty seems to have lacked insight where certain other girls were concerned. One pupil (later a doctor) gained one of two annual Clothworkers Scholarships on the basis of GCE O-level results, which paid her fees in the Sixth Form. She writes in a recent letter: 'Dame Kitty made it clear that she was furious that I had won this rather than someone more deserving' ... 'my Testamur [school leaving report] was one of the cruellest put-downs that I have ever suffered.' Dame Kitty, apparently, was not aware of relevant facts and did not enquire into them before voicing her opinion, which in any case was most intemperate. This former pupil feels that Dame Kitty took this view because she had external music tuition, albeit with an extremely eminent musician. She mentions the serious likelihood that without this Clothworkers Scholarship she may well have had to leave NLCS; and she mentions that the family had suffered trauma due to the war and illness. She summarizes: 'despite my training and working in a profession, it took me years to regain my self-confidence.'

From her research into the history of girls' education, in *The Best Type of Girl* Gillian Avery suggests that 'more anxiety and fear is likely to be caused by disapproval, than by corporal punishment administered to boys'. In the same vein, in *Counselling in Schools* (Ebner-Landy, Gill and Brace) the authors note that pupils may experience problems as a consequence of 'carrying the mantle of being difficult or bad', and that this is often a circular and cumulative process, involving actions and reactions of staff and pupils towards one another. From several examples during Dame Kitty's time, it does seem that once a process of misunderstanding or ignoring of difficulties got under way it seemed hard to reverse. Echoing Dame Kitty's comments on social problems in education, some girls at NLCS had experienced the death of people close to them or had discord in their personal or family life. At least three of those quoted travelled quite a distance to school or may have joined the school later than normal — so finding integration more difficult. In addition, some parents who had chosen NLCS because of its reputation for academic excellence made sacrifices to pay fees (such as the parents of the musical girl quoted above).

All such factors seem to have laid a foundation for academically able, independent and rather prickly girls to cause irritation or to be misunderstood. One such girl (later a business executive) with some of these problems reported that she just kept her head down, but was never happy at school. In retrospect or even at the time, several such pupils have said they realized they had been depressed (two girls who became doctors, another a business executive, one a psychologist). It is rather surprising to find that until the 1970s 'depression' was not fully accepted in psychiatry and related professions as an illness or as a condition requiring attention in children and adolescents, and as one contributor has pointed out, it would be unreasonable to expect the school to have dealt with individual problems exactly as a school counsellor could today.

Yet, in principle, Dame Kitty had shown her awareness of pressures on girls in her 1951 talk and there seems to have been an expectation among pupils that their educational concerns, in particular, would be treated seriously and impartially. Several girls, apparently at odds with the school's expectation in achievement or behaviour, have said in the course of giving information for this chapter that 'no one thought to ask what was the matter'. Thus it seems that the attention given to such problems was uneven at best.

Sources of pastoral advice included Dame Kitty who was available after Assembly for girls with specific requests of all kinds. Miss Senator sometimes worked pastorally through known friends of a girl about whom she was concerned; on one occasion, for instance, asking a friend (later a lawyer) to keep an eye on a girl who was not working hard enough; and she sometimes gave special lessons to those falling behind, or helped with personal advice. However, Miss Senator and another former member of staff (Modern Languages) have said that it was difficult to know when to approach girls who seemed to have problems. The school doctor was available; but her potential pastoral role was probably not very clear.

It may be fortuitous that several of the reminiscences that have come to me involve problems with fees, either explicitly or as background when a pupil was aware of her parents' hopes and expectations as fee-payers. There had always been provision for remission of fees in cases of hardship, and all parents were informed of this initially, but how well this operated in practice is not readily known. These were anxious times for the school financially, as discussed below, and this may have caused tension, the source of which was not fully recognized by staff or girls. It should be noted that Dame Kitty's father and two brothers were accountants, likely to be a background influence on her prudence in management.

I had an uneasy mix of problems myself, stemming from the type of social profile mentioned by Dame Kitty: a background of a working mother who paid my fees, and divorce plus tension in my mother's second marriage. This laid the ground for me to become entangled in an academic problem that was never resolved while I was at school.

Dame Kitty had known for two years prior to 1950 that some pupils would be under-age to take Matriculation, and other successive years would contain some pupils too young to take GCE O-levels. Miss Senator confirmed my recollection that neither parents nor pupils were given details until almost the last moment, just before the mock examinations in February 1950. The Ministry of Education outlined these changes in Circular 168, in April 1948. The aim was to increase the general school leaving age to sixteen by the incentive of offering pupils the chance to take fewer subjects at General Certificate of Education O- and A-levels in place of the fixed requirements of Matriculation. In later changes from GCE to GCSE examinations a good five years warning was given. In 1950, which was the last year of Matriculation, a very small handful of pupils not sixteen by 1 December 1950 were barred from sitting the exam. (The key date after 1950 was 1 September.) The NLCS circular to parents in 1950, the last year of Matriculation — *Notes on New General Certificate of Education*, — confirms that girls who were under-age (of whom I was one) carried on into the Sixth Form and studied both O- and A-levels at the same time.

One pupil (later an academic) was advised to sit for Oxford Responsions instead, as part of Oxford Matriculation. Other pupils would have liked to do this the following year, but were not advised when to apply. At NLCS, another effect for all under-age pupils was that they would not be eligible for the two annual Clothworkers Scholarships into the Sixth Form. My own hope of winning a Clothworkers Scholarship was suddenly dashed. I had calculated previously that this Scholarship was a realistic aim, given my grades and the fact that many of the girls with higher grades were not fee-payers. Also lost was the opportunity to relieve my mother of the burden of paying fees from a salaried job (as a teacher!) that she said she hated. We were not advised about this change until the last moment before we were due to sit mock examinations. The shock and disappointment of not being able to help my mother by means of this Scholarship and the loss of subjects from the broader curriculum due to timetable constraints, led to a depression. This became more serious because of my feeling that no one noticed or cared, though very much later I learned this had not been the case. Efforts I made at the time to obtain help were unsatisfactory. I lost a sense of identity and of direction that was very pervasive despite relative career success and academic success. In summary, my experiences were similar in effect to those of the pupil quoted earlier, and as indicated by her and some other contributors, slippage and difficulties of communication at the time could lead to prolonged and complicated problems.

As Dame Kitty mentioned in her 1951 talk, it is possible to separate educational problems into those more social and those more educational — 'but this is not entirely satisfactory, as one category overlaps with another', she added. I tend to think that at times Dame Kitty mistook one category for the other, rather than thinking clearly about each separately. After the pupil's Clothworkers' Scholarship success, for example, genuine congratulations were in order, and only separately mention of concerns about outside study or financial issues. In the case of decline in academic work, an exploration should have taken place, rather than assumptions about incapacity to do the work.

Indeed, in addition to some pastoral failures, Dame Kitty did not always explain herself well. At times she seemed illogical, inconsistent or even punitive without explicitly stating this. A pupil (later a lawyer) whose sister was at a leading university, but who herself did not work hard academically, was put down to the bottom stream of her year 'so that she could experience what it was like to be top'. It seemed to her that this would require even less work than she was doing at the time. A number of decisions seemed to be made for expediency rather than intellectual clarity, and were not expressed in terms of the sympathetic concern described in Dame Kitty's talk.

I believe that a good case can be made for believing that Dame Kitty was more able to empathize and communicate with girls who were extrovert like herself, even if they were high-spirited and rather a nuisance, than with more introverted girls with difficulties of the kind referred to in her talk.

In Dame Kitty's time and even much later, behaviour tended to be considered a direct reflection of character, and problems that pupils encountered were considered something of a test of character. As early as 1963 school counselling was recommended by the Newsom Report for pupils failing to meet their full potential, and the 1989 Children Act required pastoral supervision in schools. A former NLCS pupil, Jo Ebner-Landy, teacher and psychotherapist, is co-author of the recent book *Counselling in Schools*, quoted earlier, which explains the importance of considering all factors affecting human interaction in an interconnected 'system'. This style of counselling is known as Systemic Counselling. In schools this approach might involve the pupil and family, the school and the staff, friends and other significant influences. Like Dame Kitty, the book mentions that pupils 'in some areas make decisions like an adult, but in others they may feel insecure and childlike'. Their problems included among others 'death of loved ones, overload of schoolwork' and 'the mantle of being difficult or bad'.

The book notes that with all the demands on teachers' time nowadays, it is helpful to hand over the traditional staff counselling role to a specialist. This would also have been true, in principle, in Dame Kitty's time. However, it also seems that the lack of attention to certain problems could have been remedied without too much effort. For instance, the achievements of those pupils leaving to train as teachers or nurses might have been celebrated more or given greater prominence. Individuals might have been given more understanding or support. Dr Sophie Bryant commented, in a research study of the character of schoolchildren, that 'the impulse to criticize [oneself] is the basis of accurate habits of thought'. In her many enthusiasms, Dame Kitty may not have paused to do this, despite her reputation for canvassing opinion about developments within the school. According to Nigel Watson, Miss Drummond, a previous Headmistress, 'had a particular interest in girls deemed disruptive by others whom she preferred to consider difficult and wanted to remain in the school'.

This chapter has aimed to show that in a number of respects Dame Kitty's dealings with girls were not always as Utopian as is often presented, as in many of the reminiscences in this book, for example. As Gillian Avery comments: 'schools are reticent about their failures, which undoubtedly do occur.' Dame Kitty must have experienced stress and worry at NLCS, especially in the early years. The school had serious financial difficulties; reading the Archives, the pain attached to reducing staff salaries to four-fifths is palpable. It is salutary to read from Miss Shillito's record of staff meetings that salaries at the time were £260 per annum, and a term's fees at full rate £14. An attempt by the School to raise fees in 1952 was partially thwarted by the Ministry of Education. It must have been all the more important to advance the school's recognition academically, to help secure its future.

As part of the process of advancing girls' education in general, and improving entry quotas for university and medical schools, it was proper for Dame Kitty to be Honorary Secretary of the Headmistresses' Association, then Chairman of the Executive Committee and finally President. The 1950 Centenary celebrations and attendant publicity were important to the school, and required much attention. There were also significant staff shortages, especially in Science; these were a constant anxiety in some schools. Some staff members felt the demands of the school were all-encompassing, and may well have found it frustrating when girls did not appear to respond to what was expected of them. Later, Dame Kitty joined the governing Council of the Institute for Human Relations from 1963-69, but it has not been possible to find anyone who knew her in this context. It may be noted that like Frances Mary Buss, Dame Kitty was the eldest child and only daughter with two or more brothers, and was encouraged by her family from the earliest days. There is every reason to think her family life was harmonious, but this could make it somewhat difficult for her to understand or probe more complex situations. Dame Kitty's PhD thesis concerned early efforts to help individuals and stabilize society by providing suitable work. I am sure that overall her intentions were constructive and compassionate. However, to conclude: Dame Kitty had admirable objectives, but was human enough not to be able to fulfil them all.

I am very much indebted to many individuals for reading various drafts, including several authors of chapters in this book, and for their observant comments. Also to Jo Ebner-Landy, co-author of 'Counselling in Schools' *for reading a late version, for her helpful comments, and for permission to quote from that work, and to Mrs Karen Morgan, Senior Librarian and Archivist at NLCS and her staff. In particular, I thank all contributors of reminiscences, whose willingness to be forthcoming is much valued. Any faults of the final version are entirely my own.*

Erica Brostoff (Rees) 1946-53. Married with one son. MSc Social Psychology. Executive in market research and advertising, Researcher in psychotherapy and health care. Research Fellow, UMDS, University of London, 1990-92. Personal research interest: social intuition.

References (in order of appearance in text)

Anderson, Kitty, *On the treatment of vagrancy and the relief of the poor and destitute in the Tudor period, based on the local records of London to 1552 and Hull to 1576*. A thesis submitted for the degree of Doctor of Philosophy, in the University of London, 1933

Watson, N., *And Their Works Do Follow Them: The Story of North London Collegiate School 1850-2000*, James and James, London, 2000

Anderson, K., *The Education of Girls*. An Address delivered on 5 October 1951 at the Annual Conference of the National Association of Inspectors of Schools and Educational Organisers, NAISEO, 1951. (NLCS Archives)

Bremmer, C. S., *The Education of Girls and Women in Great Britain*, Swan Sonnenschein, 1897 (quoted in Avery, G., see below.)

Avery, G., *The Best Type of Girl: a history of girls' independent schools*, Deutsch, London, 1991

Uglow, J. (ed.), *The Macmillan Dictionary of Women's Biography*, Papermac, London, 1999

Various contributors, *The Class of '71: Twenty Years On*, 1991. (NLCS Archives)

Notes on New General Certificate of Education, North London Collegiate School, 1951 (NLCS Archives)

Bor, R., Ebner-Landy, J., Gill, S. and Brace, C. *Counselling in Schools*, Sage, London, 2002

Peck, W., *A little learning*, Faber, London, 1952 (quoted by Avery, G. see above)

Bryant, S., *Testing the Character of School Children*, Journal of the Anthropological Institute, vol. 15, pp 338-49, 1886

Goodyer, I.M. (Ed), *The Depressed Child and Adolescent*, Cambridge Child and Adolescent Psychiatry, Cambridge University Press, 2nd ed, 2002

Lee, R.M., *Researching Sensitive Topics*, Sage, London, 1993
Chandos, J., *Boys Together, English Public Schools 1800-1964*, Hutchinson, London, 1984

The quick firm footstep

My memories of Dr Anderson are vivid and treasured. I was in the Lower Fourth when she became our Headmistress. I recall the amazing change of atmosphere in the school. Dr Anderson wanted to know us all by name, even to talk to us. As she passed by in the corridor her smile was warm and one felt happy to be part of the school.

Her enthusiasm was always infectious — whether from the platform at Assembly, or visiting our form room to share a new plan with us, such as the launching of the School Advisory Council. Representing our Upper Fourth Form with fellow monitor Elaine Surtees on this North London version of the medieval 'Witan' was my first experience of democracy at work. School lunches and eating sweets or ice-creams outside school in school uniform were among the sensitive subjects on the Advisory Council's first agenda!

There was a new awareness of political events and life outside school. Dr Anderson made sure it was not only members of the Current Affairs Society who became knowledgeable. I remember attending the Commonwealth Conference for Schools as a representative for NLCS. Sir Lancelot Gibbs fired us all when he spoke about the change from Empire to Commonwealth. In our discussion groups we recognised the significance of the change and ourselves as part of the hope for the future. Although my interests at that time were centred on the Literary and Dramatic Society, Dr Anderson had encouraged me in a more socially responsible direction.

In my Sixth Form years, Dr Anderson told me that her past three Senior Prefects had taken up places at Manchester University in order to read Social Administration. It was an exciting new course and she thought I was ideally fitted to follow in their footsteps. Such was her influence that I did, becoming the fourth Senior Prefect to do so. My friends and contemporaries shared Dr Anderson's continuing friendship and encouragement in the years that followed. Some of us had tea with her in her new flat near

Canons, meeting again during our first year at University. There is no doubt that we all loved and honoured her for the profound influence she had exercised on our 'growing up'.

I remember so well her small gowned figure, with lisle stockings that always wrinkled round her slender ankles, the quick firm footstep, the bright expectant light in her eye, the attractive wisps of hair that escaped from her bun and softened her scholarly brow. She was a woman of amazing energy, deeply committed to the cause of education for all. Her days at North London were dynamic for my generation. Her gentle humanity is a lasting memory. I was privileged to be her Senior Prefect from 1948-49, feeling that I was supporting her and the school. I am sure that the reverse was the case but I had an unforgettable year in daily counsel with her.

Dear Dame Kitty, you will never be forgotten by me nor I am sure by those who followed us.

April Halton (Rogerson) 1942-49

'With admiration, gratitude and affection'

Reflecting on what I could say about Dame Kitty, this eminent yet down-to-earth woman, I decided I wanted to try to write from reality — hard to establish at a distance of sixty years, rather than simply the warm glow of nostalgia. As a Historian I think that is what Dame Kitty would have expected. I contacted people I still know, who were at school in Dame Kitty's time, and I have incorporated many of their comments.

The fairly general view is that we were very fortunate to have been at NLCS during Dame Kitty's headship. We were 'fantastically lucky'; she 'epitomised the perfect Head'. Many people used the words 'approachable' and 'friendly'. Her personality was such that doing the job well came naturally to her. However, allied to this warmth she 'radiated authority'. In the Hall every day she had a 'commanding presence'. Yet she could come to the front of the platform in relaxed fashion to share with us her excitement at some success, large or small, or else to admonish some among us for causing a local resident to complain about talking loudly on the bus. She had the great gift of being able to combine authority with putting people at their ease. Even when dealing with someone who had done serious wrong, she was felt to be reasonable and kind.

She had a great interest in girls as individuals. Her aim was to know every one of the approximately 1000 girls at school, a characteristically hard target. She was never satisfied except with the best. Some of the people who expressed opinion felt that she did not know them and there are examples of her confusing the names of sisters. On the other hand, others felt that she did. On many occasions I heard her address girls by name as she moved around the school. She took lessons down to the Upper Thirds, so plainly she would have known better those she had actually taught. I can only say from my experience that I know she knew a great many of us, not just prefects and the high academic achievers. Importantly, when giving advice she realised the implications of decisions on individuals, even when perhaps the individual herself would not realise her far-sightedness.

Dame Kitty was clearly a woman of great faith. The school she ran was a recognisable descendant of the Bible-based establishment watched over by Septimus Buss, the brother of the founder. She believed that true happiness stemmed from a religious belief, a view that naturally was not shared by all the girls. I never heard her proclaim her own beliefs yet I believe they sustained her and enabled her to give so generously of her scholarship and energy. She did of course say prayers every morning with the whole school. An insight into her hopes for us is given by a small, but I think significant change she made to one of the prayers. Previously we had prayed to be saved from vanity and pride. Given her own lack of self-importance, I do not think she could be accused of encouraging anything approaching cockiness. I think true self-confidence was something she hoped we would develop in her school.

She was fiercely proud of the history and traditions of the school and greatly admired Frances Mary Buss and Sophie Bryant. I think Dame Kitty consciously and by nature worked to follow in their footsteps as a pioneer of education for girls. An ardent believer in democracy, she started the School Advisory Council which even today one reads of as an innovation in other schools. I remember her enthusiasm in her classes on the United Nations Organisation, which was just being set up — what would she say now? I think her remarks might be regretful but positive. She invited all the candidates in the local constituency at the General Election to come to talk to us. Some parents complained at the inclusion of the Communist, but she insisted. Afterwards her comment was: 'He was much the nicest man!'

Founder's Day was a great occasion for her each year. Many of the people I spoke to recall her on that Day in the magnificent red gown of a London University PhD. (One girl found it a source of inspiration and indeed went on to earn one for herself.) I can see it flying behind her as she toured the school with the monitors, firmly holding the hands of the two smallest girls in school.

Now I shall indulge my own nostalgic memories. I remember Dame Kitty's laugh, her ready smile, her ever-ready enthusiasm. I remember her earnest, thoughtful response to questions on both large and small matters. I see her with Professor Richardson at the opening of the Done Gates, with the Duchess of Gloucester at the opening of the swimming pool. I see her leading the children from the East End of London through the darkened corridors at Canons to their meeting with Father Christmas beside the lit tree in the Hall, and her delight in their joy. I see her selling at the Frances Mary Buss House stall at the Grosvenor House Charity Fair and sharing everyone's enjoyment at the School Dance. I hear her reading the Founder's Day prayers, especially the piece: 'O Lord, Who has taught us that thou dost require much from those to whom much is given...' To me that was the principle with which she imbued the school; it could be followed by everyone, religious and non-religious alike. To me she was a great lady and one of the most important influences of my life. I was most fortunate to have been at school in her time. In the phrase from the Service of Thanksgiving for her Life and Work, held on 23 March 1979, I do indeed remember her 'with admiration, gratitude and affection'.

Margot Edmonds (Hassell) 1942-53

Dame Kitty teaching Current Affairs in the Drummond Library

Dame Kitty's extended family

In 1945 the decade was neatly divided by the end of World War Two. Dr Anderson, who arrived at NLCS in 1944, was a total contrast to her predecessor, Eileen Harold. Miss Harold was a woman of profound Christian faith, a distinguished scholar of donnish wit. She had a beautiful speaking voice. Many girls, especially the younger ones, perceived her as remote and unapproachable. Yet as a junior I established a rapport with her that would endure for years. Dr Anderson was a stark contrast: she embodied the warmth and good sense one associates with her Yorkshire upbringing. Spiritual or aesthetic dimensions did not loom large within her personality. One of the most admirable facets of her Headship was her response to the very junior members of the school, who all adored her.

In 1945, my form of Sheilas, Jeans, Joans and Valeries — names seemed different then — moved out of junior school. Senior school began for us in a grey utilitarian room that matched the grey utilitarian postwar years. Our form mistress was typical of many of the older members of staff. She was the sole support of elderly parents. Teachers in those days were badly paid, and often family savings had been lost in the Depression of the 1930s. Many teachers spent years repaying money loaned for their education. No wonder some looked shabby and defeated. All our older members of staff were unmarried. Not by choice: countless hopes of marriage were dashed by the slaughter of 1914-18. Some had no other life besides their work at NLCS. However, the other aspect of this situation was that the older staff members gave a wonderful loyalty and sense of stability to the school, and many generations of pupils remember them with respect and affection. Dr Anderson herself was unmarried, but would one family have satisfied her? No, we were her large, varied family.

Young teachers brought a wider outlook from the outside world. They were bound to become favourites. There was Miss Hume, a pretty, vivacious Science teacher, and handsome, serene Miss Beaumont, who had seen war service in Bible lands and who wonderfully enlightened New Testament Greek. There was great excitement when they both married and left us. Schoolgirl 'pashes' were rife, soppy but innocent. The private lives of all our teachers were subjects of great curiosity, and what we failed to find out we made up. The 'jolly hockey sticks' image of girls' schools in old-fashioned school stories was founded on the theories of Dr Arnold of

Rugby: sportsmanship was the Christian Platonic ideal. During my time at school, girls who were no good at games had a rotten time. Today's girls would never support the baiting that Games mistresses occasionally inflicted.

Today's children have a far more sophisticated and varied life than was possible in that age of rationing and restrictions. Unlike us, today's young people often fly to the continent at half-term, eat exotic meals in restaurants, have plenty of boyfriends and enjoy entertainment provided by state-of-the-art technology. In 1947 even a tv set was a rarity. Clothes were rationed, and so were a host of other things. This meant that treats at school had greater significance. They were like family gatherings. (I make no apology for my emphasis on Dame Kitty's 'family'.) At Founder's Day in the 1940s there were Old North Londoners who remembered Miss Buss; we held open days, exhibitions, and the Christmas Carol Service with the splendid processional carol *Personent Hodie*. Some of us were invited to parties at the Hampstead studio of Mrs Cowles, who taught pottery. Another Christmas treat was the staff play. In those days staff members were far more formal. We enjoyed the absurdity of seeing them all dressed up. The plays were usually Shakespeare, with Shaw's *St Joan* a notable exception. Olive Gabriel, our young, inspirational art teacher, took the title role and gave a marvellous performance. A fierce Maths teacher renowned for her mannish suits and ties was the executioner — later she was Herod in a staff Nativity play that caused a great deal of ill-will in the staff room. Rumour had it that everyone wanted to be the Virgin Mary. Then we had the school dance, held in the hallowed precinct of the Hall (one girl was seen kissing a pimply youth during the foxtrot and the scandal kept us going for weeks). The dance has long been abandoned in this modern age of discos and night clubs. Despite very infrequent visits abroad, we were very well informed about the state of the world, especially from the current affairs lessons and meetings encouraged by Dr Anderson. Paris was still the cultural centre in the 1940s. Girls anxious to make a good impression at university interviews learned by heart reviews of French films from the *Observer*.

There were an awful lot of us in our extended family at NLCS. Many races, many creeds, girls who were naughty, good, clever and not so clever. Some were left out in the race for success in their school careers. The criticism that Dr Anderson's obsession with university placements caused the less bright girls to be neglected is just. Most went on to lead solid, ordinary lives. 'Let not ambition mock their useful toil.' There were, of course, far fewer career openings for girls in those days — and the return of the ex-servicemen after the war encouraged the notion of domesticity. And schools did not have professional career advisors in those days.

I write with profound gratitude to my dear old school, and the tolerance and Christian example that was shown me. I was a difficult youngster. Today I have no unhealthy nostalgia. It wasn't a bad thing that we did not grow up too fast. Yet I believe that beneath the cool sophistication and abundance of material goods today, there is a greater care for the environment and a real sense of compassion. In 2002 I saw North Londoners wearing the national dress of our multi-faith, multi-racial school. Everyone was friendly and helpful. Dame Kitty would be proud.

Barbara Dorf, 1939-51

∼

What mattered

When King George VI died, one grey day in February 1952, Dr Anderson decided that we, her girls, could not be allowed to set off to our homes and teas in ignorance of this event of such national importance. She was, after all, a Historian. Looking back, her manner of relaying the news to us seems to me characteristic. She did not delegate the job to our form mistresses, within the day-to-day familiarity of the form room. We were not assembled in the Hall, to await a grave, remote announcement that would, literally, go over our heads. Instead she decreed something out of the ordinary that made the ordinary memorable. We had to 'wait quietly' until she herself came to each form in turn to make known the sombre story, as well as the fact that there would be a day of public mourning to mark the Monarch's death. Inevitably, being of tender years, we later reinterpreted this as a 'holiday' and, nervously, rejoiced — but only after we had already absorbed from our Headmistress a proper sense of the gravity and sadness of an occasion that ought to touch us all.

Her voice was light, spoke of the North, of Yorkshire, a place without fanciness, full of independent folk who spoke their minds, a down-to-earth place of windswept moors, where you could breathe deep and speak true; and where, below the earth, men hacked out coal for our hearths, turning our highfalutin' North West London air into fog and worse. It would have been hard to imagine a circumstance that might cause that voice to rise up and become loud, shrill, complaining.

She was yet to become Dame Kitty, a title with cuddly overtones and hints of skittishness. I don't think we ever saw the skittish side — though her eyes could certainly twinkle and beam and her physical form would have offered plenty of purchase for cuddles. Those were days when corsets still counted and bodies were reined in. Her emanation was of an august being, firmly upholstered in a stern grey suit designed (if such a level of planning could be imagined for it) simply to be overlooked. Dr Anderson must surely have worn dresses in summer, but my memory never abandons her tailored jacket. Her hair — not scraped, not pulled, but simply taken back and caught up in a bun at the nape — held to tradition also.

Such mannish outfits abounded in the staffroom, sported by Miss Shillito, Miss Scrimgeour, Miss Senator, Miss Paneth, Miss Gossip among others. A possible more casual alternative was the pale blouse with long cardigan in neutral tones: Mrs Condliffe, Miss Ellis, Miss Dass … The bright smocks and dashes of colour Miss Keightley sported scarcely counted: she taught Art. Two other singular embodiments of style existed. Youthful Miss Canham, who arrived to teach us Classics, was a sartorial sensation. She fascinated us by teaming with her pencil skirts a range of hand-knitted cap-sleeved sweaters in offbeat tones — a veritable gust of fashion. And of course there was Miss Clay. No confining suits for her. She would sit on the edge of the form room table in crumpled knits and plaid skirts, swinging her legs in dark un-mended stockings (those were the years before the coming of tights) and convey to us in her swooping voice that English was exhilarating, as yet beyond our reach but there to be discovered.

But these were not things that mattered.

What did matter? Dr Anderson once described to us a gathering she had attended. It had been, she said, eyes alight, speaking with the greatest possible relish, full of 'lively minds'. She conjured up for us a hundred shapeless cerebella, skipping and fizzing somewhere up among the chandeliers. What mattered was that as many as possible of her girls should be of and among those lively minds, up there amid the tinkling glass, reflecting light for all we were worth; that we should have more and better chances than she and her colleagues had ever had, to obtain which they had done such arduous battle on our behalf: that we should be granted as much right as our brothers to the best education available.

The best — in those days — had been practically denied to her generation, and was represented by Oxford and Cambridge. (In Cambridge women were only admitted to University degrees in 1949.) So the girls who showed any spark or gleam that might admit them to those hitherto male meccas were singled out as they passed into the Sixth and Upper Sixth, myself among them. We took part in 'lively' and potentially enlivening discussions held in Dr Anderson's room, at which we poured forth our views on what was and what should be: the phrase 'But surely … !' rang out loud and clear and often.

The path that led me to be included in this throng was a not uncommon one, taking me gradually from rebellion against authority to absorption in the system as I moved up the school and attained such lofty offices as Chairman (!) of the Litt & Dram and Editor of the magazine, as well as into the slidier position of Prefect. My waywardness had not gone unnoticed; but nor had it ever, I think, been despised or dismissed. It must have been regarded as representing an energy that might be channelled towards more fruitful goals.

I was called into Dr Anderson's office for one of the most crucial conversations of my life, which alas I cannot remember. It took place after some transgression or other, I forget exactly which one. I was aware that this was a woman who had seen into the whirlpool of my nature and was trying to save me from myself, that what she was telling me was entirely for my good, and of great import for my future. I remember an urgent question and I remember gazing out of the window across dark trees blowing at the edge of Canons Park. I remember my moody, insufficient reply: 'I don't know …' Yet I cannot remember what that vital question was. Sometimes I think that (though to the outward eye perhaps things did not turn out too badly) had I not evaded that question and wiped it forever from my mind — having become, as I think I did, sitting there, overwhelmed by the blighting sadness of the situation — I might, all in all, have achieved what my father would have called 'a better result'.

Whenever I look back at that time I find myself wondering whether the singling out of a few pupils as being to some extent 'golden girls' — that is to say, capable of high academic achievement — did not in some way diminish things for the rest; whether it might have engendered in a particular sense that getting to Oxford or Cambridge was the only really worthwhile option. When I meet an Old North Londoner of that epoch I always conduct my own personal poll to discover whether this might be so. Some deny it, but most have backed up my feelings. If it is true that there were casualties of the drive towards academic excellence it is to be regretted. Specialised amenities had been erected — swimming pools, a theatre, for example — importance was given to Art and the Arts, to Sport as well as to the world of academe. Certainly I can hardly complain.

On another occasion Dr Anderson called me to her room to discuss what direction I might take. I wanted to go to drama school. She expressed the view that that would be 'a waste of a good mind' (and presumably, one of those lively ones). Of course I was flattered. She went on, with great astuteness, taking into account the mighty contrariness of my nature, to assure me that 'all young girls' go through a period of wanting to go to drama school. By this stratagem she persuaded me to avoid at any cost doing what 'all girls' wanted to do but to think instead about trying for University.

As it turned out, Cambridge University at that period was probably one of the best drama schools around. Among my immediate contemporaries were Margaret Drabble, Clive Swift, Roger Hammond, David Buck, Derek Jacobi, John Bird and Peter Cook. I think it very possible that had I gone to drama school I should never have become an actress at all. The experience of going to university changed my life in all sorts of large essential and wonderful ways and I never stop being grateful for it.

In the midst of telling us, on that grey February day, that the King had died, Dr Anderson suddenly stopped speaking. 'Who broke that window?' she asked, in mild surprise. I had to own up. In fact while we were all waiting for her to arrive I had — whilst giving a fairly excellent imitation of the Maths teacher, Miss Hogg — flung open the window with such force that it had cracked. It may be that this personal element, abruptly introduced into the solemn occasion, is one further reason why I shall always remember where I was when George VI died. But Dr Anderson had the great gift of seeing the whole without losing sight of the detail. Her grandness lay in her great simplicity — her ability never to diminish the personal, the human scale of things, the difficulty of life as well as its joys.

I still have the postcard sent from her holiday on Crete with warmest congratulations on my A-level results and comments on the tremendously exciting archeological findings being made in the vicinity.

Eleanor Bron 1949-56

Dr Anderson had the great gift of seeing the whole without losing sight of the detail

Shakespeare in the garden — A Midsummer Nights' Dream
Celia Nottage as Puck in the Rose Garden

7

'If it ain't broke don't fix it' —
The Teaching of English During Dr Anderson's Headship

KAY MOORE

For several decades, the obvious distinctive feature of the English department was the three splendid women who led it, whilst a variety of younger teachers came and went in its lower reaches.

Ruby Scrimgeour came to NLCS in 1934 and from 1962 was Dr Anderson's Deputy Head; Miriam Shillito, Head of Department when I arrived in 1964, had been a pupil at the school during the First World War — in the same group as the writers Stella Gibbons and Stevie Smith; after taking her degree she returned to NLCS to teach. Margery Clay was the 'baby' of the triumvirate, arriving in 1942, but in her intellect and passion she was unmatchable. They liked, stimulated and supported one another, despite clear differences in style and approach, and were united in their kindly non-judgemental care of the younger teachers who served under them.

The three leaders kept the teaching of the Upper Third forms to themselves so that they could be trained in the 'right' Canons ways: as the 1958 HM School Inspectors commented admiringly, 'in the lower forms habits of work, attitude and skills are being formed that [will be] most valuable in the sixth form.' Letters in the Archives recall: 'Greek Legends with Miss Shillito ... magical'; 'English with Miss Scrimgeour was always a joy'. Loving Canons as they did, the triumvirate made full use of the varied stages the grounds offered for drama: *'Midsummer Night's Dream* was perfectly suited to the Rose Garden' — 'I remember *Gay Goshawk* on the Terraces'. One Old North Londoner found the play-acting out of doors, both in lessons and with her friends during breaks, so much the high point of later memories that in the 1980s she left a prize for Middle School Drama in her legacy.

The triumvirate: Margery Clay, Miriam Shillito and Ruby Scrimgeour

It comes as no surprise, then, that the English syllabus as it was written down shows that it was very 'child centred' — well ahead of the coinage of that phrase. The work in each layer focused on the girls' development and sought to play to their strengths at each stage. In the Upper Third, the department aimed 'to keep imagination alive in every possible way ... to stimulate the powers of observation ... to give opportunity for appreciation of every kind of story'. This involved 'much learning by heart ... particularly of good lyrical poetry'. (Remember *Young Pegasus?*)

In the Lower Fourth the girls' growing awareness of their own world was guided by 'a careful study of character in the novel, short story and drama' and their sharp young intellects were exercised on their first Shakespeare play, *A Midsummer Night's Dream*. When the play had been read each form was divided into five groups. Each chose an Act to prepare, and at the end of term, gloriously clad in Miss Kitching's costumes from the jam-packed drama cupboard, in outfits purloined from home or constructed from cardboard (Wall, anyone?) the five Acts were performed all over the place. In the Upper Fourth year, in December and March similar treatment was given to *The Merchant of Venice* and *Twelfth Night*, and in July, Julius Caesar staggered, sheet-wrapped, to his bitter death in the Rose Garden. No wonder 'Acting Outside' is vividly recalled by Old North Londoners.

It may be that some of the other chosen texts, though designed to develop desirable skills — in the Fifth Form the aim was 'to provide a cultural basis for taste and judgement' — in practice gave less real pleasure.

Cranford, Junior Modern Essays, The De Coverley Papers and the largely incident-free *Travels With A Donkey* may still have some Old North Londoner fans; however, the child's-eye view in *Kidnapped* and *David Copperfield* was more readily accessible and exciting.

Yet that ambitious Fifth Form syllabus was unbeatable; as a young graduate in 1964 I was excited by its drama content: Greek theatre and *Antigone, Oedipus Rex* and *Oedipus at Colonus;* medieval drama from its church origins with *Everyman;* Elizabethan theatre and *Macbeth,* and the progression to *The Rivals.* I learnt so much! The O-level syllabus had an inevitable flatness after this heady home-brew, apart from the Shakespeare — we studied two plays and the girls chose which one they wished to be tested on. But the examiners' choices of *Far Away and Long Ago* and *Lepanto* caused headaches and tears of frustration in private. And the substitution of Précis and Noun Clauses for the excitement of frequent debates and impromptu or prepared speech-making felt stifling.

Naomi Perry (Freedman, left 1968), now a barrister, recalls that even in the Upper Third pupils were asked to give a speech on any subject and illustrate it as they liked — she talked about a holiday in Rome and handed round postcards. On one occasion, excitingly, when their English teacher was needed elsewhere, a prefect came into the classroom, instructed to hold an impromptu debate. 'Magic!', Naomi comments. In the interests of truth and balance, it should be added that she thought those eighteenth-century essays were 'really interesting' and no doubt she was not alone.

Helen Lloyd (left 1968) sent these memories:

September 14th 1961 was my eleventh birthday and my first day at NLCS in Upper IV 14 with Miss Clay as form teacher. Whenever I hear someone refer to 'opening Pandora's box', I remember Miss Clay's Greek story lessons, my brown exercise book, and the drawing of many horrors flying out of a box, with which I illustrated the myth. I can't remember if she read the stories to us or retold them from memory, but I know that they were laid down in our memories, by her telling, our writing, our drawing and most of all by our acting of key scenes. In most subjects, we were not allowed to draw in our exercise books, so these lessons provided a welcome link to the freedoms of primary school and a series of vivid images that remain with me forty years later.

I don't remember grammar and vocabulary lessons, but we must have had them: why else would I be one of the last people in Britain to shudder every time I see a split infinitive, or read 'disinterested' in place of 'uninterested'? My memories of English teaching in the Lower IV and Upper IV are of dilapidated prewar copies of such 'major' literary works as *Travels With a Donkey*, *Cranford* and *The De Coverley Papers*. We did read one genuinely major work, *David Copperfield*, but only managed to cover ten chapters in a term, due to the slow pace of reading round the class. I remember the plays much better, because we acted them out in class. I read parts in *The School for Scandal*, *The Rivals* and Shakespeare plays and learnt some of the more famous speeches by heart. I think we did *A Midsummer Night's Dream*, *Twelfth Night* and *The Merchant of Venice* — more Shakespeare than my son read in the whole of his secondary education.

My only memories of reading poetry in those first three years are of Ballads and an anthology that included *The Lady of Shalott*. We certainly had the opportunity to write poetry and stories as well.

O-level exercises tended to instruct: *Write a sentence to bring out clearly the meaning of 'a pig in a poke'* (I was as baffled as the girls); *Write an essay on 'Grass'* ... *Explain clearly the two possible meanings of the sentence, 'Two girls went for a tramp on the downs'*. (At least they might have had some fun with that one.)

In the Sixth Form all the girls had English lessons, whether they stayed for one year (a slowly decreasing number), two years or seven terms, and whatever other subjects they studied. In 1958 the Government Inspectors commented on the unusually large sizes of Sixth Form groups — 'sometimes up to 29 ... [we saw] 26 and 24'. This may have been partly because of the demand of all those non-specialists' English lessons: four a week for general Arts students, two for girls leaving after the Lower Sixth, Literature for Scientists (and from the early 1960s the scientists also studied Use of English). This surely reflects the confidence the triumvirate felt in their crowd control and their commitment to lively, informed discussion and student presentations.

The Inspectors seemed to feel that 'the less able might be at some disadvantage' and suggested tentatively: 'it might be worth considering ... more provision for guided individual study, or work in smaller groups.' But their marvellous compliment 'there is no suggestion of any dividing line between formal and informal education' suggests a regime buzzing with inventiveness, ideas and energy that must be the envy of tests-beset teachers of the present day. Certainly the aims of the syllabus for non-specialists made no concessions. They studied 'the form of the epic/lyric novel/short story ... the history of the English language' while the one-year General Arts students had 'the development of the novel (*Otranto, Northanger Abbey, Jane Eyre, Under the Greenwood Tree, The Mayor of Casterbridge, Mr Polly*), two Shakespeare plays, *Murder In the Cathedral* and *Under Milk Wood*, and sixteenth, seventeenth and nineteenth-century poetry ...'. Again, in the face of this uncompromising enthusiasm for the best of the canon, the Inspectors had a few reservations: 'not at present entirely successful; perhaps the main need is to relate the work more closely to the girls' own interests.'

Meanwhile, for the scientists at least, the 1900 barrier was broken through far more frequently. Janet Haffner, one of the two young teachers in the English department from 1961 to 1964, recalls that Willis Hall, Wesker and Pinter went down very well, as did plays by Shaw and Ibsen about ideas and issues — including women's emancipation. In Use of English (prescribed by C.P. Snow), which influenced government to cause boffins and medics to write properly, contemporary journalism was used to trigger discussion and analysis of differing styles and choice of detail in broadsheets and tabloids. This topicality did little to allay the irritation of a seventh lesson once a week and staying in school until four o'clock!

The prevailing width of the school's curriculum was to be found in the A-level course as well. For much of the first year, in four lessons a week we cantered through texts and material related to the prescribed exam texts: *Romeo and Juliet* and *The Winter's Tale* before *Othello*; the History of English and life in medieval England before Chaucer's *General Prologue* and one of his *Canterbury Tales*; poems of every kind before Gerard Manley Hopkins (Miriam Shillito's favourite). As in the Fifth Form syllabus, there was a range and intellectual excitement in what we studied that delighted me, at twenty-four, as well as many of the girls; working through the Triumvirs' enthusiastic and ambitious program did as much to provide me with 'a cultural basis for taste and judgment' as had my three years at university.

The three leaders of the English department, too, felt that their syllabus had the stamp of excellence. Scholarly and uncompromising in their passion for good writing of every kind, they rarely altered what was taught. When I researched for this essay I was amused, envious and impressed to see that the typewritten pages of the 'English Syllabus' submitted to the new

Headmistress in 1964 were absolutely identical to those sent to the HM Inspectors of Schools in 1957. The axiom 'If it ain't broke don't fix it' may have brought about some limitations during the Dame Kitty years, but English departments at the start of this twenty-first century may well wish that their Whitehall controllers would treat that notion with more respect and give back to them and their pupils the joys and satisfactions of a stable curriculum based on excellence, enthusiasm and scholarship.

∼

Not somebody to be trifled with

In one of my Trebizon school stories the heroine, Rebecca, after some seriously bad behaviour, is sent to the Head. Later, she finds her friends are envious. 'Why, you lucky thing, you didn't even get a punishment!', they say. To which she responds: 'Oh yes I did. I'd rather have had a detention any time.' *She would have preferred almost anything to Miss Welbeck's cold and justifiable anger,* I noted as author. Although I wrote those words some thirty years after my own schooldays (and memorable summonses to Dr Anderson's study) I knew only too well how Rebecca might be feeling. Our real-life Headmistress exuded not coldness and anger but North Country warmth and kindness — but that didn't make an interview any easier. As one school friend, Sarah Flower, vividly recalls: 'There was the ghastly occasion when I was sent to her in disgrace. She seemed baffled. "Are you happy at home?" she asked, perhaps anxious to find some excuse for me. I had no such excuse and wept buckets. Her disappointment in one was the ultimate disgrace.'

In an era when the lash of a plimsoll or the sting of a steel ruler were standard fare (I had sampled both at my previous school) rather than solicitous inquiries about one's home life, Dr Anderson was ahead of her time. On arriving at NLCS I was surprised to discover there was no punishment regime for bad behaviour. Yet neither was the regime permissive. My eleven-year-old persona, pretty untamed after an early childhood spent running wild in wartime London, father away at the Front, could see at once that DA was not somebody to be trifled with. Each morning in Hall, as soon as we were all sitting quietly, the tinkling of the piano would stop as one watched that doughty figure, calm, purposeful, sheaf of papers in hand, walk towards the stage to take Assembly, with the whole school rising to attention as she entered. It was clear who was the Captain of the ship.

'To say that I thought of her as the Queen cannot be right' — Sarah Flower again. 'Dr Anderson totally preceded her in my experience ... or rather, the Queen was just a lissom young girl at the time. No, it must be that I think of the Queen now as I did of Dr Anderson then, the epitome of quiet authority: dumpy figures that exuded majesty and for whom one could have nothing but respect.'

I had my first private audience with DA at the age of thirteen. I cannot remember what I had done, only that the shock of her disappointment in me stung more sharply and lingered longer than any steel ruler, let alone a mere detention. At fourteen, the full force of her disappointment on another occasion comes back to me clearly. I had been editing and circulating 'Bright Sparks', an unofficial magazine for the Upper Fourth. It contained one or two scurrilous poems that lampooned members of staff. It only ran for two issues. One day, both copies had been found, confiscated and sent to the Headmistress — next day, so was their editor. — 'You say you want to be a writer, a journalist?', asked DA mildly. It was a rhetorical question for I had more than once confided to her my life's ambition. In spite of the trouble I was in I blushed and nodded enthusiastically. With a small frown and North Country directness, she simply handed the magazines back to me. 'Then you won't want to be writing this sort of thing', she said. That was all. In the years that followed, doing all kinds of writing jobs including, as Oxfam Press Officer, reporting on conditions in refugee camps, I hoped that now I was doing better and might be less of a disappointment to DA.

When we let Dr Anderson down, it mattered to us because we could see that it really mattered to her. It was never faked. She would shake hands with every girl in the school at Christmas time and knew each one of us by name. 'From my very first meeting with Dr Anderson', writes another ONL friend, Gillian Seal (she came to North London in the Sixth Form), 'I can remember wanting to go to her school. She always spoke directly to you and looked into your eyes. She was such a kind considerate teacher.'

Dr Anderson had a dry sense of humour and was very astute. In spite of a passionate belief in women's education, her approach was not inflexible. When, in the middle of my O-level year, I was offered my dream job (as a trainee writer and sub-editor with the Amalgamated Press in Fleet Street) she could see that I had made up my mind to take it. She gave me her blessing, on one condition. 'You must come back in the summer and sit your O-levels. You'll have to study for them in your spare time, of course. But I won't hear of you not taking the exams. They may come in useful, you never know.'

In that era five good O-levels as a passport to the workplace were the equivalent of a general arts degree today. She was possibly concerned that I might one day change my mind about wanting to be a writer. I never did change my mind, but it was the right advice. It was not the O-levels themselves but the very rewarding experience of studying independently that was to give me confidence and proved of value over the years. How wise she was. Kitty Anderson's outlook was thoroughly modern. Once she spoke to Gillian Seal about a problem confronting teachers in Africa. The problem there, she explained, was providing a creche for the older pupils' babies. 'This information', recalls Gillian, 'inspired me to ask for a creche at the afternoon pottery class I was attending in the 1960s. The male principal of the Further Education college was horrified at my suggestion, but the time would come.'

DA never needed a creche. She had no babies of her own. But we were all her children. In 1978, hundreds of us came together for her Memorial Service at St Margaret's Westminster and said our last good-bye.

Anne Digby 1946-51

Two reprimands

I was summoned to DA's office to be told that a senior member of staff had spotted that I wasn't wearing my beret on my way to school. My impression was that DA herself felt bound to act because it mattered to that member of staff, but that her heart was not in her reproof. School uniform rules were not really strict in Dame Kitty's time — far less strict than at my daughter's State grammar school, thirty years later. At NLCS in the 1960s we were allowed to wear, for example, any dark brown (called, amazingly, 'nigger brown') skirt or coat.

On another occasion I was reprimanded by Dame Kitty for introducing a chain letter that threatened a terrible fate to anyone who broke the chain. This time I felt she seriously disapproved and that her disapproval was entirely justified. I'd only introduced the wretched letter to please the boy who gave it to me. These two encounters bore out the impression I'd received from school Assemblies that Dame Kitty was both liberal and fair.

Helen Lloyd 1961-68

∼

The School Dance Outrage

'Never forget', Dame Kitty said to us, 'that there are people of your age paying tax so that you can go to university.'

Of all the things I heard her say during my time at NLCS, that made the deepest impression. It summed up the ethos of the school. Growing up surrounded by the beauty of Canons, we might have considered ourselves as a privileged elite, separate from the rest of the world. She never let us fall into that trap. It was made clear that we were fortunate people with obligations to others. Our visits to the Frances Mary Buss House at Bromley and the gifts we made for Founder's Day may have been of varied usefulness (I was never much good at looking after children or knitting) but the emphasis given to such things reinforced the message that we owed a debt to society for making our education possible.

One way of repaying the debt was, of course, to become well informed and effective members of that society — not at some time in the future, but *now*. Dame Kitty was committed to the teaching of Current Affairs in school and we learnt that in common with those people of our age who were taxpayers, we had a duty to understand what was going on at home and abroad. The School Advisory Council existed not merely to give advice, but to teach us about democracy and representation.

Theory and practice didn't always marry up, of course. The School Advisory Council taught us about voting but it was a body with no power. All I took away from my Current Affairs lessons was a nodding acquaintance with the structure of the United Nations Organisation. I never got into the habit of reading newspapers. But I did learn the importance of being involved in the community where I lived, and of looking beyond national boundaries to see our own country as part of a community of nations. Much of that derived, I am convinced, from Dame Kitty herself. She was a member of the Robbins Committee during my period at school, and her contribution to the world outside NLCS was acknowledged when she received the DBE. Although that work must have taken a lot of her time and attention she always remained central to life at school.

Her style of leadership was intensely personal. Even though I was in awe of her and rarely spoke to her, it never occurred to me that she might not know who I was. Her concern for all of us was obvious and she took an interest not only in our academic attainments, but in our ordinary lives. What was important to us was important to her too. When the O-level results came out, we were summoned to her office one by one, to be told our grades in individual interviews. In those days, the Headmistress's room was in the new part of the building, in the heart of the school. I was so eager to reach it that I ran up the steps from Red Square, slipped over and gashed my knee open. I was taken to the Medical Room to be patched up before going to Casualty at the local hospital and lay there dripping blood and fuming with frustration at missing my results.

I needn't have worried. Before I was whisked off to hospital, Dame Kitty appeared in the Medical Room to give me my grades, so that I shouldn't have to go off without knowing them.

Maybe that experience gave me the courage to knock on her door a year later, to complain about the School Dance Outrage. Going to the School Dance was one of those privileges (like being part of the Latin carol procession at Christmas) that was open only to girls in the Sixth Form and Upper Fifth. We couldn't wait for our turn to come round. A certain degree of anxiety was involved because buying a ticket for the Dance meant inviting a partner. We waited for our turn with longing and trepidation.

When it came at last, we gathered our courage and invited partners so that we could sign our names on the list. Then came the bombshell. We'd been told that the dance couldn't go ahead unless 100 double tickets were sold. Naturally, because there was always a School Dance, we never gave that a thought. However, by the cut-off date only ninety-six people had signed the list. The Dance was cancelled.

We were outraged. There was an indignant meeting in our form room. We were furious that we were to be deprived of something that all previous years had enjoyed. I remember a lot of shouting and talk about rights and a petition. (Any ONL will have no difficulty imagining this scene.) After a while, I realized that nothing was actually going to *happen*. Without saying anything to anyone, I left the form room, marched off to Dame Kitty's office and knocked on the door, shaking in my shoes but filled with righteous indignation.

When she asked why I'd come, I told her about the fury in the form room and said that it wasn't fair to cancel the Dance. I had no real argument except that it would be embarrassing to tell the boys we'd invited that it had been called off. And I pointed out that ninety-six wasn't very far short of 100.

In retrospect, I can see that I said nothing to change anyone's mind. Yet Dame Kitty did change her mind. She listened to me gravely and then she said the Dance could go ahead so long as the ninety-six people who had asked for double tickets would commit to buying them. They did. The Dance went ahead.

I'm not a natural protester, but that experience taught me that it was worth speaking up. It also taught me something about listening to other people. I'm grateful to Dame Kitty for those lessons and for all I learnt from her about society.

And I'm grateful, too, for a very happy evening spent dancing the waltz and the Gay Gordons!

Gillian Cross (Arnold) 1957-64

∽

Please try something different next week

Things that stand out: for a child who was shy, remote, and thought she was no good, a wonderful year in the Lower Fourth when Miss Wayneforth allowed me to write a short story instead of an essay. 'Allowed', perhaps, is not the right word. I just wrote the story using her essay title. She gave me an 'A' and wrote: *Please try something different next week.* I never did. It was always a story, occasionally a long poem, and she always, bless her, despite her teacherly instincts (or perhaps they told her that writers needed confidence) went along with it. It was the first time I found I could do something I really liked — and that other people liked too.

Then there was the great day Miss Godden came to teach singing. The choirs blossomed; there was also a tiny extra madrigal choir at 8.30 on Friday mornings before school. I had an hour and a quarter journey — walk, bus, train, long walk — and on Madrigal Choir mornings I got up very early, wrapping my thick school scarf round my mouth in winter to keep out the fog. That weekly half-hour which Miss Godden gave out of her own time laid the foundation for me, and I am sure many others, of knowing that wonderful body of work produced by the English madrigalists, who were of course poets too.

In the Fifth Form the school introduced a Greek class taught by Miss Flemington, and since I was the only girl who wanted to do A-level Greek, she and Miss Chandler taught me that too. Gentle Miss Chandler suffered deeply in having to teach Horace and Tacitus to a class of thirty Bolshie sixteen-year-olds who did not want to do Latin A-level but had to in order to enter university. I always felt guilty for being part of that rowdy, obdurate class, when Miss Chandler was so kind and relaxed towards me in our Greek studies.

The greatest joy of A-levels was discovering new writers: Homer, in Greek; in English, Chaucer, Marlowe, Ibsen, Virginia Woolf, Gerard Manley Hopkins, T.S. Eliot. One memorable lesson, just before lunch, a new English teacher, Miss Haffner, did something extraordinary: she started to read to us Katherine Mansfield's short story *Bliss*. When the bell went for lunch we begged her to go on to the end. What did we care about lunch? We were hearing something magical, read with passion and care. I shall never forget it.

These are the things I remember most: formative discoveries in music, poetry and creativity which I might never have made but for individual teachers giving, generously and imaginatively, exactly what was needed at the right time. And, of course, Dame Kitty was the inspiration behind such wonderful teaching.

Ruth Padel 1957-64

8

A Hiatus in Tradition —
Dame Kitty Anderson and Science Teaching at the North London Collegiate School

MARGARET GHILCHIK

It was Frances Mary Buss who incorporated Science in a prime position in the curriculum of her school. In 1868 she wrote to a teacher in New Zealand:

> After my many years of work, if I were to found a school … I should include … viz. English thoroughly, with Elementary Science … French, Latin, … and thorough arithmetic, with geometry and algebra … and no school ought to omit physical training.[i]

In 1878, when the University of London made every degree, honour and prize accessible to students of both sexes on perfectly equal terms, it did so because the limited access granted eleven years previously was a scheme designed in a manner considered suited to female students; however, it was found that women particularly gained distinction in Classical Languages and in Science.[ii]

By the time Dr Kitty Anderson was appointed Headmistress in 1944, there was a tradition of respect for the subject of Science at NLCS and there was no lack of precedent for Old North Londoners who had become scientists.[iii] Previous headmistresses included Dr Sophie Bryant, the first woman to obtain a DSc, and Isabella Drummond, who took First Class Honours in the Natural Science Tripos at Cambridge and herself taught Science at NLCS.[iv] Miss Drummond was eager to dispel the notion that girls found Mathematics a difficult subject, one that only clever girls could manage.

Thus there was a sound historic basis for Science being perceived as a valued and important part of the curriculum at the North London Collegiate School.

Dr Bryant's first degree was from Dublin, and it is interesting to note that at the time Miss Buss was founding her school in the 1850s, it was from

Ireland that Richard Dawes obtained the secular Science reading books for his village school children, when he carried out his astonishing experiments in elementary education, which included teaching 'the science of common things'. While Dawes pioneered the practical teaching of Science, John Stevens Henslow achieved similar success but gave greater emphasis to the intellectual training of the mind that was achieved by the study of Science.

Both Dawes and Henslow were Cambridge scientists who left their research and college professorships to pursue a different way of life in which they could marry and become a force for good in rural communities. They both founded schools and had a profound effect on the teaching of Science and subsequent development of the Science curriculum by Kay-Shuttleworth and Moseley, not only in the elementary schools of the day but in teacher training colleges as well. At Cambridge, Henslow was tutor to Charles Darwin (as a student, Darwin was dubbed 'the man who walks with Henslow'). He was astonishingly class-unconscious, teaching the same science to the Royal children, when invited by Prince Albert, as to his village children. Most importantly, Henslow emphasised the potential of Science for training the mind. As Professor David Layton points out,[v] this led to controversy that raged throughout the next century. Underscored by the necessity to avoid ruffling religious sensibilities by the teaching of Science, the concept arose that teaching elementary school children too well might give them an education superior to upper-class children who received only a Classical education. Above all, there was heated debate as to whether Science was a philosophy and an intellectual discipline or solely a technical and factual practical subject.

In 1944, the year Dr Kitty Anderson became Headmistress of the North London Collegiate School, many students with first-class brains still had their training rooted in a Classical education: this was true, for example, amongst the echelons of the Administrative Civil Service. A hundred years previously, Dr Arnold of Rugby had declared: 'It is not right to leave boys in ignorance of physical science.' (In 1859 a later Headmaster of Rugby, Frederick Temple, sent his Science Master, the Rev J.M. Wilson, to learn Botany in the summer holidays so that the younger boys could be taught Botany before the Chemistry laboratory was opened the following year.)

Yet if some boys' education remained over-biased towards the Classics, this was no excuse for a foremost girls' school to neglect Science. Kitty Anderson was a Historian. She did not perceive Science as a significant part of girls' education. Committed as she was, in the tradition of Frances Mary Buss, to the notion that girls were entitled to the same education as their brothers, Dr Anderson nonetheless tended to disregard the wider breadth of knowledge that Mathematics and Science brought to the development of the mind. Her own educational background had given her no feeling for Science as an academic discipline. She felt that girls who wished to pursue careers in Physics, Chemistry, Medicine, Engineering, Mathematics or any other branch of Science could pick up such disciplines later, after receiving a general education in the Arts and Humanities. She had no sense of Mathematics as a language or a philosophy. Nor did she understand the necessity of a firm grounding in mathematical principles as a prerequisite for moving into the fields of Chemistry and Physics. C.P. Snow and The Two Cultures — Arts and Science — still lay in the future.

The failure of NLCS to provide a reasonable level of education in Science and Mathematics during Dame Kitty's headship rebounded on many girls as they struggled to attain the scientific and medical careers they had set their hearts on. Some were honed by their failures and strengthened in their resolve, finding in their experience at NLCS useful lessons of survival strategies that could be used in dealing with the wider world later on. Many more abandoned their planned careers, losing self-esteem and confidence when they failed what should have been possible for them. All of them had to struggle unnecessarily to attain a reasonable standard.

For example, from 1950-53, half a dozen girls who were determined to be doctors experienced a lack of support that amounted to discouragement. This, in addition to the school's lack of awareness of what was required to obtain a place in a medical school. But most importantly, there was a common experience of totally inadequate teaching in the Science subjects. At the start of the second year Sixth Form, one girl wrote to the University of London for a copy of the curriculum for A-level Science subjects. The school took great exception to this, deeming it to reveal a lack of confidence in the school's authority. The lack of confidence was unfortunately entirely justified when it was revealed at the time of the 'Mock' exams, a few months before A-levels, that only one-third of the Biology syllabus had been covered. There was not sufficient Mathematics to support the A-level Physics, and only half of that syllabus had been taught when exam time came round. Six girls passed Physics out of a class of thirty-six. Chemistry teaching had been largely based on the inorganic, learning by rote, with insufficient emphasis placed on the Organic Chemistry syllabus. The teaching was muddled: two former students recall the teacher exclaiming, following a double lesson of note-taking, 'Girls, have I been saying "Arsenic"? I meant Antimony!'

One girl who had joined the Sixth Form at NLCS in order (as her parents imagined) to receive better Science teaching than her small Convent school could provide, withdrew from all classes. She was tutored at home, passed her exams, went on to medical school and became a doctor. Another girl flatly declares: 'the science teaching was grim.' She found a place in a medical school where she could take First MB, in fact studying the Sixth Form Science subjects again, and she too became a doctor. It was suggested to a third girl that she was not sufficiently bright to become a doctor; however, she too found a medical school that still offered First MB and later qualified.

Yet another of this group failed her A-levels; she had been affected by the anti-elitist stance of the Government of the day, which disallowed pupils to take O-levels until they were sixteen. The school failed to deal with this situation and this girl went into the Sixth Form with all her O-levels to take at the end of first year Sixth. She passed, but her A-level studies suffered, and she subsequently failed her A-level exams. Dr Anderson was not helpful. She did, however, reveal what had happened to her at the end of her own first year at university. She had been devastated to learn that she had failed and was to be sent home. Having to repeat that first year at university, she told this girl, was one of the best things that could have happened, as it consolidated her learning so much. In spite of her own experience, she offered little to the unhappy failed Sixth Former who had lost her place in medical school. Dr Anderson refused to allow her to sit for the exams again in the autumn, or to use the rest of the year to attempt Oxford or Cambridge entrance. The girl left NLCS, took five A-level subjects at evening classes at a technical college, got a place at another medical school and went on to a distinguished medical career.

She had a sister at school. Four years later, her sister spent a third year in the Sixth Form in order to add Mathematics to her A-level Physics and Chemistry. Somewhat reluctantly, Dr Anderson allowed her to try for Oxford entrance to read Chemistry. At her Oxford interview she discussed Jane Austen with the Chemistry Tutor, and Science and the Two Cultures (by this time a hot topic of the day) with the Morals Tutor. Back at school from her interview, before she could speak, Dr Anderson said: 'Never mind! At least you got an interview.' — 'But Dr Anderson', the girl replied, 'I've got in!'

Apart from such examples of poor teaching and lack of understanding, the scientists at NLCS in Dr Anderson's time felt marginalised. They were, for example, usually excluded from the Headmistress's Discussion Group, when Sixth Formers met each week in her room to discuss topics — a useful preparation for Oxbridge interviews. The girls who did attend enjoyed the warmth of Dr Anderson's smile, the twinkle in her eye, her unique enthusiasm, and appreciated her sane view of Current Affairs. The scientists were excluded from her warm human qualities. One of the scientists decided to found The Science Club. At the first after-school meeting of the Club, the invited speaker, an eminent medical scientist and mother of one of the girls in school, arrived very late to give her talk; it transpired she had been waylaid by Dr Anderson when she arrived at Canons and given tea in her study with the Head Girl. One Founder's Day the Club organised an exhibition — it was noted that the Headmistress did not go up to the labs to see the display.

Why did Dr Anderson have this attitude towards Science and the scientists at NLCS? In such an outstanding school, how did it come about? Why was it not put right? There was, as I have outlined, no lack of tradition for Science subjects in the school.

NLCS had Science and Mathematics teachers of a high calibre, but there were not enough of them to cover the whole school. Too much was asked of them in the attempt to teach every pupil. The lower classes were divided, the bright girls studying Chemistry, the not so bright taking Biology. What sort of message does that give to future scientists? No one studied much Physics. It might have been better to organise the curriculum so that Chemistry and Physics were taught in the first two terms of a school year and Biology in the summer term — or to rotate the subjects in some other way. Too few lesson periods were allotted to Science.

The Art Department was allowed to occupy space on the Science labs level for far too long, and the 1958 Inspection of NLCS criticised the lack of technicians to service equipment. The school acknowledged the problem. In order to present a better impression to the Inspectors, the Science and Mathematics teachers were listed together, which had the effect of concealing the scarcity of Science staff. Perhaps the inadequate provision of labs and equipment held back Science at NLCS. During the war, evacuation of part of the school to Luton made Science teaching very difficult. (It is on record that one Chemistry lesson was held in the teacher's bedroom at Luton.) All the Science teachers were at Luton except for Miss Raeburn, the

Biologist. In 1944 everyone was back at Canons, occupying the buildings erected alongside the Old House just before the outbreak of war in 1939. It was a new beginning with a new headmistress. However, the laboratories on the top floor of the new Richardson building were empty spaces. The Biology lab was in the Games changing room; there was one Bunsen burner. Dr Anderson did not appear motivated to fight hard enough for extra funds for lab equipment.

The Science teachers Dr Anderson inherited as Headmistress remained on the staff almost throughout her time at NLCS.[vi] The subject of Chemistry had undergone profound change during the decades since 1930, when the well qualified and experienced Miss Harker had joined NLCS to teach Chemistry. Dr Anderson, generous in her treatment of staff where Grace terms or a year's leave of absence were concerned, should have organised the re-training of Science staff. She probably did not appreciate that unlike History, where new ideas and theories can be acquired through reading and at seminars, nothing short of a year's practical re-training would have been adequate to bring Chemistry teaching up to date for the 1950s and 1960s.

Miss Parks, whose subject was Physics, was also highly qualified and an experienced teacher. She taught her subject well, but one person was quite inadequate to teach Physics throughout the school. In addition, the Mathematical structure was inadequate to support the Physics. Her subject had also developed over the years, and she did keep up with the advances.

Miss Gare, Miss Raeburn, Miss Horder and Mrs Gagarin were other Science teachers who remained at NLCS for several decades. Other, younger teachers were appointed for shorter periods. There was potentially a good Science staff. What went wrong? There were simply not enough Science teachers, yet Dr Anderson was reluctant to appoint more. (There is a note in the Archives dated 1958 from DA: *I have decided not to appoint 2 Chemistry teachers for next year.* There were currently two Chemistry staff members, one within a year of retirement, the other, just married, in her first teaching post.) There was no organisation or teamwork amongst the Science staff, and no Heads of departments to ensure standards were upheld. Dr Anderson had a phrase: 'Each member of staff is the custodian of their subject.' She failed to appreciate the interrelation of different branches of Science — for example, the dependency of Physics on Maths, already cited. The provision of a sufficient number of lessons throughout the school years for Science and Maths was never achieved. When queries

Some children clearly enjoyed Science

were raised, the full weight of authority turned its head away and refused to listen. The pupil, it seemed clear, had no right to question or to be heard.

In 1955, seventy-five years after the first women doctors had obtained their degrees, fifty years after the Royal College of Surgeons opened its doors to women as Fellow Surgeons, the Headmistress of the foremost Girls' Public Day School was setting the sights of girls throughout the land towards the traditional careers of nursing, teaching and domestic science. Was Dr Anderson ignorant of the achievements of so many women by that time? Did she underestimate the potential of the girls in her school?

She can hardly have been ignorant. In her first headship at Kings Norton Grammar School, the Biology teacher on her staff was an Old North Londoner, Betty Underhill. At Somerville College, Oxford, Betty took First Class Honours in Zoology and added a research degree in genetics and cytology before she obtained her Diploma of Education. She then taught for more than ten years. It had always been her burning desire to be a doctor. By 1943 she had saved enough to support herself through medical school, and she obtained a place at the London School of Medicine for Women. She qualified in 1947, became a surgeon in 1953 and worked for the rest of her life as a consultant in Britain and abroad.[vii] Dr Anderson must have been aware of the pathway towards a medical career that her brilliant Biology teacher was taking.

As Dr Anderson left Kings Norton, she was invited to the Boys' School to present prizes.[viii] She commented that the Sixth Form boys were surprised to find that so much 'Mathematics, Pure and Applied, and Physics and the like' were studied in the Girls' School. What did they expect, she asked, sewing and knitting? She did draw attention then to the importance of a solid basis of factual knowledge. Interestingly, having taught in a mixed school of boys and girls in her first teaching post in Hull, Dr Anderson recognised that girls at first develop more rapidly than boys, have a greater responsiveness and readiness to learn, are more conscientious and better at self-expression — a most percipient observation for that time. It has been re-observed by others many times. Nevertheless, she persisted in recommending careers for girls that were limited, badly paid and often inferior to those chosen by boys.

Again, in 1951, in an address to the National Association of Inspectors of Schools and Educational Organisers,[ix] she said there were four careers especially appropriate for girls which afforded scope for their natural gifts: teaching, nursing, domestic sciences and institutional management, as well as branches of the social services. She made the extraordinary statement that at NLCS at that moment, twenty-nine girls were taking A-level Physics, but they were not future scientists! The previous year she had admitted in a lecture to the Institute of Education that girls, with their late specialisation in the Sixth Form, were finding it difficult to compete with boys who seemed to have done so much more Science training. She did not seem to understand it was the responsibility of the school to provide that adequate scientific and mathematical background.

In her 1956 address as President to the Association of Headmistresses,[x] Dr Anderson recommended a General Course in the Sixth Form, not purely academic, stressing the openings available for scientific technologists and technicians. She iterated that Science was a natural part of a general education that could lead to careers in nursing, as medical auxiliaries and in domestic science, and that there were opportunities for social service. She remarked: 'the shorter training periods required for technician posts offer attraction to those whose interests lie in an admittedly narrower field but one which can be resumed more easily after breaks due to marriage or family chores.' A depressing statement of her lack of ambition for the future of her schoolgirls. She went on: '...in my view the growing tendency for early specialisation in science may be the real stumbling block to a recruitment of girls for scientific work.' She then referred to the popular belief that girls cannot do Maths and stated that research was needed to help overcome this position.

During the 1960s Dame Kitty travelled throughout Britain to address schools of the Girls' Public Day School Trust and other prominent girls' grammar schools as they celebrated their Centenaries. Her speeches related the history of Frances Mary Buss and Dorothea Beale, founder of Cheltenham Ladies' College, of Bedford College, London, and Girton, Cambridge, founded by Emily Davies, and passed on to later developments in education for girls and women.[xi] The story of the struggle for the right of education for girls is an important subject.[xii] However, in every speech, she concluded with the same message, that there were three careers particularly suited to girls: nursing, teaching, and Domestic Science. In truth, three admirable careers. But the horizon she presented was far too limited.

It is a commonplace that women who have achieved positions of eminence sometimes fail to imagine that other girls and women could do likewise; they perceive themselves and their position as unique. Dame Kitty Anderson appears to have lacked a vital belief in the great potential, academic and otherwise, of which her girls were capable. It was her limited attitude towards the future possibilities open to her girls in general, not only in Science, that coloured her opinions; possibly this spread across Arts subjects as well. One can but ask — did she not meet with high-achieving women in the rest of her life? Or were they so few in those days? In researching the NLCS Archives, the most depressing discovery has been the absence of a crusading feminist spirit in Kitty Anderson, a desire to clear a path for girls' education and claim equality for their future.

Dame Kitty seems to have held a deeply felt disbelief in Science as a philosophy and as an academic subject worthy of study and capable of training the mind. She did not believe that the study of Science was part of a general education; rather, it was something to be added later by those who wished or needed to pursue it. In short, she did not really approve of the study of Science.

[i] Ridley, Annie K., *Frances Mary Buss and her work for Education*, Longmans Green & Co, 1895
[ii] *Ibid*

[iii] *The North London Collegiate School. 1850-1950. A Hundred years of Girls' Education,* Oxford University Press, London, 1950
[iv] Watson, Nigel, *And Their Works Do Follow Them. The Story of North London Collegiate School 1850-2000,* James, 2000
[v] Layton, Prof David, *Science for the People. The origins of the school science curriculum in England,* George Allen & Unwin, London, 1973
[vi] NLCS Archives, Staff Files
[vii] Ghilchik, Margaret, *Women Fellows. The lives of the first 100 women doctors to become Fellows of the Royal College of Surgeons in England.* (In preparation)
[viii] Prize-giving Address to Kings Norton Boys' School by Miss K. Anderson, 1944. NLCS Archives, Kitty Anderson Biography
[ix] Address to the National Association of Inspectors of Schools and Education Advisers, 1951, by Dr K. Anderson. NLCS Archives, Kitty Anderson Biography
[x] Address as President of the Association of Headmistresses, 1956, by Dr K. Anderson. NLCS Archives, Kitty Anderson Biography
[xi] *Ibid*
[xii] Glenday, Nonita and Price, Mary, *Reluctant Revolutionaries. A Century of Headmistresses 1874-1974,* Pitman, London, 1974

Margaret Ghilchik (Childe) decided at the age of twelve to become a doctor. She trained at St Bartholomew's Hospital and qualified in 1947. In 1953 she became a Consultant Surgeon, FRCS, one of only seven women in the UK. Her book 'Women Fellows', which recounts the lives of the first 100 women doctors to become Fellows of the Royal College of Surgeons in England, is in preparation.

'DA's coming!'

I started at NLCS in the Upper Thirds in 1956. Whenever Dr Anderson appeared in our vicinity, a reverent whisper: *'DA's coming!'* would rapidly spread through the ranks. We certainly stood in awe of this Headmistress whom we always held in the utmost respect. She smiled when she spoke to us and even knew our names. For someone who felt overshadowed by the large number of very clever girls in my form, this was particularly comforting. When she became Dame Kitty, we found it difficult to address her by her first name, although we did of course get used to it.

I remember my days at NLCS with affection — as do all my immediate circle of friends. At the reunion I organised for our fiftieth birthdays in 1995, it amazed us to find that some of our number were not so full of praise for our school. They were, however, the minority. The rest of us fondly reminisced about compulsory swimming in the outdoor pool when the temperature reached 60°, rushing to play tennis for fifteen minutes before school after a twenty-minute walk from the station and learning our French vocabulary for a test on the train, and still playing tag on the terraces in our O-level year. Such sophistication!

Dame Kitty made school a memorable and happy experience for me and so many others. She was a unique and highly individual person who contributed enormously to education both at NLCS and in the outside world.

Angela Cannon (Hunt) 1956-63

The University of Life also had much to offer

I was fortunate to be taught by Dame Kitty, who gave me a lifelong love of English history. If I could have had History for every lesson it would not have been too much. She was a gifted teacher with a love of her subject that brought every lesson alive. I was not academic, but through her enthusiastic teaching I got a credit in History in my General School Certificate — two credits, in fact, as I did not achieve GSC on my first attempt.

Although Dame Kitty was such a talented teacher, I did not feel she had much time for those pupils who were not going on to University. It was understandable to some extent, as academic prowess would obviously bring reflected glory on NLCS, but the less gifted girls felt they were somewhat underrated. Success in their chosen careers proved the University of Life also had much to offer.

Mary Coulter 1941-48

She was always 'DA'

She was never Dame Kitty to us — she was always 'DA' amongst ourselves, and 'Dr Anderson' more formally. In many ways she *was* the school, epitomising values that would remain constant in the changing world we inhabited as children, adolescents and young women. She told us to remember that her delight in our achievements and her expectations for us set standards for life, not just the years we were at Canons.

Two anecdotes: in the Lower Fourth one wet afternoon we drove our History teacher to distraction; mid-lesson she left us in disgust. Into the general mayhem that followed walked Dr Anderson. There was an instant, embarrassed silence. She proceeded to teach us about the medieval wool trade and the Lombards. We listened as we had never listened before. She asked questions and we answered them; she set homework and we wrote it down assiduously. The bell went. She bade us 'Good afternoon' and left. Nothing was said about our appalling behaviour. It did not need to be.

A few years later, when I headed the Current Affairs Society, we invited Tony Benn (then Anthony Wedgwood Benn) to be our guest speaker. It had simply not occurred to us that because he was a prominent politician, all kinds of security arrangements would need to be in place. Dr Anderson, after gently pointing out that 'Wedgewood', on the poster pinned to the Society's noticeboard, was misspelled, suggested that I come to see her to discuss the arrangements. At that meeting, matters were very tactfully taken out of my hands. The meeting was transferred to the Hall because a lot of people would want to attend. I would want to give our guest tea, and I would be welcome to use her room — and she would very much like to be invited. Perhaps I would like to show him round the school, and maybe she could accompany us? The only hint I received that I was being managed came after tea, when I was gently ushered out of DA's study and she and Tony Benn settled down to talk.

Beyond the anecdotes and the memories, what remains? The knowledge that we were all known, understood and valued by an exceptional woman and an outstanding teacher. It was a privilege to have known her, to have been known by her and to have been a North Londoner during the time of her Headship.

Rosemary A. Rees (Dawson) 1950–60

We were well prepared for the modern world

Dame Kitty was my Headmistress for the whole of my school life and later a friend, as I had a six-year friendship with her nephew David during his medical school days, when he lived with her. (I lived opposite Dame Kitty in Lake View.) As an intellectual academic she was surprisingly appreciative of those who did not excel academically. She was equipped with lots of commonsense and appreciated the spirit of adventure.

Dame Kitty believed in me as someone of value and later arranged for me to work in the school office. I did not take A-levels but left after a term in the Sixth Form and entered retail distribution, feeling at the time that I was failing the school I loved so much. My father insisted that if I did not know what career to follow, I should train in something. Lillywhites in Piccadilly Circus employed me as an apprentice. Margot Hassell, a former Senior Prefect and a Cambridge graduate, was working at Harrods so it did not seem such a bad career. A secretarial course and a secretarial job followed (as was the custom for non-academics at that time) and then I was employed for a year at NLCS. It was during this time that Dame Kitty helped me to find a real career path: Nursing. She wrote a glowing reference to Charing Cross Hospital which accepted me. She followed my training days closely and it was Dame Kitty I rang first to let her know that I had passed my Final examination with very good marks. She appreciated the hard work and effort I had made and encouraged me to pursue my chosen career further.

The romance with David finished, leaving me with a broken heart; it was Dame Kitty who once more urged me on my way. I went to Edinburgh and did both parts of Midwifery, loving the home deliveries. Later on I migrated to Australia on my own. Dame Kitty's advice was always to give your best and to have integrity — and I guess we all had the school motto touching our lives.

In an address to the school in 1950, Dame Kitty said that when one's eldest child reached the age of ten, 'most young women will be back in full-time or perhaps part-time work. Our future will be different from our Mothers.' Our education will continue.' She was certainly correct as far as

I was concerned. I was working as a full-time Community Nurse when my first child turned nine. I continued to study and have become a Child and Family Health Nurse. I have always maintained a continuous interest in my local community and been extremely active in obtaining better educational and social conditions for my local area. Today it is quite usual for mothers to return to work three to six months after their children are born. We were well prepared for the modern world.

Dame Kitty was well ahead of her time. Without her guidance and the school's philosophy I would not have become the person I am now. My children have had the benefit of my education that taught us self-esteem and to be aware of the unique contribution we can make to our communities.

Philippa (Pip) Robinson (Bradbury) 1946-57

∾

Pure and Applied Maths, Physics and History

Like so many people, I owe an enormous debt to Dame Kitty. It was thanks to Dame Kitty that I was admitted to NLCS at all, and certainly that I was allowed to continue, one year and six days too young, at the level I'd reached at my previous school. I had spent the war in Leeds, where my father's laboratories had been relocated after the London Blitz. We returned to London in spring 1946, after the normal admissions procedures for NLCS for that autumn had finished. He persuaded Dame Kitty to allow me to sit a special entrance examination of my own, although she did explain to him that the Upper Third was already full, but said the Lower Third might have a space. So I sat my solitary examination, supervised by her secretary. I remember that I wrote an essay about 'The Clerk of the Weather', describing all the different kinds of weather he supervised. I don't recall the Maths exam at all, which probably means that I found it easy. Anyway, the upshot was that I was admitted to the Upper Third. My parents said Dame Kitty was 'as pleased as Punch' when she told them about my result.

She continued to take a personal interest in my development beyond the normal call of duty. The first example of this is her handling of the problem caused by the fact that I was two years too young to take O-levels (to be precise, one year and six days, but those six days would have led to a further year's delay). I remember the glee with which she discovered that I could in fact take Oxford Responsions or Cambridge Previous instead. The reasons why others did not take these exams were twofold: firstly, the need for me to wait two years made the problem more serious than for others; secondly, although Oxford accepted Previous and Cambridge accepted Responsions, no other university would accept either. So NLCS needed to be fairly sure that you were going to Oxbridge before following that route.

For Responsions, I had to take five subjects. (For Previous, I would have had to take a paper in English History as well, six subjects in all, which is why NLCS and I chose Responsions.) The five subjects were not very different from the London Matric requirements: English Language, Maths, a foreign language, a Science subject, and Latin or Greek. The only one of these that caused any problem was the Latin, not because it was particularly difficult, but because I was required to write a Latin prose piece, something I had not been taught to do. So I had six weeks of coaching in writing Latin prose from the young teacher who was our Latin mistress. (Soon after she left to become a policewoman, which I remember seemed very odd to us then. I don't think it would seem so odd now.)

To take the exam I stayed in Oxford for a week. I expect it was Dame Kitty who arranged for me to stay in St Anne's College, where the students were all amused by and kind to this shy fourteen-year-old, dressed up in the black and white Oxford *subfusc* compulsory for those taking examinations. The exams -- English, Maths, French, Latin and Chemistry -- all took place in the Oxford Examination Schools, like any other University exams. Except for the Chemistry practical, which took place in one of the University laboratories. Like the obedient, well-trained North Londoner that I was, I asked the examiner's permission to switch on the apparatus once I had set it up. He was astounded. I don't think any student had ever thought it necessary to ask his permission before!

For me, the main excitement of the week was when some of the St Anne's students took me punting on the river.

But that is about me and Oxford rather than Dame Kitty and NLCS. Back at school, preparing for the following September, I caused consternation by my choice of A-level subjects. I remember we each went in to see Dame Kitty about these, one by one. She said to me: 'Pure and Applied Maths, Physics (needed if I were to sit the Cambridge entrance exams) and Chemistry?' I said: 'No. I want to study Pure and Applied Maths, Physics and *History.*' I already sensed that I wanted to become a social scientist of some kind, rather than a mathematician or a physical scientist.

The combination of Maths and Geography was already well accepted at NLCS, but the combination of Maths and History was unprecedented. Dame Kitty took it in her stride. She explained that it might be difficult, but she would see what she could do. The following September, Dame Kitty told me proudly: 'I managed it. I had to rebuild the entire Sixth Form timetable around your Maths and History.' I had to miss out one or two of the general lessons, but indeed I did study the subjects of my choice.

Later, after I had won my Oxford scholarship, Dame Kitty took me with her to central London one day. We had lunch at the University Women's Club, and then she showed me The London Library, with its open stacks and borrowing facilities, recommending it strongly.

I certainly owe Dame Kitty an enormous debt for the mind-broadening experience of her special class for Oxbridge entrants. For someone coming from the rather narrow experience of Mathematics, and the cram of going from nowhere to A-level in Physics in five terms, it was especially and immensely important to experience the broader worlds of history, literature, art and even philosophy. I remember the enthusiasm with which she announced one day: 'I know almost nothing about Japan. Why don't we all study Japan this term?' And we did. I also recall reading Empson's *Seven Types of Ambiguity,* becoming excited about the Italian Renaissance, reading Plato's *Republic* for myself and writing a big essay to discuss the statement 'Progress is only achieved through heresy', and reading J.Bury on progress (although not, I would now say, with a sufficient degree of criticism!). Altogether, her class was much the most stimulating intellectual experience of my pre-University days and I'm sure I owed my Somerville scholarship to it.

Judith Marquand (Reed) 1946-54

9

'In spite of the many other claims on your time ...' — The Robbins Committee and Dame Kitty's contribution to other national bodies

JOAN CLANCHY

> '...I hardly need to point out, however, that the outcome of this most important enquiry must largely depend on the qualities and experience that the members of the Committee bring to it. You would make a most valuable contribution and I therefore hope that, in spite of the many other calls on your time, you will not be deterred by the work involved from undertaking this public service.' Prime Minister Harold Macmillan to Dame Kitty Anderson, 26 January 1961.

The invitation Dame Kitty received to join the committee being formed by Sir Harold Robbins to enquire into the state of Higher education was the greatest honour that could have been paid to her. There were twelve members: she was one of only two women, the other being Helen Gardner of St Hilda's College, Oxford, who was an Old North Londoner. The only other serving Head was Anthony Chenevix-Trench, later to be Headmaster of the young Anthony Blair at Fettes.

Just four weeks earlier, Dr Kitty Anderson had been awarded the DBE in the New Year's honours list for her contributions to national educational development. It was because she had already done so much that she was asked to do more. Thus, before describing the Robbins Committee and its work, it seems appropriate to discuss Dame Kitty's former public work.

Kitty Anderson came to prominence largely through the Association of Head Mistresses (AHM), in which she held almost every office including that of President. The AHM, founded by Miss Buss in 1874, was famously dominated by her as President, and by Miss Beale of Cheltenham Ladies' College as Secretary, for twenty-three years. Together they built a strong, inclusive association. At the time of Dame Kitty's membership the AHM was at the height of its power and influence. There were about 1000 members. They included Heads of independent schools (in those days confusingly called Public Schools), direct grant schools, maintained and voluntary aided grammar schools and maintained secondary schools. The AHM could rightly claim to represent the full range of secondary education for girls. After Dame Kitty's time, the Association lost its impact: gradually it was eroded by the growth of co-educational schools (with Head Masters) and by the polarisation between independent and state maintained secondary schools, and in 1976 the AHM was amalgamated with the Head Masters to form the Secondary Heads Association. (A smaller association of the Heads of 200 independent girls' schools, the Girls' Schools Association, was founded and does distinguished works, but cannot have the range of the AHM that Dame Kitty headed.)

During the period after World War Two, the AHM had made continuous contributions to the evolving debates on education. The 1944 Education Act brought in by the then Minister for Education, Conservative 'Rab' Butler, had made the provision of secondary education compulsory. Many changes followed from that legislation. There was debate about the division of pupils at age eleven and also about the curriculum. The AHM made many submissions, often drafted by Dame Kitty, who had been elected to the executive committee after only six years as a Headmistress. These made an impact. In 1946 she was invited by the Minister for Education in the post-war Labour government to serve on the Carr-Saunders Committee on Education for Commerce, which made recommendations for increase in the provision of technical education. In 1953, she accepted an invitation from the Minister for Education in a new Conservative government to join the National Advisory Council on the Training and Supply of Teachers.

The issues around the training and supply of teachers had long preoccupied Dame Kitty. There was a constant shortage of teachers in the 1950s and 1960s, as there has been, on and off, ever since. To her generation this was a new phenomenon. In the 1930s there had been an over-supply and jobs had been hard to find. Women then had been required to resign on getting married: remember Miss Jean Brodie's proud boast to her girls that she had preferred them over marriage?

In the 1950s, married women continued to teach, though not until after they had a family — that revolution did not really take place until the 1970s. The easy way to fill the vacancies was through short training courses and minimal qualifications. Dame Kitty constantly warned against such a solution. The role of the Advisory Council she joined was to monitor the different training colleges and their certificates. Two-year diploma courses were accepted, but only as a temporary measure; Dame Kitty was in favour of three-year courses and of having as many graduates as possible in the profession. Her contribution to this Advisory Council led her to be invited in 1959 to serve on the University Grants Committee (UGC).

It often comes as a jolt to realise how recently any real equality for women has been gained. In 1959 Dame Kitty (or Dr Anderson as she then was) was newsworthy as the first woman ever to serve on the UGC. She was described as having 'an unusual head for accounts', the implication being that women could not manage sums — exactly the same attitude that had exasperated Miss Buss 100 years earlier. Dame Kitty wasted no time on indignation over such matters and worked at the equable application of criteria in the complex matter of university finance. The warmth of the tributes paid to her when she later resigned from the UGC suggests that she was much valued.

By 1961, therefore, Kitty Anderson's proven experience and expertise as a government committee member lay in teacher training and university finance. In addition, she was Headmistress of a school of acknowledged excellence. It was these qualifications that led Harold Macmillan to write to her in January 1961 and invite her to join the Robbins Committee to consider 'the long term development of universities, colleges of advanced technology, certain other colleges of further education and teacher training colleges'. His letter explained that the claim on her time would be considerable for at least two years, which meant that it would be necessary for her to stand down from the University Grants Committee.

It would be hard to overstate the importance of the Robbins Committee in the history of Britain's education systems. Committees, each with its own often confusing acronym, come and go more quickly now. They report and are forgotten. The National Curriculum Council, which in 1991 was vaunted as about to change schooling root and branch, was housed in a portentous building with its acronym woven into the carpet. The Robbins Committee sat from 1961 to 1963, had no acronym, logo or mission statement, and made an impact that has lasted to this day. Many of us recall vividly the excitement generated by the publication of its report and the brave new world of education it promised.

The remit of the Committee was wide and long-term. It was accepted wisdom that there had to be some expansion of places in Higher Education, because of the pressure of numbers of eighteen-year-olds with A-levels, but where, and to what extent? What should be deemed affordable? Should there be an additional level of degree-awarding institution introduced, with all its resources devoted to teaching undergraduates and none to research, as an economical way of funding the pressure for degree courses? Should the sharp divide between the two-year diploma teacher and the graduate remain impassable? What was likely to be the demand for places ten years hence? Twenty years hence? The Committee was asked 'in the light of national needs and resources to advise Her Majesty's Government on what principles [Higher Education's] long-term development should be based'.

The methods of the Committee represented the reverse of what is now — apparently admiringly — called 'blue skies' thinking: that is, bright new ideas without basis in evidence. Harold Robbins was an economist from the London School of Economics. He had been the author of reports on fiscal policy for the Treasury and was, perhaps, a surprising choice for the Committee on Higher Education. By all accounts he was a brilliant and extraordinarily hardworking Chairman, preparing all drafts and many memoranda himself. The Committee met 115 times over thirty months; in the first sixty or so meetings it took oral evidence from all interested parties as well as considering a pile of written submissions. In addition, its members visited seven countries on research missions.

Dame Kitty went on three of those visits, to the USA, the Soviet Union and Holland. (Other Committee members were impressed by the warm welcomes she received from Old North Londoners in each of these countries.) In a letter written from her hotel room in Washington on 2 May, 1962, addressed to Miss Gossip at NLCS, she begins: 'I shall be thinking about you all at Canons tomorrow starting off the new term. ... My travels in the States are now drawing to a close — I seem to have travelled thousands of miles at great speed ... I enjoyed my stay in California very much indeed and was much impressed by the "State wide" plan for education.' After visiting San Francisco and Los Angeles, the Committee members travelled to Chicago — 'city of enormous skyscrapers which I found bewildering', Dame Kitty writes, and goes on to describe her time in Boston: 'Here I visited Harvard and the famous Massachusetts Institute of Technology ... in my spare time I visited the places of special interest to me — the site of the famous "Tea Party", Paul Revere's house, Bunker Hill ... '

A meeting of the Robbins committee — Dame Kitty does not look happy with the discussion

She continues: 'Now I am in Washington and my hotel room has a huge number of gadgets. I can get hot coffee at any time of day or night ... of course there is also television and wireless. I heard today that there is a special programme of instruction for teachers at 6.30 am!!' In Washington there was another visit to an Old North Londoner — 'Yesterday I went to dinner with Sheila Gulard (née Cooper) ... Her eldest son is going to the local primary school, so I heard all about the first stages of education.' This visit was made after 'we had a long session with the Teachers' Association and discussed examinations, entry to colleges, text books, methods, and I began to feel I was back with the problems I know so well. Soon we shall be flying off to New York — the Committee ends its work next Tuesday, but I shall be staying on for an extra week and hope to visit Princeton University and a New York school.'

The Committee meetings that did not take testimony from outsiders were largely spent considering the dramatic statistics produced by the young Professor of Statistics, Claus Moser. He laid before the Committee evidence of the build-up of demand for Higher Education and how it was likely to increase. The appendix to the report of the volume containing his statistical evidence became a model of its kind. Dame Kitty wrote that a blizzard of information was coming at her and she felt like the Red Queen in *Alice In Wonderland* — ' "Now! Now!" cried the Queen, "Faster! Faster!" And they went so fast that at last they seemed to skim through the air, hardly touching the ground with their feet, till suddenly just as Alice was getting quite exhausted, they all stopped.'

The only long paper submitted to the whole Committee by Dame Kitty on file concerns the future of Teacher Training Colleges. She wrote it in partnership with fellow Committee member Professor James Drever, of the University of Edinburgh. The paper highlights concern for the prospects of young men and women who trained as Primary or Secondary school teachers on two- or three-year Certificate in Education courses in one of the multiplicity of small training colleges in England, entered the profession and then found they could rarely progress. University graduates in an academic subject, with a one-year diploma in Education, would almost always be promoted over them. Dame Kitty knew there were excellent teachers caught in this unfortunate position, and that the opportunities for them to undertake later top-up degrees were few. All teachers in Secondary schools in both Scotland and Northern Ireland were graduates, so the problem was less acute there; however, in Primary schools the same divisions between graduates and certificated teachers existed.

The solution outlined by Dame Kitty and Professor Drever was a fairly radical one. Small, stand-alone Training Colleges would be phased out, and they should all be affiliated to Schools of Education in Universities. This would facilitate contribution from the Universities to the academic content of the College courses. It would also enable the institution of a new degree: the B.Ed (Bachelor of Education). Students who showed themselves to be very able during the first two years of the Certificate course could undertake a further two years of study for a B.Ed, under the auspices of the University. Dame Kitty recommended a light-touch approach from the Universities and used some telling metaphors. The association between Universities and Training Colleges should be 'close enough for the stimulus of scholarly breadth and ongoing research to reach the Training Colleges, but not so close as to be stifling'. The aim should be 'to foster new and relatively independent growth ... [not] a topiary intervention, and clipped, unnatural habit'. The two authors dismissed the argument that the introduction of a four-year degree was no way to solve the urgent teacher crisis of the day. (The memorandum refers to the 'current crisis', which, in view of the fact that the same 'crisis' seems to have existed intermittently ever since, now appears touchingly naïve.) They reminded the Committee that the remit was to think long term. Their arguments prevailed and their recommendations for the introduction of the four-year B.Ed degree appear in the Committee's final report largely as they formulated them.

The other written record of Dame Kitty's personal submissions is on the topic of pastoral care in Universities. It was a theme repeated by many witnesses: Universities must not be allowed to increase their ratios of teachers to students beyond one to nine (or one to ten in the 'current crisis'). There must be good accommodation for students. There must be good libraries. Universities should not expand simply by increasing the number of laboratories and lecture halls.

The Robbins Committee reported to the government in October 1963, making 111 recommendations. The essence of its report may be summed up in its answer to the question 'on what principles should development [of Higher Education] be based'. The Committee's forthright reply was 'that courses of Higher Education should be available for all those who qualify by ability and attainment to pursue them and who wish to do so'.

These were bold, clear words. The statistics showed that they implied a massive increase in Higher Education places. In 1962, 8% of the 18 – 22 age group were in Higher Education; the Committee recommended that provision be made for 17% of the babies currently in their prams. As the population was rising and expected to continue to rise (which in fact it did not do again until the end of the century), the calculation was that the 1962 number of Higher Education places of 216,000 should be increased to 560,000 by 1980. It was stated that provision should be dictated by demand.

A large part of this expansion, the report stated, should be in the University sector. The Committee recommended not only the foundation of six new universities but considerable expansion of all the existing ones. Notions of a second level of University that would only teach undergraduates, give degrees and carry out no research, were firmly rejected. It was recognised that Universities already had and would continue to have varying status: inevitably new hierarchies would be formed. The shadow felt in other English universities by the pre-eminence of Oxford and Cambridge was acknowledged. The recommendation, however, was to allow free competition to take place. The Universities should be funded and left to battle it out for their standing academically and from the viewpoint of the potential undergraduates.

Strong recommendations were given for the creation of prestigious Universities of Technology, along the lines of the Massachusetts Institute of Technology, which had impressed the Committee. The existing Colleges of Technology in Glasgow and Manchester were recommended for immediate upgrading in addition to the case being made for the foundation of a further four such Universities.

Expansion was also recommended in places for teacher training in new, larger colleges grouped around Schools of Education in the Universities, very much as Dame Kitty and Professor Drever proposed. The new B.Ed degree was proposed. Degree courses for Colleges of Advanced Technology were also a strong recommendation, as well as an increase in the number of those Colleges. Only two schools of Art were recommended as degree-awarding colleges: this comparative meanness was less well explained. A Council for Academic Awards was proposed, to coordinate the accreditation for all the new degree-awarding institutions. Dame Kitty was eventually appointed to this Council and served on it in her retirement.

The section on finance in the report was large and thorough. It acknowledged that what was being proposed was very expensive, but the argument was advanced that it would prove a false economy to do otherwise. In 1962, 0.8% of the Gross Domestic Product was being spent on Higher Education; at the prices then current, the report's recommendations would require 1.6%, but the Committee argued that the existence of so many more well-educated people meant that it was likely more wealth would be created, and therefore the percentage of the GDP would be less. Even if that were not the case, the presence of so many more educated people would greatly enhance the cultural life of the country and its sense of unity. There is the assumption here that education improves morality and that 'high' culture would automatically increase. One is reminded that only fifteen years previously the Third Programme had been introduced by the BBC on the radio, with the stated ambition that it should become the preferred station for 33% of the population. There seems to be a certain puritanical idealism in the arguments advanced ... as well as the usual pragmatic realisation of a country's economy needing a skilled workforce.

The Committee had considered all the arguments for student loans and rejected them. The members were convinced that such a system would deter the very students they wanted to attract, the sons and daughters of manual workers, and they deplored the notion of recent graduates starting professional life with big debts. Another argument was put forward. It was hoped that many more girls would now go on to University: if they were to finish their degree courses with large debts, just at an age when they were likely to get married, it could prove very difficult for them. Such a prospect might deter girls from going forward as was hoped. There is no written evidence to confirm the idea, but perhaps those paragraphs carry a strong echo of Dame Kitty's voice.

The Robbins Committee reported in October 1963. That summer Harold Macmillan had resigned as Prime Minister because of ill health. There was some turmoil: his successor, Lord Home, had to renounce his hereditary title to get himself elected to the House of Commons. Parliament was resuming after the summer break without a Prime Minister in the House of Commons. Nevertheless, the Robbins report was received by the government with warmth and the commitment was given that its recommendations would be carried out. Ten months later the Conservatives were defeated. It fell to Harold Wilson's administration to carry out the reform and expansion of Higher Education. In that respect, the Robbins report resembled the Beveridge report of 1944: both reports were commissioned by Conservative administrations and subsequently came to be identified with the Labour governments that implemented them.

In the days following publication of the report, the newspapers properly reflected its importance, although the excitement of having a new Prime Minister who was fighting a by-election to enter the House of Commons pushed it from the headlines. The *Times* and the *Daily Telegraph* both compared it in importance with the Beveridge report and praised its thoroughness. Both gave prominence to a recommendation that now seems of lesser importance — that there should be two ministers in charge of education instead of one. Both newspapers considered that unnecessary 'empire building'. Nobody had even suggested that Education should have a Secretary of State with a seat in Cabinet. The *Daily Telegraph* said the six volumes of the report gave the most complete picture possible of Higher Education in Britain, and praised the Committee's clarity concerning the importance of leaving a large measure of academic freedom within Universities. The *Times* said the report would provide the raw material for 100 Doctorates of Philosophy in the future. The comment was generally favourable, but the *Times* struck the first notes of scepticism. Its leader expressed surprise that such a 'hard headed' Committee should recommend such rapid expansion. It feared that in the future, 'students of questionable academic bent' would gain admittance to Universities and that there would be a 'thinner spread of first rate teachers' leading to a 'certain dilution of academic standards'.

A few weeks later, in the *Spectator*, Kingsley Amis encapsulated that view in an article with a headline that became a slogan: MORE WILL MEAN WORSE. The author of *Lucky Jim* had not enjoyed his year at Swansea College; as a result, he had a poor view of all provincial Universities. Some rallied to his side and to some extent that debate has rumbled on ever since. This argument was anticipated in the Robbins report: the Committee had discussed the dangers of an increased number of places leading to students coming forward to study for degrees simply for the prestige of acquiring letters after their names, and not for love of learning. If 17% of the population had Higher Education rather than 7%, would that mean that the additional 10% would prove less able and more frivolous? Gently but robustly the Committee expressed the view that there were plenty of frivolous students among the current 7% and the percentage was unlikely to rise.

After the Committee had reported, Dame Kitty's involvement was not fully over. She, along with other members of the Committee, had to undertake many speaking engagements to sell the proposals to different audiences. She broadcast on the World Service, gave the annual Fawcett Lecture at London University, spoke to the Association of Headmistresses and to her own domestic audiences of the ONLA and the Parents' Guild. Dame Kitty often began these talks by describing the 'crisis' of the huge pressure on University places and the anxiety this created for her Sixth Formers. She was fond of adding that in the current bottle-neck she doubted whether she herself would have won a University place. (It is doubtful if any of her audience believed her.)

Her broadcasts for the World Service were very successful. The producer wrote to her to tell her of the response: 'There was a Spanish police officer who liked your talk particularly because you touched on new aspects of education and "enriched it with most valuable personal views and experience of your own". A Danish schoolboy was interested to hear about the place of women in English education. A French engineer thought you dealt too much in generalities, but an assistant lecturer in Holland said you kept him interested all the time. And there was this from a Belgian teacher: "Dame Kitty Anderson's comment had a very pleasing sensitive touch. One feels she has much comprehensive love for the needs of her pupils".'

That Belgian teacher showed considerable perception.

Joan Clanchy was Headmistress of the North London Collegiate School from 1986 to 1997. An historian, she came to the school from being Headmistress of St George's School, Edinburgh. She served on the National Curriculum Council from 1991-94, where she experienced some of the same pressures that Dame Kitty knew.

~

She was a Labour supporter

Dame Kitty came into our lives like a gale of fresh air. Not only from the academic point of view: she introduced new ideas into the school, and even affected our social lives. She immediately grasped and became involved with whatever subject of interest to oneself one brought up — a trait which must have stood her in very good stead in her work on the Robbins Committee on Education.

I was just starting my Sixth Form year when she introduced Current Affairs classes — discussions, really, which I am sure caused many of us to think more deeply about what was going on in the world. She started the School Advisory Council so that the girls had some say in what went on in the school; and certainly not least she instigated the School Dance — boys from Mill Hill and Aldenham Schools in the hallowed precincts of the Hall! I remember my mother nobly donating me her only pair of nylons, sent from the US, for the occasion. Then there was the affair of the University College School performance of the Messiah. I was asked if I could bring a party of altos and sopranos from NLCS for rehearsals and performance. Regretfully, Dame Kitty had to refuse. It was the time of the 'Doodlebugs', the V1 and V2 rocket attacks, and she felt she could not take the responsibility of agreeing to a party of girls from the school being gathered together in one place where they might be hit ... nevertheless, I am sure she must have known that a few of us sneaked off privately, particularly as Miss Gabriel, the Art mistress, also turned up to sing.

Dame Kitty was a Labour supporter — I shall never forget her assuring me that the world would still continue when she saw my face as the overwhelming vote for Clement Attlee rolled in in 1945. Nevertheless she was furious when the new Labour government abolished the charge for school milk — 'pauperising us all' she called it.

Academically, of course, she was an inspiration — and not only in her enthusiasm for her own subject, History. Her interest in one's other subjects led one on. Though she did lean on me slightly to take History for Higher School Certificate ... however, I did avoid reading it at University!

I was fortunate to maintain social contact with her when she retired to Northallerton, because we were living in Yorkshire by then and she came to visit us. My husband and children thought she was wonderful, and her interest extended to my elder daughter's pony — we have a photograph of this. When we moved to Roundhay she attended a very successful ONL meeting at our house, to which Miss Senator and Dr Leese also came.

Dame Kitty had a vivacious and bubbling personality and it is a joy and privilege to have known her, and to have had the benefit of coming under her influence in one's early life.

Vera Woolf (Norris) 1937-47

We basked in her reflected glory

Dr Anderson was Headmistress when I started at NLCS aged nearly eight. We saw her most days at prayers in the Hall. A small woman, neatly dressed in a dark costume with a loose hair bun and a brisk chin-up walk. We also saw her Deputy, Miss Gossip, a lot as Dr Anderson was often away, sitting on Government committees on education and travelling on official business. We were immensely proud when she received the DBE and we admired her gown and maroon ribbon and decoration. Rosemary Bechler wrote a description in the school magazine about expecting her to come swooping into prayers in long robes — we basked in her reflected glory and honour.

In the 1950s the idea was quite often expressed that higher education for women was a waste of time, as so many women eventually took up the role of housewife. Dame Kitty was able to convince and silence the doubters by reminding them that an educated woman means an educated family. We didn't feel let down by her taking this line, we knew she passionately believed in education for its own sake and ours.

I'm sure it was her status in the educational world that enabled her to exercise her philosophy that whilst one should work hard, there is no point in working harder than necessary. Whilst we maintained a broad education with thirteen subjects on the timetable until 'Mocks' at O-level, we took only five subjects at O-level, the minimum University entrance requirement at the time. My children are envious and incredulous!

Linda Williams (Parr) 1959–70

The atmosphere at Canons

I arrived in the Modern Languages department at NLCS in 1952 with just five years teaching experience behind me. The atmosphere at Canons seemed to me enormously exhilarating, with so many new things happening in all directions, including the opening of the new Drawing School and a wonderful feeling of being part of a friendly, encouraging team of very gifted people who swept you along with them and enabled you to be more creative than you would have thought possible. To me it seemed that Dr Anderson was likely to appear on the scene in any situation, bubbling with enthusiasm, or else solemnly discussing how some improvement could be made.

In my first year we had a General Inspection and I was impressed by the good organisation and the emphasis on the positive side: that we were delighted to welcome these good folk, the Inspectors, and show them our great School with pride. (This attitude was inspired by Dr Anderson.) Of course at the same time we were willing to learn. Ours was a staff that taught with skill and enthusiasm, never letting the dead hand of academic testing gain the upper hand. For this reason we recorded secretly the actual percentages in examinations, only publishing grades representing bands of marks.

Dr Anderson encouraged the postwar contacts that began with France and Germany and the exchange visits that became permanent links — the link with the Goethe Mädchen Gymnasium in Ludwigsburg is a shining example. I remember Dr Anderson saying to me that she would think her Modern Languages staff 'not worth their salt' if they did not take a full part in these exchanges. Dare I say it, the reason for our conversation had been financial, as we were then expected to receive and entertain the visiting staff in the same way as the families of the girls did. In the 1950s and 1960s teaching salaries were exceedingly modest.

As a form mistress, I was impressed by the custom of the weekly form meeting run on democratic lines. This, and the idea of an educational theme in each form room to accompany the exhibition of Founder's Day work and a special blackboard display, was the creation of Dr Anderson. The form mistress had a difficult task trying to allow a certain amount of freedom but at the same time avoid complete anarchy.

It was the custom for end of term reports to be written in triplicate and grades to be copied on to lists, reports and into permanent second books. All this had to be done in a trice over the busiest weekends towards the end of term. A young colleague of mine caused a sensation by taking her reports to the GPO in London to have them Gestetnered. Any attempt to ease the system was frowned upon in those days. Endless copying showed dedication.

Dr Anderson's Testamurs for the school leavers were, and still are, highly prized. A tiny vignette occurs to me: Dr Anderson dancing for joy in the corridor outside her study, with a girl who had just received the news she had won a scholarship to Oxford.

It was of course Miss Shillito, Miss Scrimgeour, Miss Clay and Miss Lewis who organised those wonderful Christmas parties for the children from Tottenham. These took place after the end of term and girls from every level of the school contributed specific aspects of the parties. For example, the Upper Fourths held a competition to write a pantomime which I believe the Lower Fourths acted. Dr Anderson was always radiantly present, enjoying the company of the little ones. She always said she loved a party and she had a great sense of fun.

She also famously coined the phrase 'Everyone Matters' which became the title of the film made about NLCS in the mid-1960s. Quite recently I was at a meeting of a regional group of Old North Londoners. One who belonged to DK's time harboured a bitter memory: although she had been right through the school, at her final interview with the Headmistress it was clear she was not known by name or achievement, but confused with her sister. In her case, she felt 'Everyone Matters' to be a mockery. This revelation produced a very negative reaction among those present. I am sure that Dame Kitty kept that phrase very much before her. However, one of the reasons for the honour she received was her arduous work in the wider field of education. By this stage she was not always in the best of health and great as her ability was to remember people's names, interests, achievements and problems (which she dealt with in a motherly way) she did not always succeed. Had she done so, she would have been superhuman.

In 1965 I was granted a Grace term which I took in the summer. It was Dame Kitty who pointed out to me that a Frances Mary Buss travelling scholarship was advertised in the Times Educational Supplement. She suggested I might apply for it. Apparently the scholarship had been unused throughout the war and beyond; interest had accumulated and £500 was available. In the end this was divided between myself and another teacher from Bristol. I opted to study 'Modern Methods of teaching Modern Languages including the use of machines'. It was the beginning of language laboratories and the audio-visual method that had recently been introduced.

That Grace term — and the holiday on either side of it — was a high spot of my life. I travelled to seven countries in Europe, including Russia, and eventually wrote my thesis. Without Dame Kitty I would not have had this fantastic experience.

This contribution is written out of admiration for a wonderfully warm-hearted Yorkshire woman who rose from a modest background, was the first from her school to go to University, became a stimulating teacher, a positive influence in the wider world of education, and a brilliant Headmistress.

Joy Taylor, Staff, 1952-68

10

'Trust schools which I feel are my schools' — Dame Kitty and the Girls' (Public) Day School Trust

JANET SONDHEIMER

As Dame Kitty approached retirement, she looked forward to enjoying the leisure to engage once again in historical research and to accept 'invitations to undertake some university lecturing'. Yet when the moment arrived, in July 1965, she had committed herself to a further stint (in the event ten years) of strenuous activity in the cause of girls' education, this time as Chairman-elect of the Girls' (Public) Day School Trust.

Founded in 1872, the Trust was currently responsible for twenty-three schools divided almost equally between London and the provinces and modelled initially on those of Frances Mary Buss. Like NLCS, the schools' Senior Departments enjoyed the status of Direct Grant Grammar Schools and were thus vulnerable to the threat to schools which selected on grounds of academic ability contained in the Department of Education and Science Circular dated October 1965, addressed to Local Education Authorities.

The magnitude of the problem facing the GPDST and its incoming Chairman was thus clear at the outset; so, equally, was the promptness of Dame Kitty's reaction, which was to call a special meeting in November 1965 of Council members and headmistresses, the first of many such gatherings and typical of her modus operandi.

To Dame Kitty, former Chairman and President of the Association of Headmistresses, it seemed only natural to take erstwhile colleagues into her confidence, perhaps without fully realising that she was creating thereby something of a precedent. Her own contribution to the meeting (held at Sydenham High School) was to review the various schemes proposed by the government for creating Comprehensive secondary schools, of which she considered that only two would even remotely make proper use of the Trust's educational expertise. 'It would be best,' she concluded, 'to offer via unrestricted social entry a good academic type of education to children within a wide range of ability.'

A month later she departed on her world tour, visiting former NLCS colleagues and pupils along the way. This tour was the sole survivor of her original plans for retirement. During her absence a small room at the Trust's offices in Queen Anne's Gate was redecorated and furnished for her exclusive use, filling a need not felt by her exclusively male predecessors who tended to use their own offices and clerical staff for the conduct of routine Trust business.

Dame Kitty, by contrast, took a friendly, even maternal interest in the clerks, young accountants and junior staff members she daily encountered, and is still gratefully remembered for her approachability. Beyond the office, she carried out an exacting program of school visits, during which she spent time with all sections of the community, starting with the youngest. Typical was the timetable she proposed for a day at Portsmouth High School in 1967: 'I will come by the early train arriving at 11.20 a.m. All the plans you suggest seem admirable to me. In the evening when I talk to the parents may I speak about "Girls' Education in the present and future"?' She apologises for her plan to leave by an early train the following day: 'I am going to make a speech at a Dinner ... I must say that "retirement" hardly describes my way of life!! But I love coming to Trust schools, which I feel are my schools... ' Her interest was not purely sentimental. As a guide to future planning, she initiated the systematic collection, school by school, of historical and current data (pupil numbers, site areas and so on) as reference points for building and other developments as soon as the times were appropriate for these to proceed.

Meanwhile, in 1966 and while she was abroad, Dame Kitty had accepted, presumably in her personal capacity, an invitation to serve on the government commission being set up under Sir John Newsom 'to advise on the best way of integrating the public schools with the state system of education'. At this stage the Commission was concerned only with the independent boarding schools and she was disappointed that its recommendations (from which she and two other members dissented) were concerned more with 'reducing socially divisive influences' than with increasing the scale and scope of boarding provision in general.

Publication of the Newsom Report in 1968 was followed by the partial reconstitution of the Commission under a new Chairman, Professor David Donnison, with the brief of considering 'the means by which Direct Grant

The Trust Council Procession, Westminster Abbey 1972 — the celebration of the Trust's Centenary: Lady Johnson (Finance), Mr. Leighton Irwin, Dr.C. Hardie (Education), Dame Kitty Anderson (Chairman), Mrs G. Woodcock (Deputy Chairman)

Grammar Schools could participate in the movement towards Comprehensive reorganisation'. But Dame Kitty was no longer a member, having made clear her wish 'to be closely associated with presenting the evidence to the Commission on behalf of the Trust and the girls' Direct Grant schools'.

Within the Trust, and via the newly-formed Direct Grant Joint Committee, this task was carried out with great thoroughness and largely under Dame Kitty's direction, together with input from officers and members of Council, amongst them one or two novices who 'had caught the Chairman's eye'.

Outwardly Dame Kitty remained optimistic about the outcome, but to one correspondent (a member of the Commission) she admitted to deep feelings of apprehension, clearly not completely assuaged by her resolve 'to live "in hope" as Frances Mary Buss did'. In the event both premonitions proved correct: when the Donnison Report was published in mid-June 1970, its recommendations were patently unacceptable to the GPDST; by contrast, the largely unexpected return of a Conservative government at the General Election two weeks later ensured the continuation, at least for a while, of Direct Grant status on the familiar pattern (but not at the expense of Comprehensive systems already agreed upon).

For the Trust this reprieve could not have been better timed, since it enabled its Centenary in June 1972 to be celebrated in an unfeignedly joyous mode. The high point was a service in Westminster Abbey, to which Dame Kitty made a point of inviting, amongst others, former pupils, 'old girls' whose schooldays dated back to the nineteenth century. She took advantage, too, of the unique opportunity offered by the Trust's Centenary Cruise to become acquainted as a fellow-passenger with some fifteen hundred current pupils and staff, who greeted with 'deafening cheers' her loudspeaker address to the entire party when *SS Uganda* and *Nevasa* met at Vigo, the halfway point.

Respite from political pressure lasted only until the second of the two General Elections held in 1974; but the interval served to strengthen Dame Kitty's conviction, which she imparted to her colleagues, that the future for the Trust's schools lay in the direction of independence. This was the message conveyed during 1975 to parents, staff and local governors by members of a touring 'Chairman's Working Party' which Dame Kitty, until prevented by an accident at an early stage, had looked forward to leading in person.

Support for the Council's policy proved well-nigh overwhelming, enabling Dame Kitty to relinquish the Chair with a clear conscience when she moved to Yorkshire in the summer of 1975. Although in poor health, she delighted in her new role as Local Governor of the Central Newcastle High School GPDST, the more so since the Headmistress, Catherine Russell, had been educated, like herself, at Saltburn High School.

Of all the tributes paid to Dame Kitty as Chairman of the Trust after her death in January 1979, she would perhaps have been most gratified by the endowment of a History prize named in her honour, to be competed for annually by Sixth Formers at all Trust schools. The donors, the Governors of Howell's School, Llandaff, had reason to be grateful to Dame Kitty for her help in starting the process which eventually brought their school into a close association with the Trust; Dame Kitty herself might also have welcomed the gesture as a fair compensation for her frustrations as a historian manquée.

Janet Sondheimer (Matthews) was educated at Bromley High School (a member of the GDST) and Girton College, Cambridge, where she gained an MA and PhD (History). She is married and has one son and one daughter. She has worked as a part-time university lecturer and academic translator, and is a contributor to the 'New Dictionary of National Biography'. She is currently a Member of Council, Girls' Day School Trust, and served as Deputy Chairman, 1985-2001.

11

'*I love retirement*' — the last years

BARBARA KER WILSON

Dame Kitty was sixty-two when she made the decision to retire in 1965. She had been Headmistress of NLCS for twenty-one years, spanning several schoolgirl generations.

I was at school from 1938 to 1948; my first Headmistress was Isobel Drummond, who was succeeded by Eileen Harold. When Kitty Anderson was appointed Headmistress in 1944 — that penultimate year of war, the year of the dreaded 'Doodlebugs' over London and the 'D' Day landings in France — we knew her as 'Dr Anderson' ... just as Sophie Bryant had been known as 'Dr Bryant'. After she received the DBE Award in 1951, at first it seemed almost impertinent to address her as 'Dame Kitty' ... but she was indeed christened 'Kitty', not 'Katherine', and everyone soon became accustomed to her new title. 'Dame Katherine' would not have seemed half as appropriate: it has a slightly formidable, almost Tudor resonance. 'Dame Kitty' seems to conjure up the essence of her warm, outgoing nature and lack of self-importance ... though she could certainly exude dignity on formal occasions, and her clear-cut reprimands were all the more effective because of their contrast to her usual friendly style of communication.

I had a particular sense of empathy with Dame Kitty, because we both belonged to the north of England. My family moved to the south in 1937; in retrospect, the trauma of that emigration, from the country of the North to the country of the South, seems to have impressed itself on my mind far more than my later removal from England to Australia. At school, I found it somehow reassuring to hear Dr Anderson's homely-sounding voice, with its Yorkshire intonation, at morning prayers. I loved the way she pronounced 'coat-hanger', for example (with a hard 'g') when she read out the list of Lost Property. My sister and I had made a conscious decision to talk 'Southern' after our own northern accents aroused derision amongst our new schoolmates, who shrieked with laughter when we said, for instance, 'pass the glass' at dinner time. With diligent practice our voices came to sound just like *theirs:* 'Parse the glarse' we learned to say. It was almost like learning an extra Modern Language.

Dame Kitty spent thirty-nine years as a teacher, twenty-six as a Headmistress; before coming to NLCS, she was Head of Kings Norton Girls Grammar School, Birmingham, for five years. Teaching, especially with the additional huge responsibilities of managing a large school, is an arduous profession. And Dame Kitty, of course, served the wider educational world in so many other notable ways. Little wonder that by 1965 she was ready to retire without regret, although she was to retain a number of her public commitments and take on new responsibilities.

The *Times Educational Supplement* published a Profile of Dame Kitty soon after she left NLCS, and it was in that interview with journalist Elizabeth Willatts that she exclaimed: 'I love retirement!' — 'with all the enthusiasm of someone starting out on a new career', as Willatts added.

The spontaneous letter she wrote to those who organised the ONLA Retirement Dinner held at the Criterion Restaurant, Piccadilly, on 6 April 1965, certainly expresses no regrets about her retirement. 'What a wonderful party!', she writes. 'It was the high spot of my life and I shall never forget it. ... I loved and appreciated every moment, from being brought up in style by Daisy and her husband ... the quiet room in which to leave my coat, the magnificent flowers, the reception, the grand toast master, the delicious dinner, the speeches and so on. But the best present of all was seeing so many Old North Londoners from Miss Buss's days right down to the leavers from 1964. It made me very proud and also very humble to think that so many should have come to do me honour. I wished that I could have done so much more than I have to be worthy of all this. The two presentations gave me great happiness ... nothing could have given me greater pleasure than to be a proud life member of the London Library as this personifies my academic interests which are deep and abiding. ... Then there was that tremendous cheque ... which will give me infinite joy to plan the application to some permanent benefit for the school we all love so dearly.'

'All this you have given to me and so much more that cannot be put into words — support, encouragement, friendship and affection. I am the most fortunate of women.'

The presentation of the cheque to Dame Kitty was made by two former Senior Prefects, Mavis Greathead (Cosgrove) and Caroline Askew. To commemorate her twenty-one years as Headmistress, Dame Kitty handed the sum of £750 to the school, with a letter to the Chairman of the Governors, Archdeacon Carpenter:

It gives me great pleasure to ask you to accept for North London Collegiate School the enclosed cheque for £750 with which I would like to establish a fund in my name. The greater part of this money was given to me by Old North Londoners on my retirement and I have added to it something from the cheque given to me by the parents ...'

So the Dame Kitty Trust Fund was set up.

Dame Kitty told her interviewer from the *Times Educational Supplement* that she wanted to do some writing during her retirement; however, Williatts reported, she 'complains without too much concern' that no one would let her get on with it — 'there was so much else to do'.

Her writing ambitions seem to have focused on two main subjects: her lifelong interest in vagrancy and vagabondage in the sixteenth century, and an autobiographical account of her life in relation to the contrasting opportunities for women in the nineteenth century. Her lifetime spanned five reigns, and was very much conditioned by the changing educational pattern for women. She was born a year after the 1902 Education Act which created the maintained secondary schools, and she always thought that perhaps she exemplified just what that Act meant. From the little elementary school she attended in Lancashire (conducted by an uncertificated teacher), she went on to a maintained grammar school at Saltburn-by-the-Sea in the North Riding of Yorkshire. Her Headmistress there was Miss Craig, later to become Head of Christ's Hospital, and she had a great influence upon her bright-eyed young pupil.

Although Dame Kitty carried out a good deal of research and made notes for these two writing projects, neither came to fruition.

During her years at NLCS, Dame Kitty lived in a house in Lake View, part of the development that was carved out of the Du Cros estate in the late 1920s. ('Canons Park', with its eclectic mix of mock-Tudor and Georgian-style houses, was redolent of past eighteenth-century glories, other roads and cul-de-sacs being designated 'Canons Drive' (tramped over the years by thousands of NLCS feet), 'Dukes Avenue', 'Chandos Close', 'Handel Close'...) For a few years Dame Kitty shared her house with her nephew David, who was studying medicine. She had always been a beloved and loving member of a close, affectionate family. After her retirement she moved back to her 'calf country', as the northern saying goes, and settled in a one-storey house, Number 35 Hutchinson Drive, Northallerton.

Here she was fortunate indeed to have as opposite neighbours Wendy Jameson, her husband John and their two boys. Wendy clearly remembers the day when 'from my sitting-room window I saw a car stop and out stepped three grand ladies, all in fur coats. [They had come to inspect Number 35.] Shortly afterwards I answered a knock at my door ... the smallest of the three ladies introduced herself as Dame Kitty Anderson. She informed me she hoped to buy the bungalow. I recall a delightful little chat — guess I was being vetted! All these years later I can still vividly recall the scene — my first meeting with a Dame!'

Dame Kitty made a few additions to her house, including a good-sized study that looked out onto the playing fields of the local Grammar School. Wendy recalls a football game on the Grammar School pitch organised by her sons Chris and Tony and their friends. Dame Kitty was most enthusiastic about it, and at half-time passed refreshments over the hedge. 'Just a little thing', Wendy comments, 'but typical of her thoughtfulness and an example of the pleasure she got out of her later life.'

The distinguished retiree soon established herself as a notable newcomer to the area. 'I believe people were fascinated to have a Dame in Northallerton', Wendy says. 'People did feel intimidated by her title — until they met her.'

Like so many women of her generation, Dame Kitty did not drive. She used a local taxi firm whenever she did her shopping, and the proprietors always chauffeured her themselves. Her house-cleaner had the appropriate name of Mrs Bright, and a Mr Kilvington tended her garden, in which she always took a great interest. She enjoyed her new home immensely. She especially enjoyed her baking days — always a proud achievement of

At home in Yorkshire Dame Kitty greets Heather Macmanus

northern housewives. There were many visitors to the Northallerton house: I recall visiting Dame Kitty there one day, and taking afternoon tea with some of her delicious cherry cake while I was staying nearby with one of my aunts.

Her friendship with the Jamesons progressed gradually. 'We were somewhat in awe of her at the outset', Wendy writes, 'but we soon found ourselves at ease in her company. "DK" did the chatting! I was the ever-willing listener. She would ring me up …"I say, Wendy, I've had this splendid letter, do come over and I'll tell you about it." I cannot emphasise strongly enough the joy she obtained from her Old Girls' letters. They came from all corners of the world.'

'One recollection still makes us smile', she adds, 'a tip from "DK". "When you are invited to a Garden Party at Buckingham Palace, go in the side entrance, this way you don't have to queue up for something to eat."' The Jamesons still await the royal invitation.

During the week of the Silver Jubilee, the Jamesons won an award for the Best Decorated House in Northallerton; Wendy spent hours with her two sons toiling over the decoration ... yet it was her husband who was duly presented with a certificate of congratulation from the local Council, presumably on the principle that an Englishman's home is his castle. '"DK" thought this as hilarious as we did', Wendy says.

At one point Dame Kitty asked Wendy Jameson where she was educated. — 'At Bridlington High School for Girls', was the reply, whereupon Dame Kitty told her that she had presented the Speech Day prizes there one year. 'Great excitement', Wendy remembers. 'I dug out the only school magazine I had kept, this being for 1951, my first year ... and lo and behold, that was the very year Dr Anderson presented the prizes!' She showed the Speech Day Report to Dame Kitty:

> Dr Anderson, the Headmistress of the North London Collegiate School, distributed the prizes. Last year Dr Anderson's school celebrated its centenary, thus it was natural that she should tell us a little about the great work of Frances Mary Buss, who founded the school ... Dr Anderson stressed that it is largely to the work of Frances Mary Buss and of Miss Beale that we owe the admission of women to our universities and she urged that this work should be carried on by encouraging girls who, after obtaining their School Certificate are tempted to leave school, to extend their education if not to university, at least to Higher Certificate standard. In this way they would be the better fitted to take up their duties in the world, the chief of which should be to become good citizens.

I am reminded of Dr Anderson's Current Affairs classes, which she taught to the Sixth Form — she was a pioneer of the study of Current Affairs and Civics — and of our enthusiastic participation one year in a 'Mock Election', when the real-life candidates for the Borough of Harrow visited Canons to address us.

The same issue of the Bridlington School Magazine reported: 'A kind invitation from Dr Anderson, the staff and girls of the North London Collegiate School made it possible for 36 of us to pay a visit to London ... and see something of the Festival.' [This was the 1951 Festival of Britain, on the South Bank.] The Bridlington girls also visited Canons. '... at four o'clock we were deposited at the end of the school drive and a delightful party was held in our honour ... [including] large slices of ... amazing strawberry tart.'

Dame Kitty would leave the key of her house with the Jamesons whenever she went away on one of her many trips, and Wendy would take in her daily piles of mail. Dame Kitty used to leave courteous notes of instruction: *'Do not put anything on night store radiators as they are on. Back on Tuesday. Many, many thanks for everything.'*

She left home on two particularly auspicious occasions, to play a leading role in academic ceremonies. In 1967, the University of Hull awarded her the Degree of Doctor of Laws, *honoris causa*. In 1926, Kitty Anderson had attended an interview for her first teaching post, at Craven Street Secondary School, Hull. When she arrived and saw the old unprepossessing building, she went into the interview with mixed feelings. However, having met her interviewers, Mr Shoosmith, the Head Teacher, and Archdeacon Lambert, Chairman of the School Board, she decided that human beings were more important than buildings: she accepted the post and began her life's work in Hull. At Hull on 8 July 1967, Mr Shoosmith, a member of the University Council, was present at the Degree ceremony to honour the young woman he had interviewed forty-one years ago as Head Teacher of Craven Street School.

On 9 July, 1971, the University of York conferred upon Dame Kitty the honorary Degree of Doctor of the University. Her fellow honorary graduates included composer Aaron Copland and the Australian painter Sidney Nolan.

In December 1965, accompanied by Dr Margaret Yates, the friend she had known since her college days at Royal Holloway, Dame Kitty embarked on an adventure she had looked forward to for a long time, a world-wide visit during which she would meet many old acquaintances and former pupils.

She had made several visits abroad in past years, including an extensive tour of the USA as a member of the Robbins Committee, to review American educational methods and establishments. That was a very high-pressure trip, taking in California (where she was 'much impressed by the "State wide" plan for education'), Chicago (where she visited the leading High School, which had over 4000 pupils), Boston (Harvard and the Massachusetts Institute of Technology), Washington — a long session with the Teachers' Association there, as well as meeting up with an Old North Londoner and former School Captain, Sheila Gulard (Cooper), and finally New York. No wonder she wrote in a letter sent from Washington to the NLCS staff: 'I seem to have travelled thousands of miles at great speed. The journey I shall remember most vividly is the one by South Pacific train from San Francisco to Los Angeles.'

Her latest adventure was to take her halfway round the world and back again, a journey of six months. Margaret Yates was a lively, entertaining and very efficient travelling companion. She, too, had recently retired: her life's work had included a stint at the Foreign Office, another in the Civil Service, where she was in charge of implementing wartime conscription, two posts as Headmistress (one as inaugural Head of a large new grammar school at Gateshead), and more recently she had been Personnel Manager at the John Lewis Partnership. Seated at the Captain's table on board *SS Southern Cross*, bound for New Zealand, these two intelligent and competent women who had accomplished so much must surely have added spice, savour and good humour to the conversation.

Their route to New Zealand took them across the Bay of Biscay and the Azores to the West Indies. '...we had a tremendous gale in the Bay of Biscay and the ship performed every antic possible. It pitched, tossed, rocked, shuddered; I was one of the fortunate ones ... able to be up and about and was not laid low', Dame Kitty reported with a hint of pride, then added: 'My admiration, already great, for the early 16th-century sailors, is now unbounded when I think of them adventuring through seas like this in their little boats.' The ship called at Trinidad, where she and Dr Yates spent the day with the parents of former NLCS pupil Jacqueline Sealey ('Jacqueline now at the Royal Academy of Music', Dame Kitty notes) and visited the fast developing university campus. The next landfall was Curaçao, then *Southern Cross* entered the Panama Canal. 'From Balboa', she reported, 'we set out to cross the Pacific to Tahiti — over 7 days of ocean and still more ocean — no land and not a single other ship in sight, only lots of flying fish.'

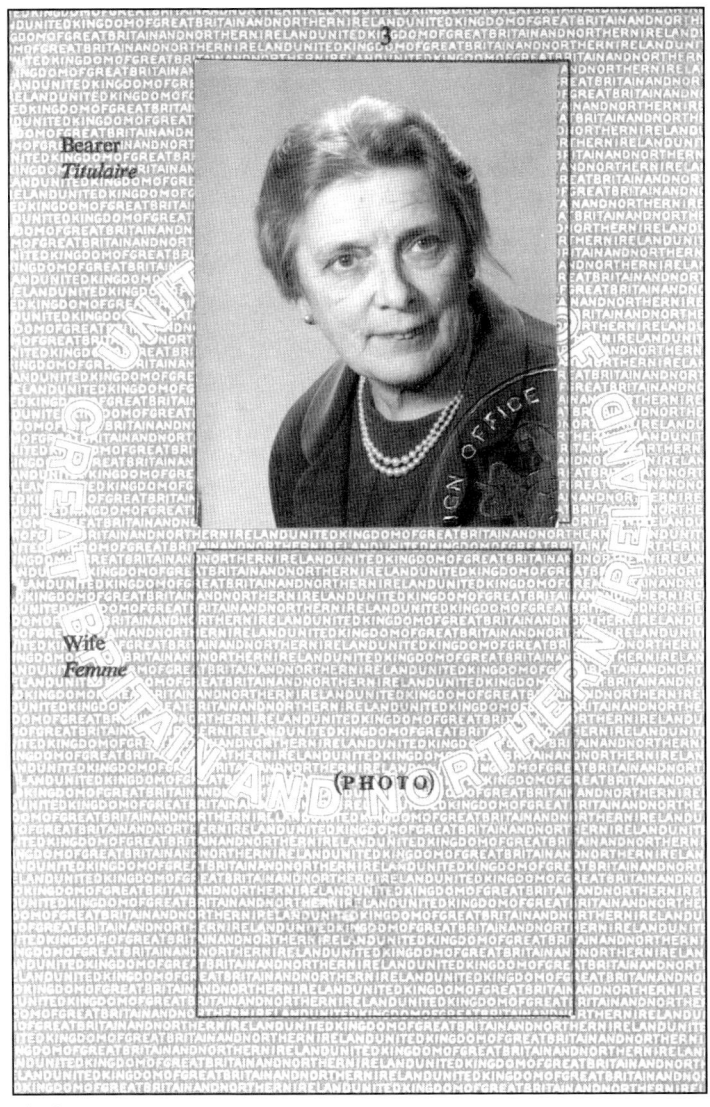

The last passport

During this leg of the journey, covering 450 – 500 miles each day, Christmas was celebrated on board ship. 'In the evening we had Christmas dinner with crackers, paper hats — elegant ones, and mine was a mortar board in gold with gaily coloured tassel!', she wrote delightedly in a letter to Miss McLauchlan. (Dame Kitty's propensity for acquiring new hats was well known: one close friend referred to them as her 'meringues'.) In a letter to the Parents' Guild, she reported: 'Life on board is full of interest and I have met many people with whom I have some link through NLCS or mutual friends. ... I have judged the Children's Fancy Dress party and so the children all know me and talk to me and there are 130 of them!' On 2nd January, she was 'up at 5.30am to see the sun rise over Tahiti' and to watch the ship dock at Papeete. 'The island is out of the world', she wrote enthusiastically, 'with its palm fringed lagoons, exotic vivid flowers, thatched houses and friendly colourful people, incongruously using motor cars and motor cycles! I loved it all ... I can understand why Paul Gauguin made it his home.'

After calling at Fiji, the voyage to New Zealand ended at Wellington on 12 January. They travelled across to the South Island, and spent time with Old North Londoner and former Head Girl Helen (Murray) Aitkin, her husband George and their two young sons, on their large sheep station inland from Pegasus Bay. 'As you can imagine we talked and talked', Dame Kitty wrote in a letter dated 1 February to the Staff at NLCS. The Aitkins took the travellers for a few days to the Wairakei thermal area — 'with its steam which shoots out of the ground alarmingly and its boiling mud pools', Dame Kitty reported. (Helen Murray was a year or so ahead of me at school: I clearly recall watching her play in a hockey match one sports weekend, and Miss Gossip walking onto the pitch at half-time to give her the tremendous news that she had won a place at Oxford.)

After a brief visit to New Zealand's North Island, the two world-hoppers flew from Auckland to Melbourne, Australia, where the summer temperatures were in the 100°s. It was now eight weeks since they had left England. There were NLCS ex-staff members in Melbourne as well as some former pupils, and Dame Kitty was guest of honour at a gathering of the city's school and university representatives.

The next stop was Adelaide, where I was then living with my husband, Peter Tahourdin and our two very young daughters. I recall being worried because we had only one double guest room, which the intrepid travellers would have to share. Luckily it had an en-suite bathroom. All these years later, it has been touching to peek over Dame Kitty's shoulder and read the letter she sent on 6 February to Miss Cross: 'First, greetings and love from Barbara and me. I am having a delightful time staying in her lovely house and look out into the garden with its vines, grapefruit and orange trees and passion fruit — now gloriously ripe, and the sun is shining and the sky is blue.'

The Australian Broadcasting Commission rigged up cables on our tennis lawn for an outside interview with Dame Kitty that came across on the 6.30pm news program, showing her standing against a hedge of opulent Golden Chalice flowers. As a result of this broadcast we were contacted by an Old North Londoner who told us of another former pupil in Adelaide, then in her nineties, who had been at school in Dr Sophie Bryant's time. She had qualified as a dentist and emigrated to South Australia. We were delighted to be able to visit her and take her flowers. There were other contacts, too: Old North Londoner Alison Bailey, engaged on genetics research at the University of Adelaide, allowed us to look down her row of microscopes, and Dame Kitty was especially excited to meet Sister Gabrielle, Headmistress of St Peter's Collegiate School, another friend from her college days at Royal Holloway. She also addressed a joint meeting of all the Adelaide Headmistresses, and was given a conducted tour of the brand-new Flinders University of South Australia by the Vice-Chancellor, Professor Karmel.

More relaxing was our shopping trip to the Adelaide produce markets, where Margaret Yates could not resist buying a large quantity of deep purple, shiny eggplants. That evening she cooked us delicious stuffed *aubergine gratinée*.

At this time I was Managing Editor of the children's books department of the Australian publisher Angus & Robertson, based in Sydney. I remember Dame Kitty's interest in the huge, padlocked mailbags of manuscripts and correspondence that were flown over from Sydney each week, and returned after I had dealt with their contents. 'Just like despatch boxes!', she exclaimed. At this time Dame Kitty was a director of Constable Young Books, the list started by the legendary editor Grace Hogarth: she and Dame Kitty had joined forces to launch me in the world of publishing, after I failed to gain an Oxbridge scholarship in the Upper Sixth. (Dame Kitty persuaded Dr Helen Gardner to grant me an informal interview at

Oxford, after which that distinguished Old North Londoner wrote to Dame Kitty: 'On no account should this girl enter a university'. At the time I was taken aback by such a forthright reaction, but I now realize she was quite right: I was essentially a 'hands-on' person who needed to engage with the hurly-burly of the real world.) A few years later, Grace Hogarth published a few of my teenage novels at Constable. I realise with hindsight that it was thanks to the influence of NLCS and Dame Kitty that an ongoing theme of these stories, set in different periods, was the changing role of women in the world.

On the final night of our visitors' stay, the Federation of University Women gave a grand dinner in Dame Kitty's honour. Regretfully we farewelled them both at Adelaide airport, and they flew off to Sydney. It was sad to watch their plane become a mere speck in the sky.

Diana Wynne (Langley) was Dame Kitty's hostess in Sydney. (Dr Yates stayed at an hotel.) Like me, she was concerned about accommodation: the only room she could offer Dame Kitty was her son Davydd's bedroom, but Dame Kitty assured Diana that she had quite happily slept in ONLs' children's rooms for most of the trip. At that time Diana was editor of the *Australian Home Journal,* and we used to meet whenever I visited Angus & Robertson's Sydney offices. She told me that Dame Kitty was absolutely wonderful with Davydd (he was aged two at the time) and he was enchanted by her. When he got up each morning his first words were: 'Where's damn Kitty?'

Dame Kitty was interviewed by the Sydney *Telegraph*, which published a rather sombre photo of her, and the journalist reported: 'when Dame Kitty returns to London she'll face a welter of work that would send the average woman back to a 9 - 5 job just for a rest. She'll take up her duties as Chairman of the Girls' Public Day School Trust — the first woman to hold the post. The Trust administers 23 of England's biggest schools.' ...Interestingly, Dame Kitty expressed her first regret upon her retirement in this interview. '"I miss teaching terribly", she said. 'I miss the children — this is the only sadness in my retirement."' In a previous interview, she had stated her firm belief that teaching was one of the greatest professions, declaring: 'If I was starting all over again then I know that I should make the same choice for my career. *I am proud to have been a teacher.'*

Now it was time to join *SS Oronsay*, bound for India via Hong Kong. In India the travellers were to be guests of the Indian Council of Cultural

Relations. On Easter Saturday Dame Kitty wrote to Mrs Cowie from the 'comfortable Edwardian hotel' where she and Margaret Yates were staying: 'The official part of my Indian visit is over … I have had a heavy programme of lectures and meetings in Bombay, Madras, Calcutta, Benares and Delhi.' The Delhi visit included a meeting with Preeti Kaul, yet another Old North Londoner. 'I have stood up to the intense heat very well and am now revelling in the fine air of the Himalayas. The Indian Council for Cultural Relations have been wonderful hosts and I now have many new friends all over India. The problems [of India] are immense; one cannot really appreciate the magnitude until one actually is here. … We are in Simla for Easter … We return to Delhi for a farewell dinner on 12th April and the next morning fly to Israel. When once we arrive in the Mediterranean area we shall really feel we are on the way home. The journey here was adventurous — overnight sleeper from Delhi to Kalka and then rail car (narrow gauge) for 5 hours and through 103 tunnels up into the mountains. … I'll soon be home now and telling a rare traveller's tale!'

In Calcutta, Old North Londoner Maya Ray (Battacharya) was practising at the Bar; her husband, also a barrister, was a member of the West Bengal Legislative Assembly, representing the Indian National Congress. Maya was worried because her house was not air-conditioned, so she organised for the travellers to stay at the Ram Krishna Mission International Hostel. One of the most memorable engagements in Calcutta was a visit to Mother Patricia at Loreto House School, which had an exchange program with NLCS.

After India came the eagerly anticipated visit to Israel, where Dame Kitty made contact with yet more Old North Londoners who had settled there. On 20 May, writing from Rome, she reported: 'The contrast between India and Israel was most striking — from the large to the small; from apathy and from poverty and famine to vitality and new exciting development. In Israel I saw many Old North Londoners … I stayed with Shelia Kritzler (Oster) at Kibbtz Lavie, with Ruth Lowenthal in Haifa and Lisa Thaler (Pollak) in Netanya.' There were other former pupils in Upper Galilee, Jerusalem and Tel Aviv.

'I really think my great adventure could be called "Around the world with Old North Londoners"', Dame Kitty declared in a letter written from Rome, where she was 'revelling in the antiquities' before going to Venice to join a Hellenic cruise. 'After the intense heat of the East I find Rome quite cold', she wrote, 'so expect I shall resort to my fur coat in Edgware! I look forward immensely to seeing you soon.'

Clearly, she was eager to be back home, and to tackle the new workload of public service that awaited her. It had indeed been a great adventure, and one that might have taxed the strength of a much younger woman.

On her return, she remarked that the new and fascinating horizons she had seen put England and its educational problems into a more sober perspective. With vivid memories of the plight of schools in India, she was left with the feeling that England's problems were really rather small, and with a concern, as she expressed it, 'that we may have reached a level of refinement of problems at which the essentials begin to be forgotten.'

During the next decade, Dame Kitty continued to work as a member of the various bodies to which she had been elected. Her Chairmanship of The Girls' Public Day School Trust continued until 1975, when she became Vice-President. During those years she went tirelessly about the country visiting all the Trust schools, opening new buildings which often owed their initiative to her; speaking at centenary celebrations, declaring her faith in the future and bringing fresh heart to parents and governing bodies and particularly to Headmistresses, to whom she was wise counsellor and most welcome friend. She also served on the Executive Committee of the Association of Governing Bodies of Girls' Public Schools and on the Direct Grant Joint Committee. In addition, she served on various other Councils and was a member of the Governing Bodies of a number of colleges until 1969.

During these last years, Dame Kitty's health gradually declined. In 1976 she suffered serious illness and was admitted to a Northallerton Hospital. She recovered and was able to return home to resume her life at a gentler pace. In 1977 she was at Canons for Founder's Day — she sent a card to Wendy Jameson on 28 March in which she wrote: 'I am feeling good and sleeping well. I had a lovely Founder's Day and saw crowds of people.' Her nephew David, his wife Chris and their son Simon accompanied Dame Kitty on this journey.

Her death was very sudden — 'a tremendous shock', Wendy Jameson says. Dame Kitty had just enjoyed a visit from Margaret Yates and was planning her next small holiday. Lately, she had been in the habit of phoning Wendy most mornings, and the Jamesons always glanced across the road each morning to check that her curtains were drawn back. On 15 January, 1979, a Monday, the curtains remained drawn, and so they knew something was wrong. Dame Kitty had died in her sleep.

Her funeral was held at All Saints Parish Church, Northallerton. Besides her dearly loved family members and representatives of her professional life, a very large number of local people came to show their respect, including all her neighbours. As Wendy Jameson writes, 'This simple funeral service contrasts sharply with the splendour of the magnificent Service of Thanksgiving for the Life and Work of Dame Kitty Anderson held in St Margaret's Church, Westminster, on Friday, 23 March' (Founder's Day). In her heartfelt Address, Madeline McLauchlan, Kitty Anderson's successor as Headmistress of the North London Collegiate School, described this as 'the right day on which to try to pay tribute' to Dame Kitty. For, as she said, 'Dame Kitty's last words of her earthly life, at the end of a happy visit from members of her beloved family, and repeated later on the telephone to a dear friend, voiced her eager hope of coming to the Founder's Day Service.' Miss McLauchlan spoke of Dame Kitty's 'liberating, creative leadership of rare quality' and her 'infectious enjoyment of life'. To Dame Kitty, she said, 'Everyone mattered and continued to matter for all her life after she had left school.' She ended her address by quoting Dame Kitty's own words from her Founder's Day address of 1965:

'The challenge to each one of us is to see to it that our individual contribution to the whole is worthy of ourselves and is the very best that we can give. Let us never forget that "we are members one of another".'

Barbara Ker Wilson was at NLCS 1938-48, and was Editor of the school magazine; during wartime paper shortages, each edition was displayed on a board. It became known as 'The Wall Magazine'. She trained as an editor at Oxford University Press and subsequently worked for other leading publishers in the UK, Australia and the USA. As a writer, she has published over forty books, mainly for younger readers.

Not the kind of remark you expect to hear

The memory of Dame Kitty I would like to share is of a visit Joan Goldring (Collins) and I paid to her at her bungalow in Northallerton some years after she retired.

We talked about school, of course, and about various Old North Londoners with whom she had kept in touch. We got the impression she didn't remember us very well, but she was very interested in hearing about our current careers — Joan as a nurse, myself as a civil servant. When she discovered that Joan lived only a few miles from her childhood home in Saltburn, on the North Yorkshire coast, there was a lively discussion about places they both knew. We were fascinated to learn that Dame Kitty remembered an incident in World War I when the German navy shelled Hartlepool, Scarborough and various coastal towns in between. At the time of our visit Dame Kitty had only recently recovered from major abdominal surgery. We were amused (and a little embarrassed) when she confided in us that for some time after the operation she had not been able to wear her corselette. Not at all the kind of remark you expect to hear from your former Headmistress, but perhaps typical of her Yorkshire forthrightness.

Barbara Faux (Lousley) 1948-55

∽

'She was our friend at all times'

Dame Kitty Anderson was one of the most wonderful and remarkable women I have ever met. I had the good fortune to be able to take advantage of her teaching and advice for the last four years of my school career, until I went up to Oxford in 1948.

All through the Sixth Forms we had one Current Affairs lesson a week, and when Dame Kitty could spare the time she took us for these. The times were stirring. They included the end of the Second World War and the formation of the United Nations. Dame Kitty's lessons were fascinating.

She had the talent of inspiring interest in whatever subject she was dealing with. Her audience was always totally attentive and there was always time for us to discuss whatever subject we were dealing with. Although we were very busy preparing for A-levels and University entrance examinations we had other fascinating outings with Dame Kitty, sometimes totally unconnected with the subjects we were studying. She took us on a tour of the bombed-out City churches of London and explained their history. We went with her on a most interesting tour of the London Library. She also invited two or three of us at a time to take tea with her at her pleasant house in Lake View. On these occasions there were never any uncomfortable silences, in fact time passed all too quickly! In those days we were all very sad indeed to leave school. Dame Kitty kept in touch with many of us, always interested in our progress and always ready to help and advise. She was our friend at all times.

I have spent the past fifty years in Israel and there are also many other Old North Londoners living here. On her retirement from School in 1965, Dame Kitty went on her world tour, accompanied by Dr Margaret Yates. Their last port of call was Israel. Dame Kitty asked whether she and Dr Yates could make their base with us during their month's stay here. We were delighted to agree and it was a most wonderful and enjoyable month. By then, Dame Kitty was of course a well-known personality. As soon as she arrived here from India she received an invitation to tea from the British Ambassador at his house in Ramat Gan. She insisted I should accompany her (Dr Yates preferred to stay with our children here in Netanya). Dame Kitty said she thought we should wear white gloves and she would wear a hat. As it turned out, the Ambassador came into the room in his white tennis outfit, perspiring from his recent game. It was an interesting, entertaining and most informal teatime together.

Another Old Girl, Sheila Kritzler (Oster), is a long-time member of Lavie, a religious Kibbutz situated near Tiberias, where Dame Kitty was invited to spend a few days. While she was there she asked to take a class of kibbutz children. These children, in a completely different part of the world, with a completely different outlook, were fascinated and did not want the lesson to end.

Dame Kitty also spent time in Upper Galilee and in Haifa, and of course she visited Jerusalem. Here in Netanya she and Dr Yates took our two young children on a tour of the town in a horse-drawn carriage and showed them how to wave at the passers-by 'as if they were the Royal Family'! We laughed a lot but we also had a lot of serious discussions on all kinds of matters. At one point I asked Dame Kitty why all the teachers at NLCS in my time were unmarried. She answered that in the First World War so many men were killed that there were hardly any left of that generation. Many women at that time decided to devote their lives to teaching instead of to husband and family.

I shall never forget Dame Kitty. She gave me such a lot. I am now over seventy and I still miss her. I am sure she lives on in the memories of all who knew her.

Lisa Thaler (Pollak) 1940-48

∽

A long association: England and India

I had the good fortune to have a long association of some thirty years with Dame Kitty, from the time she arrived as Headmistress. I entered school when I was eleven, two years before she came to NLCS. Until then, my youthful image of headmistresses had been awesome. At my previous school, South Hampstead High School, the Head was a stern and formidable character. Miss Harold, Dame Kitty's predecessor at NLCS, was kindly but appeared to us remote and austere by temperament. I was at once struck by Dame Kitty's warm and attractive personality. She was not at all intimidating; she combined authority with a more 'human' face; here was someone approachable, sympathetic and genuinely interested in each individual.

She created for me a happy environment throughout my schooldays in which I thrived. She showed understanding and resilience in dealing with the difficulties and needs of the girls and their families under the pressures of wartime conditions. She had shrewd insight into child psychology. She told us as seniors that the high-spirited 'naughty' girls often turned out to be responsible individuals as they grew up. As Sixth Formers, she gave us lessons in History and Current Affairs. She also held group discussion classes for those of us, then few in number, who intended to go to university. She gave us valuable advice, both academic and practical, and great encouragement in preparing for university entrance.

Later on, when I returned to England after my marriage, having practised as a barrister and lectured in Calcutta, I had an unexpected encounter with Dame Kitty in Oxford. I was acting as tutor to law students at St Ann's College, and was in the dining hall when Dame Kitty descended the stairs with Lord Robbins. They were visiting colleges and universities in connection with the Robbins Committee on Higher Education. Dame Kitty was surprised and delighted to see me and with typical enthusiasm she introduced me as an Old North Londoner to Lord Robbins.

On her retirement from School in 1966 she embarked on a world tour with her friend, Dr Margaret Yates. (I had met Dr Yates earlier at the John Lewis Partnership, where she held an administrative post and where I was employed for a short period as a legal assistant in their small, all-female in-house legal department.) The travellers were welcomed in Calcutta by my elder sister Maya, who left NLCS in 1944. In a letter Dame Kitty sent me from Simla, dated 9 April 1966, she wrote:

> A month ago I arrived in Bombay. ... I cannot leave India without writing to you to tell you how much I have enjoyed my visit — I have seen much, lectured, talked, held seminars and met many, many people so that I now feel that I have friends in many parts of India. The Indian Council for Cultural Relations ... have shown us great friendship and hospitality. We have been in Bombay (and from there went for a weekend to Aurangabad to see the marvellous caves at Ellora and Ajanta), Madras, Calcutta, Benares and Delhi (spending a Sunday in Agra to see the Taj Mahal). Now we are high up in the mountains having a rest after the heat of the plains. ... Of course one of the high spots of this tour was seeing Maya and being entertained by her in Calcutta. She and her husband were Kindness itself and we both loved being with them. Through Maya we were able to meet leaders in education, law and government. I felt very proud of Maya as an Old North Londoner, and as a High Court barrister. ... I've seen quite a number of Old North Londoners in India as well as elsewhere

as I have made my way round the world ... Only by coming to India can one have any idea of the nature of its problems — Mine is only a bird's eye view, but I have a much clearer picture of the educational scene at any rate...

On her return to England Dame Kitty invited me to supper one summer evening at Lake View and projected a large number of slides she had taken as she recounted her experiences.

Over the years I stayed in touch with Dame Kitty and sought her advice regarding my daughter Marisha's education. She entered NLCS, starting in Form I, and left in 1987. I met Dame Kitty for the last time at a Founder's Day Service when she felt unable to mount the platform and asked me to sit with her at the back of the Hall. She was eager for me to point out Marisha as the girls filed out at the end of the daffodil procession, and later she spoke to her.

In 1979 I attended the Memorial Service for Dame Kitty at St Margaret's, Westminster. A vast number of Old North Londoners were congregated there. It was testimony to the esteem and affection in which she was held by so many of us.

Chaya Ray (Battacharya) 1942-50

∼

A verve never to be forgotten

Dame Kitty was someone I have always looked upon as a role model in my life, at the Bar, in politics, as a member of Parliament and again as the wife of the Governor of Punjab, in its days of terrorism, and later still as an Ambassador's wife in Washington. She was someone who combined her teaching career with full participation in public life with great success. She was a joyous person, full of encouragement, with a verve never to be forgotten.

Maya Ray (1942-44)

Epilogue: *She was a real morning person*

Enid Ellis

In her *Prologue* to the NLCS Centenary book, Ruby Scrimgeour wrote:

The end of a hundred years of a school's life is the time to look back to perceive the pattern of the past and forward to prepare the threads of the future. It is the ideal time to do this, for the beginning is not too densely shrouded in the mists of time. We can look at these years with the excitement of the contemporary as well as the detachment of the historian.

I first came to NLCS in 1946 as a student teacher. The words I have quoted catch quite vividly my own early impressions from encounters of that time. They made the span of one hundred years contemporary to me. Dr Anderson had been Headmistress since 1944 and must have felt the same. She herself contributed the important, carefully researched second chapter to the Centenary book: *Frances Mary Buss, the Founder as Headmistress, 1850-94.*

Someone has said that we find the history we seek: Dame Kitty seems to have found her own self in her account of the person and purposes of Miss Buss. Certainly there emerge in that chapter examples of her own characteristic vocabulary: 'family', 'experiment', 'adventure'. Her merrier zeal perhaps softens the Founder's more solemn and embattled Victorian dedication. Not that Kitty Anderson lacked a profound and quite still gravity behind the sparkle. The portrait later painted of her catches this intensity, which remains my very strong recollection of one-to-one conversations with her.

Miss Buss's successors as Headmistress (apart, perhaps, from Eileen Harold) had already been grafted onto the school family. It was, therefore, significant that Dame Kitty arrived as a Historian, a proven academic, but also one for whom History was part of the philosophy of practical living and of the development of institutions. For all her academic status Dame

Kitty could empathise with Frances Mary, who had had to gather her education as she went along. They shared a kind of practical vision and wisdom learnt from experience.

Dame Kitty exercised a leadership educative not only of her pupils, but of her younger staff. I speak from personal experience. NLCS was my first and only teaching school. She took very seriously the pastoral role of form mistresses and I remain intensely grateful to her for giving me experience of that role at all levels of the main school. Her own contacts were with the youngest to the most senior pupils. The opportunity given bred in me a commitment to her ideal of a vertically responsible, caring, interactive school community. Everybody matters to everybody, and, if possible, should be known by everybody — as, indeed, everyone was to our Headmistress. This microcosm was the preparation for work and service in the wider world. Dame Kitty was reticent about her religious faith, but it could perhaps be glimpsed in the moral and social values she stressed. In 1965 she ended her final Founder's Day Address (in which the pronoun 'we' predominates) with the plea: 'Let us never forget that we are members one of another.'

Dame Kitty was not so much all things to all people as her one self to all. She initiated, but also served alongside in the implementations that arose from decisions. The nature of her authority was to accord to teachers and taught alike trust, freedom and dignity. From the beginning I noticed the respect with which she consulted her senior staff. In meetings she would listen to all views, however idiosyncratic. She would draw out and nurture less obvious gifts of staff members, so that we came to perceive ourselves as a company of peers and friends. What was true of the staff was true also of the girls, made clear in the operation of the School Advisory Council and of the Prefect body.

Even when public responsibilities claimed much of her time, Dame Kitty remained personally involved with particulars of school enterprises. In my own early, inexperienced years, I put on a pantomime at the Frances Mary Buss House in Bromley with the Junior Girls Club. There in the audience, one winter evening, sat Dame Kitty.

In April 1950, immediately after the Centenary celebrations, Dame Kitty travelled to Germany to spend a few days with the first NLCS group on exchange with the Goethe-Realschule in Ludwigsburg, near Stuttgart. It would be difficult to overestimate the importance of this exchange; together with the French link with Reims, it reconnected our school community with postwar mainland Europe. We thus laid our hands on the history of the times after wartime isolation and began the process towards healing and understanding. Friendships made then still endure. Dr Anderson on our side and the reinstated, brave and distinguished Dr Elisabeth Kranz in Ludwigsburg supported the initiative of Jewish friends Caroline Senator and Jenny Heymann. Dame Kitty was at Victoria Station to welcome the first Ludwigsburg group in autumn 1949, certainly one of the earliest of such postwar exchanges and significant by reason of those who inaugurated it. Elisabeth Kranz and her successors, Madeleine Suchail, Headmistress in Reims and later in Paris, paid visits to NLCS, affirming their faith in friendship through education.

Throughout Dame Kitty's Headship, NLCS was a Direct Grant school with a degree of autonomy, yet involved in the local free-place system — and, as the Founder had wished, in the mainstream of state education. Dame Kitty's gifts, her practical acumen as well as academic distinction, enabled her to make the very best of this status. She believed that education should have enough distance from political projects to be able to work through its own longer time-spans. When the GCE was introduced, the intention at NLCS was to limit the weight of public examinations. Five essential subjects were to be taken at Ordinary Level and intended Advanced Level subjects were to be, in general, bypassed at that stage, assuming a secondary school career to age eighteen. NLCS kept to this plan for many years and established trust in universities and other institutions in the validity of the school's internal assessments. The leaving Testamur recorded all studies of the final three years, the bodying-out of Sixth Form timetables in practical and cultural ways around the Advanced Level subjects, and included a substantial testimonial. Ideally, it was a passport from the microcosm of school to the wider world.

The Founder's Day Bidding Prayer speaks of Dame Kitty's 'tireless enthusiasm'. This was no superficial liveliness of manner, but a strong emission of energy. It inspired the hard, meticulous work in and for School which earthed her valuable contribution to education in the public arena. It enabled her to dominate fatigue and health problems and to motivate the lower-pulsed among us. Possibly it distanced a few girls and staff of different pace and temperament. I personally felt a kind of homely bond with her. We were both northerners, though from opposite sides of the

Pennines, and we shared the same birthday, 4 July, exactly twenty years apart. I recall a vivid, rueful example of her zest. As a fairly new driver, I was anxiously ferrying her along the (to me) complicated road system between Edgware and Archway in my Mini. She, meanwhile, in unaware trust, expounded some matter near her heart and patted my knee to elicit a response. Perhaps we swerved a little ... but we survived.

Dame Kitty seemed to delight in the symbiotic life of herself and her school. She loved the hymn 'Morning has broken/Like the first morning'; I see her in my mind's eye on the platform at Prayers, with pale sunlight glancing in upon our Assembly. She was a real morning person, with a spontaneous courage to carry forward any who feared the morning.

Enid Ellis read Modern Languages at St Hugh's College, Oxford. After teaching practice at NLCS she was appointed to the staff in 1946, became Head of Department in 1958 and Deputy Head in 1971. She left in 1980 and at Oxford read for the Diploma in Theology. Since 1985 she has been licensed as a Reader to St Mary's Church, Harrow on the Hill. She has a home in Harrow and a cottage in Dorset. Her mother who supported her in experience died in 1991.